Power Tools
for
REASON 3.0

Master the World's Most Popular Virtual Studio Software

BY KURT KURASAKI

Backbeat
Books

San Francisco

Published by Backbeat Books
600 Harrison Street, San Francisco, CA 94107
www.backbeatbooks.com
email: books@musicplayer.com

An imprint of the Music Player Network
Publishers of *Guitar Player, Bass Player, Keyboard, EQ,* and other magazines

United Entertainment Media, Inc.
A CMP Information company

CMP
United Business Media

Distributed to the book trade in the US and Canada by
Publishers Group West, 1700 Fourth Street, Berkeley, CA 94710

Distributed to the music trade in the US and Canada by
Hal Leonard Publishing, P.O. Box 13819, Milwaukee, WI 53213

Text and cover design by Doug Gordon
Illustrations by Andrew Hamilton
Composition by Craig Woods and Robin Kibby, Happenstance Type-O-Rama

Library of Congress Cataloging-in-Publication Data

Kurasaki, Kurt, 1969–
    Power tools for reason 3.0 : master the world's most popular virtual studio software / by Kurt Kurasaki.— 1st ed.
        p. cm.
    Includes index.
ISBN-13: 978-0-87930-861-2
ISBN-10: 0-87930-861-3 (pbk. : alk. paper)
    1. Reason (Computer file) 2. Digital audio editors. I. Title.

    ML74.4.R43K87 2005
    786.7'6—dc22

                                        2005028886

Printed in the United States of America

05 06 07 08 09   5 4 3 2 1

Contents

Foreword

It is a pleasure to have been asked to write the foreword for Kurt's book. Reason has played a large part in the process of making music for Neil Davidge (Producer of Massive Attack's *Mezzanine* and *100th Window*) and myself since it first became available, and will continue to do so in the future. Reason has taken the whole premise of the virtual studio into a new domain. With each version upgrade, Reason has become an increasingly powerful tool for creating and arranging music in a way that is spontaneous and seemingly limitless.

The graphic interface, as users will already know, makes the process of creating and using the virtual studio very simple, yet gives the user the potential for endless permutations as the piece of music he or she is creating develops. The flow of the music need never be broken while auditioning new sounds or introducing new components, as all these functions can be performed without having to stop the sequencer. Both Nell and I have found this feature invaluable when an idea needs to take shape quickly, without losing the vibe of the moment. The other key thing for me as a programmer is that the sequencing engine is as tight as anything I have used. There is little point building up layers of grooves if they are going to sound loose. Reason holds it all down, effortlessly.

One of the things that I loved about Reason's predecessor, ReBirth, when I first began using it to create drum loops in the early stages of *100th Window*, was the wealth of resources available on the web to enhance it. Makers of electronic music from all corners of the globe have given up their time to create "mods" (in essence, their version of ReBirth, which featured their favorite samples and sound effects), and posted them to the Propellerhead website. These were available for free download, and were often of a very high standard. This gave rise to a real sense of interaction with the online musical community.

This spirit of generosity and sharing has been carried on by Kurt at his website, www.peff.com. Visitors to this site will find a wide range of useful supplements to Reason. In keeping with his own musical diversity, you will find everything from lovingly multisampled 303 patches and vintage rhythm boxes to faithful representations of Rhodes pianos, Stradivarius violins, and shakuhachi. In addition to such downloadable goodies, Kurt is happy to share a wealth of tips and tricks for the creators of music in the virtual domain. It is a hugely rewarding site to visit, even if you are just starting out in the field of virtual studio technology.

Kurt's wealth of knowledge now comes to the wider stage in the shape of *Power Tools for Reason*. As I was writing this foreword, the document was only available as an unfinished draft, but even so I was amazed by the breadth of ideas and examples Kurt had put together. Each aspect of Reason's versatility as a music production tool has been revealed in great detail, with care being taken to explain why particular techniques or configurations have been used.

I would recommend that even the most avid fan of Reason pay close attention to the first two chapters, which provide invaluable guidance on the first principles of using the software. The section that deals with shortcuts is rightly described as essential, as the key commands listed will save a lot of repetitive mouse movement, leaving the user with vital headspace to concentrate on the music. Kurt's sensible advice on file management, including the use of customized songs as a starting point for each new project, is well worth understanding and implementing. Take care also to read up on copy and paste techniques with the various devices, as these again will save precious time which you can spend being creative.

Once these basics are under your belt, feel free to progress to more intricate maneuvers. Pattern-controlled vocoding and side chain compression are not just useful pieces of jargon to impress your buddies with; they can help you in your music making! By following the examples found in this book, you will learn to use the software in new and inventive ways. Not only that, but you will also have taken in a lot of very useful knowledge of music production in general, because the author has taken a lot of care to explain what is actually happening to the audio once you begin to manipulate it. In other words, you're not just getting great sounds out of your software synth, you're learning how you're doing it. I had a lot of fun trying out some of these ideas, and found myself falling in love with Reason all over again.

Therefore, I wholeheartedly recommend this book to newcomers and experts alike.

—Alex Swift

Alex Swift's programming credits include
Massive Attack's *100th Window* and Peter Gabriel's *Up*.
Alex's music appears regularly in the television franchise, *CSI*.

Chapter 1
All You Need Is Reason

Propellerhead Software Reason is a powerful virtual studio application, with the tools necessary to produce almost any style of music. Even on a basic computer setup, Reason runs solidly, making it one of the most popular applications used by music hobbyists and professionals. It's a power studio tool, and Reason is fast becoming a live performance instrument as well. Live acts rely on its synths, samplers, and drum machines, and some artists perform with Reason alone.

The focal point of Reason is the virtual rack, whose visually stunning graphic user interface balances aesthetics and intuitive control. The list of devices includes mixers, synthesizers, a drum machine, a sample loop player, sample playback instruments (compatible with the Akai S1000/3000 libraries), and a variety of effects—all with professional audio quality. Reason 3.0 introduces the MClass mastering devices, a suite that comprises a compressor, high-definition equalizer, stereo imager, and peak limiter. The most interesting addition to 3.0, however, is the Combinator, a device that allows users to create their own synthesizers and effects.

Reason rack devices have input and output jacks for audio signals and analog-style control voltages like those found on modular synthesizers. Akin to their hardware counterparts, Reason devices are connected using virtual cables. Any number of devices can be wired together in unique signal processing chains.

The virtual equipment rack is controlled from Reason's sequencer, which records MIDI note events and parameter changes. Propellerhead Software has developed Remote, a communication protocol between Reason and USB/MIDI keyboards and control surfaces. The Remote technology allows connection of multiple control surfaces, and works with the improved sequencer to record multiple tracks of controller data.

Reason 3.0 introduces the first major changes to the sound libraries with new synthesizer patches, ReCycle loops, and instrument sample sets in addition to the original samples found in previous versions. The number of sample libraries has grown, and an improved file browser system organizes multiple audio sample and ReFill directories.

Power Tools for Reason 3.0

*P*ower *Tools for Reason 3.0* presents a variety of techniques that experienced Reason users will find useful. Each section attempts to explain certain principles of audio engineering and music production. The early chapters introduce procedures and concepts to familiarize users with the terminology used throughout the book. The central chapters explain various engineering concepts and how these concepts apply to Reason and to audio production.

The first edition of *Power Tools for Reason* covered the features in version 2.5. This new edition explores the new features of the software, and many of the examples incorporate the new devices. The chapters on dynamics effects and filters (Chapters 6 and 7, respectively) detail the use of the MClass Compressor, Maximizer, and Equalizer devices, and an all-new mastering chapter (Chapter 13) describes using the MClass devices together. Because it adds a new dimension to Reason, the Combinator is given a separate chapter, in which the new control, synthesis, and effect features are discussed. The chapters on synthesizers and samplers (16 and 17) now include projects that detail methods of patch programming.

The passion to create music is as important as production expertise, and Reason provides the ideal environment to realize both. To fully understand every aspect of this application requires knowledge of music composition, computers, MIDI sequencing, synthesizer programming, sampling, acoustics, and audio engineering. This information is valuable, but cannot substitute for creative inspiration. Keep in mind the old adage, "Practice makes perfect." Reason, like any musical instrument, requires practice to become proficient, but a technical understanding will provide the foundation with which to experiment and innovate.

Prerequisites for Using This Guide

*P*ower *Tools for Reason 3.0* is not for the absolute novice. Before attempting the examples, users should understand the fundamental procedures, such as creating and cabling devices, loading patches, adjusting parameters, recording MIDI sequences, and programming patterns on the Matrix and Redrum. Anyone can follow the comprehensive directions to get hands-on experience, but this book does not cover the basics. Beginners should consult the Reason manual, The "Getting Started" documentation, or the "Producing Music with Reason" tutorial from Propellerhead Software.

Most of the examples in this book require nothing more than a reasonably up-to-date computer with a soundcard and the latest version of Reason. Some projects are CPU-intensive and require a fast computer processor with plenty of RAM (1Gb recommended). Certain examples refer to using a MIDI keyboard or a MIDI controller with knobs or faders. These procedures can be substituted by programming events in the sequencer, but a USB MIDI keyboard controller is strongly recommended.

The main requirement is a passion for technology and music. Creative use of technology has become a form of art, and different genres embrace unique production methods. The projects draw inspiration from many categories of music, especially those that verge upon the bizarre. The history of electronic music is filled with accidental discoveries, and in the spirit of experimentation, *Power Tools for Reason 3.0* carries this tradition into Propellerhead Software's virtual studio environment.

The *Power Tools for Reason* CD

Learning by example is the most efficient way to grasp the versatility of Reason, and included on the CD-ROM accompanying this book are several tracks produced by different artists. Listen to these productions and study the cabling methods and patch settings used to achieve the sound of each track. Also included with the book are a number of ReFill sample libraries, audio samples, patches, and the Reason song files necessary for the project examples.

RESOURCES.
There are many Reason-related websites where one can download more example files and tutorials: www.propellerheads.se, www.reasonstation.net, and www.peff.com.

Chapter 2
Essential Shortcuts

With only one mouse for manipulating all of Reason's controls, access to the mouse cursor is a precious commodity, especially when you're performing tasks in real time. In complicated Reason song configurations with dozens of rack devices, hundreds of control parameters are available. When accessing a menu item in real time, you have to find the cursor destination, move and click the mouse, then move the cursor back to the device in the rack. During this brief moment, the creative process is suspended while your focus of concentration shifts from the rack to the menu bar.

The essential shortcuts that help expedite the process revolve around contextual menus and Reason key commands. The protocols described in this section are referenced throughout the book and make programming more efficient.

Organization is another timesaving process. Quick access to samples and song files eases confusion as your projects become more complex. The end of this chapter describes a few strategies for organizing song files and audio samples for Reason projects.

Remote

A quietly powerful new feature in Reason is the Remote protocol, which establishes a standardized system of interfacing with different USB keyboard and control surfaces. If you use one of the supported control devices listed in the "Control Surfaces Details" documentation, then Reason can automatically set up device control. After installing the latest drivers for the control surface, connect and power the device. Launch Reason and open the Control Surfaces and Keyboards Preferences pane. Click on the Auto-detect Surfaces button, and Remote establishes the device settings.

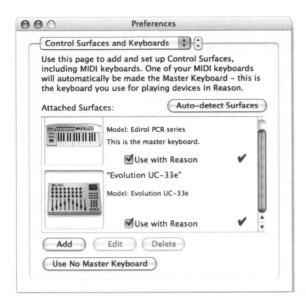

Figure 2-1
The Control Surface
Preferences pane
allows you to manage
multiple control
surfaces.

A MIDI keyboard or control surface can totally change the music production experience. It makes parameter changes faster by adding direct real-time control over the devices. Remote allows you to attach multiple USB keyboards and controllers, and several control surfaces can control many different devices in the song rack. Remote adds bi-directional communication that sends control and event data to control surfaces. On certain keyboard models, rotary controls receive parameter change updates from Reason and drum pads illuminate according to Redrum patterns.

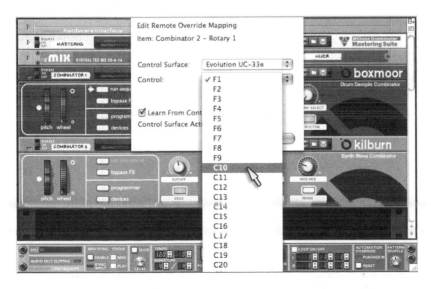

Figure 2-2
Remote Override
Mapping allows you
to quickly assign a
control surface slider
or rotary control to any
Reason parameter.

Remote Override Mapping

Remote features a standard set of knob assignments for each device. For example, slider 1 is assigned to a reMix mixer channel 1 fader. These assignments can be changed using the Remote Override feature, which lets you assign the slider to another fader, or even a parameter on another device. Right-click on the knob that you want to control. On the contextual menu, select Edit Remote Override Mapping…. Click on Learn From Control Surface Input and turn the control knob until the activity display registers incoming data. When the knob assignment is registered, click on the OK button to continue. These assignments are saved with the Reason song, so they will remain when you open it later.

On several of the default Remote settings, additional Override Mappings have useful shortcuts for surfaces with buttons. Two or four buttons control the transport play, stop, and advance. Two buttons are assigned to scroll up and down through the sequencer track list, and another two buttons are assigned to scroll through patches. With the right controller, it's possible to set up a live performance and never touch the mouse while performing because commands from the control surface can change patches and parameters and switch the sequencer track focus.

Create Device by Browsing Patches

The improved patch browser of Reason 3.0 allows you to select the specific sound you desire regardless of the type of device generating it. In other words, when a patch is selected, the sound module is added to the rack with the patch settings. This applies primarily to synthesizer, sampler, Combinator, ReCycle loops, and Redrum patches.

In the Create menu, select Create Device by Browsing Patches…. When the patch browser opens, navigate to the Reason Factory Sound Bank \ ALL Instrument Patches \ Pads directory. The patch list includes preset pad sounds for all sound modules. When you click on a patch, the device and patch are temporarily loaded into the rack.

While the device and patch are temporarily loaded, you can audition the sound by pressing keys on a MIDI keyboard controller. This functions while a sequence is playing as well, so you can quickly find a patch that fits in your track. While auditioning patches, use the computer keyboard's up and down arrow buttons to scroll through the patch list. Remember, when a sampler patch is selected, it takes a moment for the samples to load after the device is created, but synth patches load almost instantaneously.

Menus

Reason employs contextual and pop-up menus that appear at the location of the cursor. This eliminates the need to move the cursor to the menu bar and then back down to work on items in the sequencer or rack. The menu *items*, the features in the menu list, vary depending on the cursor location and selection focus, but the primary menu palettes include the Create menu items, Edit menu items, and patch and sample listings.

Contextual and pop-up menus are accessed by using the right mouse button (right-click) on computers using Microsoft Windows. Macintosh users can access the contextual menus by holding the Control key while clicking. Two-button mice are available for the Macintosh, and the software drivers can be configured so that the right button sends a Control-click.

Contextual Menus

There are several different Edit menus in Reason, and the available commands change depending on the device focus, the section, or the device selected. The Create menu is the most important contextual menu. Right click on an empty space in the device rack and the contextual menu appears for you to add a new device. A right-click on a specific device opens the Edit menu applicable to that device. Because the Edit menu items differ on each device, the contextual menu helps verify that the correct device is selected.

The features also apply to the sequencer. Right-click on various areas of the sequencer window to access menus for modifying the sequence or menus for duplicating tracks. Right-click on the track list to display a menu to quantize the events on the track or access the Change Events features.

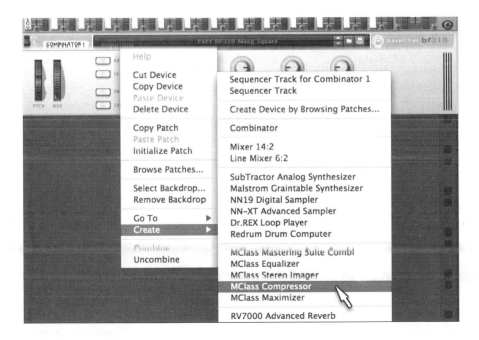

Figure 2-3

The contextual menu of the Combinator. The Create submenu opens to insert an MClass Compressor between the Combinator outputs and the mixer inputs.

Pop-Up Menus

A list of patches appears on a pop-up menu when you click on the patch name of a synth or sampler. Devices with this feature include the SubTractor and Malström synthesizers, both the NN19 and NN-XT samplers, the RV7000 Reverb, the Combinator, and the Scream 4 Distortion Unit. The Redrum Drum Computer has a pop-up menu for patch browsing and also menus on each of the drum channels for sample browsing.

If you use the Create Device by Browsing Patches feature, the pop-up Browse Patches menu in the synth panel will contain a list of patches comprised of the items from the directory you selected the patch from. In other words, if you created a SubTractor by selecting a pad patch in the ALL Instruments directory, the pop-up menu lists pad patches for Malström, NN-XT, NN-19, and Combinator as well as SubTractor pads.

ReCycle loops can be browsed using the pop-up menu by clicking on the file name on the Dr.REX Loop Player. When browsing through REX loops, click on the Preview button, which plays the loop at the current song tempo. When the new loop is loaded, preview mode automatically starts playback. This can also be done while a sequence is playing, but make sure to either delete or mute any previous REX slice data that triggers the Dr.REX.

The Malström synthesizer has a pop-up menu that lists the oscillator graintables. The graintable menus allow you to quickly select a desired graintable from the list.

Reason Key Commands

Reason key commands are keystrokes or combinations of keystrokes and mouse clicks. One of the basic key commands (one that every Reason user should know) is the Tab key, which flips the rack from the front to the rear view. Other important key commands handle the tasks of copying, pasting, undo, redo, saving your song file, and creating a new Reason song file.

The set of key commands changes depending on the mouse cursor location. The same keys may perform different functions on different devices. For example, holding down the Shift key and clicking on items selects multiple items in the rack, but this same combination behaves differently when you click on the pattern edit interface of a Matrix pattern sequencer.

Key command behavior is not consistent, but with practice, using the key commands will become second nature. The entire list of shortcuts and key modifiers is described in the "Reason Key Commands.PDF" document, which is installed when you install Reason.

Not a key command, but worth knowing about: By holding the Shift key while dragging up or down on a knob or slider, you can adjust the parameter by finer increments.

Copying and Pasting

Music has a certain degree of repetition, and using Reason's copy and paste feature to duplicate phrases helps develop a complete track more quickly. Reason's context-sensitive copy and paste features work much like those in other computer programs: There are copy and paste items in the Edit menu, but the Command/Ctrl-C (copy) and Command/Ctrl-V (paste) key command shortcuts are more convenient.

Drag & Drop Duplicate

The fastest way to copy various items in Reason is to use drag-and-drop duplicate. The drag-duplicate feature is enabled by holding down the Option (MacOS) or Ctrl (Windows) key, clicking and holding the left mouse button, and then dragging an item.

The devices have "hot spots" where dragging is enabled. The hot spot is on the rack ear at either end of the user interface. Clicking on other parts of the device interface does not enable the drag-move or drag-duplicate feature. With several devices selected in the Reason rack, the drag-duplicate feature copies all selected devices and the cables between them.

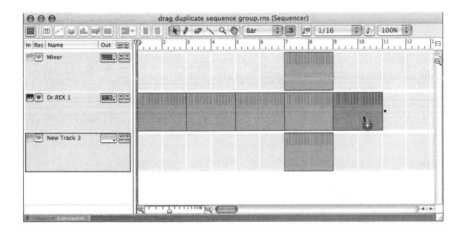

Figure 2-4
A sequencer group duplicated with the drag-and-drop duplicate feature. Groups can be duplicated along the same track or to other sequencer tracks.

The drag-and-drop duplicate feature also works on sequencer tracks and groups. Using the Option/Ctrl key while clicking and dragging on a sequencer track or group of sequencer tracks duplicates the selected track or tracks. (When doing this, click and hold first, then press Option/Ctrl.) When duplicating groups (chunks of data that you've defined using the Group command in the Edit menu) in the sequencer arrange view, it's recommended to have the snap-to-grid feature enabled with the grid resolution set to bar or 1/2 bar. The duplicate groups advance in steps according to the resolution, but the relative positions of all data within the group remains the same. With several groups from different tracks selected, entire regions of songs can be quickly duplicated.

Duplicating events on a smaller scale works well in the sequencer's edit mode. With the snap-to-grid feature enabled, set the resolution to 1/8 or 1/16 (eighth-note or sixteenth-note) steps. Groups of note events or parameter automation events can be selected and drag-duplicated.

Copy & Paste Between Files

Data from one Reason song file can be copied and pasted into another. This includes devices in the Reason rack as well as groups of devices, sequencer tracks, Redrum patterns, and Matrix Pattern Sequencer data. The effect configurations described in this book can be tedious to recreate each time one uses them in a production. Once you create the configuration and save it to a Reason song file, you can open this file alongside the song you're working on, select the devices you need, copy the devices (their connections are also copied), and paste them into a different Reason song.

Entire sequencer tracks can also be duplicated to other Reason song files. For instance, you can copy crucial timing information such as a Dr.REX slice track that is used as a quantization template. In addition, parameter automation and pattern selection data can be copied, so songs can incorporate control change information from a different song.

Redrum and Matrix patterns can be copied regardless of the song file, but it's usually easier to copy the whole device instead of the pattern. When a Redrum or Matrix is selected and duplicated, all of the patterns in it are duplicated. When a Redrum is duplicated, the sample assignments and parameter settings are duplicated as well.

Copy & Paste Automation

Reason 3.0 introduces the ability to copy and paste automation data from one control lane to another lane and between tracks as well. This is a handy feature especially when you want to copy filter sweep automation from a Malström sequencer track over to a Combinator rotary control track, or to duplicate Mixer fader automation to multiple faders.

Use the tool tip contextual menu by right-clicking on a fader and select "Edit Automation." This opens the sequencer in Edit mode to reveal the automation controller track. Using the sequencer arrow tool, select the region of automation and copy it. Click on the "Show Device Controllers" sequencer button, and move the transport position marker back to the beginning of the selected region. Click on the automation lane of the destination control, and paste the automation data into the new track.

Cable Routing

When new devices are created in the Reason rack, the modules automatically connect to sensible destination sockets. This is the "auto-routing" feature in Reason. The auto-routing feature is quite powerful, as it saves time in connecting devices. It's not a perfect process, however, and there are certain rules that should be followed when using it.

Automatic Routing Rules

Automatic routing occurs when a new device is created in the Reason rack. The outputs from the new device connect to the first available inputs above it. Creating a mixer as the first device in the rack ensures that all subsequent sound modules are automatically connected to mixer inputs. Effects, such as reverb modules, automatically connect to the mixer effect send and return sockets.

Auto-routing recognizes when an effect is applied as an insert. If you need to add a distortion to a synth output, it's not necessary to manually reconnect the audio cables. For example, click on a sound module to select it, then select the D-11 Distortion from the Create menu. The sound module connects to the D-11 audio inputs, and the D-11 outputs cable to the mixer.

When a song becomes complex, with many modules and effects, there may be times when you've deleted sound modules while their insert devices remain in the rack. New modules created below the open insert device cable to its inputs, not to the mixer. To prevent this, select the mixer before creating a new sound module.

Pasted devices are not automatically cabled. Hold down the Shift key when pasting or drag-duplicating to automatically connect the device. This also applies to duplicating groups of devices, such as a sound module with several insert effects. The last output of the signal chain automatically connects to the next available mixer input.

CV cables are only automatically cabled with the Matrix Pattern Sequencer and the Spider CV Merger & Splitter. The Matrix Pattern Sequencer gate CV and note CV sockets connect to a sound module's sequencer control inputs. With certain effects, the Matrix curve CV socket connects to a modulation input. The Matrix gate CV and note CV are also auto-routed to Spider inputs, and the Spider inserts between a Matrix and a sound module's sequencer control inputs.

Bypass Auto-Routing

On occasion, the automatic routing rules do not provide the connection required, and manual routing of cables is required. There is a key command that bypasses automatic routing: Hold down the Shift key when clicking on a device item from the Create menu. The new device will be created with no cables attached.

When a second mixer is created below the primary mixer, automatic routing connects the Aux send and master outputs of the second Mixer to the primary Mixer's chaining aux and chaining master inputs. This isn't desirable if the second mixer is used as a submixer for drum sounds, so use the bypass auto-routing feature when creating the submixer. Once the connections to the second mixer have been set, drag the second mixer above the primary mixer. New devices created at the bottom of the rack will then connect to the primary mixer, not to the submixer.

There is a second use for this feature. When connecting a cable from a device with stereo audio outputs to stereo inputs, both the left and right channels cable automatically. When the connection is made with auto-routing disabled, only one cable connects.

Auto-routing also works when disconnecting cables. If the left cable is disconnected from a stereo connection, both the left and right cables are automatically disconnected. When auto-routing is disabled, only one cable is disconnected.

Pattern Controls

The Redrum and Matrix are pattern-based devices with mini-sequencers built into them. Reason has several key commands that assist in the basic sequencer and programming functions.

Redrum Dynamics
The key to programming effective drum patterns on the Redrum Drum Computer is to use dynamic changes. Programming hard, medium, and soft events that vary through the pattern adds dynamic variation to the pattern. When programming Redrum patterns, the dynamics switch must be changed before programming a step with a louder or softer event. Once the event is programmed, the dynamics switch has to be changed back to the previous setting for a different step event. Reason key commands make this process more efficient.

Set the dynamics switch to the default, medium. Hold the Shift key and click on a pattern button to program a step with hard dynamics. Hold the Option/Alt key and click on a pattern button to program a step with soft dynamics.

Pattern Shifting
Redrum and Matrix are based on pattern sequences. The edit and contextual menus for Redrum and Matrix have items that allow you to offset a pattern. Using the edit menu or contextual menu to shift a pattern several times is time-consuming, and using the keyboard commands simplifies this task.

Shifting the Redrum and Matrix pattern left or right is achieved by holding down the Command (MacOS) or Ctrl (Windows) key and pressing "J" or "K." To shift the pattern to the right eight times, hold down the Command/Ctrl key and press "K" eight times.

The Matrix Pattern Sequencer has another set of keyboard commands to transpose the note events. Transposing the Matrix pattern up or down in semitones is done by holding down the Command (MacOS) or Ctrl (Windows) key and pressing "U" or "D."

Matrix Modifiers

The Shift key commands associated with the Matrix Pattern Sequencer provide several timesaving features. The Shift key performs three different editing functions in the Matrix. These functions differ depending where the cursor is located on the Matrix interface.

While programming gate events, holding the Shift key and clicking on gate segments creates tied events.

In the key view mode, holding the Shift key and clicking on note events enables the line tool, which is a quick way to program scale patterns. While holding the Shift key, click on a note event on any step, drag the mouse cursor to another step, and then drag the mouse up and down the key lanes until a horizontal line appears across the key view.

The line tool also applies to the Matrix curve edit mode, and works in a similar manner. Hold the Shift key and click on the curve editor on one step, set the start value of the ramp, then drag the mouse to another step and drag up or down to select the destination value of the ramp.

File Management

Like any computer application, Reason creates and uses a variety of computer files. The following tips offer ideas on keeping these files organized on your system, as well as methods for localizing files so that song projects can be moved to other systems. There are also a few file handling shortcuts that help in case there are problems.

Locations & Favorites List

The version 3 patch and song browser features two file management fields for various files. The first is the Locations field, which directs Reason toward samples, patches, and Refill file locations. The second field is the Favorites List, where users can place references to their favorite sounds and patches. Individual files or entire folders can be dragged into the Location field, then quickly found by clicking on them in the location list.

The Favorites List is like the bookmarks of a web browser. By default, there is the "Showcase" list that features some highlights from the Reason 3 Factory Soundbank. Create a new list by clicking on the "New Favorite List" button. Using the browser, find the files you want to have in the list, and drag specific patches, samples, refills, or song files into the "New Favorite List" item. Double-clicking on the list item enables the edit field so that you can customize the list name. As mentioned, you can place song files in the list to organize song projects or playlists for live performances.

Figure 2-5
The File Browser
Locations and
Favorites lists help
organize patches you
frequently use as
well as ReFills and
samples in your
sound library.

File & Patch Search

The Reason File and Patch browser includes a search field to help you quickly locate files without navigating through different directory levels. Try to make the search as efficient as possible by navigating to the directory or ReFill where the item can be located. Set the Search In item to "Current Folder" and find the file you're looking for. You can also search for file extensions like ".cmb" to find all Combinator Patches.

Organizing ReFills

Many free and commercial ReFill Sample Libraries are available, and with the introduction of Reload, users can create their own ReFills from Akai S1000/S3000 CD-ROMs. The number and size of ReFills on your hard drive can grow incredibly fast, and you may find the need to move these to another drive.

Create a folder called "ReFills" and move your ReFill files into this directory. The ReFill folder can be on any drive mounted on your system, including external FireWire devices and network drives. Reason looks within the application directory for the Factory Sound Bank and Orkester ReFills, and these Refills should remain in the application folder. Open the Reason Song Browser by selecting the "Open…" item in the File menu and navigate to the parent directory of the "ReFills" folder. Once this is located, drag the ReFills Folder icon into the "Locations" list in the Browser window.

On the *Power Tools for Reason* CD-ROM are a number of ReFill sample libraries. Copy these from the CD-ROM into your ReFill folder.

Custom New Song File

When the New Song item is selected in the File menu, the default song is opened. When you get tired of listening to the factory song, you can go to Reason's General Preferences pane and choose an empty rack for your default song. However, there's a better way. Usually, the first few items you'll create in the empty rack are a mixer, a few effects processors, and perhaps a few sound modules. You can also modify the song information. This saves time in typing the copyright, website, and email information. Save this song file in the Reason application folder so it can be easily located.

Select Preferences/General and click on the radio button labeled "Custom." Click on the file browser button, locate the custom song file saved in the Reason application folder, and click on Open. When you select the "New" item from the File menu, the customized song file will be created.

Project Folders

A Reason song can easily become quite intricate with the use of samples and ReCycle loop files, so it's wise to organize song projects in unique folders. When starting a new song project, create a project folder on your hard drive and save the Reason song file into this directory. All files associated with the song, such as patches and samples, should also be saved in this folder.

Saving Duplicate Song Files

You should save copies of each Reason song file as the project progresses. This creates a working history of the song development. If you make drastic changes and later decide they were a mistake, you can revert to an older version. Establish a numbering system to keep the history organized. For example, save the first file as "My Reason Track 000.rns," and increase the digits as the song progresses. Name the files in sequential order—"My Reason Track 001.rns," "My Reason Track 002.rns," etc. Save these files into the project folder. Don't save song files to the desktop and move them. Reason is sensitive to file paths, and moving files around may cause problems.

Patches & Samples

Patch settings are easily lost, especially when you're making several parameter changes. Since Reason is limited in the number of undo levels it supports, it's wise to save patches. Save these patches in subdirectories of the project folder. A numbering system can be used with patch names so you'll remember when they were created.

Create a sample directory inside the project folder. Reason is sensitive to file paths, so the samples should be in the project directory before they are loaded. If there's a problem, Reason prompts you to find and replace samples. To fix this, move a copy of the sample into the save directory level along with the song file. When Reason opens a song, it will scan the song file directory for the samples.

A self-contained song file includes the samples and loops imbedded in the file. If you're collaborating with another Reason user or moving the track to another computer and if you're using any audio files that are not contained in ReFills, the self-contained option is the easiest way to ensure playback integrity. The resulting song files can be large, however, and having many duplicates consumes disk space.

Back Up Song Files

Back up your files—this should be the mantra of any computer user. With the time and energy you put into creating songs, taking a little time to back up the Reason song files after each work session is the only way to prevent the loss of critical data. Saving multiple files safeguards your project if one file becomes corrupt, but backing up the entire project folder to a separate physical device protects your work in the horrible event of a fatal hard drive problem or a stolen computer. This can be considered the mother of all shortcuts. It saves time and potential trauma, should disaster strike.

Chapter 3
Control Voltages

Electrical currents called control voltages govern the processes of analog synthesizer systems. Vintage modular synthesizers manufactured by companies like Moog Music and Buchla & Associates have multitudes of connector jacks on the front panels. Some jacks route audio signals from one module to another. Other jacks connect control voltages (CVs) between the modules. When modules are connected by patch cords, control voltages from one module can trigger events or alter parameters in other modules. Complex sounds are created by using dozens of cords connected in unique modulation and audio signal routings. This is the origin of the term "synthesizer patch."

Patching CV and audio signals between devices is a powerful way to create unique sounds, and while Reason doesn't use true control voltages (it's a digital device), it operates as if it did. Understanding the theory behind control voltages is essential for developing the custom modulation routings used in patches throughout this book.

Control voltages do not directly modify audio signals. Instead, a module like a filter alters the audio signal, and the CV affects the behavior of the filter. A value change initiated by a control voltage is called a *modulation*. A typical modulation routing is a low-frequency oscillator (LFO) triangle wave output patched to the pitch control of a voltage-controlled oscillator (VCO). As the voltage level from the LFO rises and falls, the oscillator pitch increases and decreases, creating vibrato. The LFO CV is not combined with the audio signal. Instead, the CV value from the LFO is added to another value that determines the oscillator pitch.

Another common modulation is an envelope generator patched to a voltage-controlled amplifier (VCA). When a key is pressed on the keyboard, a gate CV (basically, a voltage that works like an on/off switch) triggers the envelope generator. The envelope generator's CV signal rises and falls, and this signal changes the VCA loudness level. The audio signal at the VCA's output increases and decreases in level according to the level of the envelope CV.

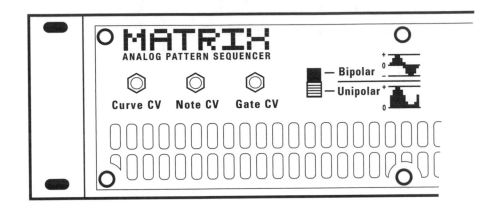

Figure 3-1
The Matrix Pattern
Sequencer's CV
outputs.

On most analog modular systems, multiple patch cords can be connected from the same source, so an envelope CV can be routed to the VCA, a voltage-controlled filter (VCF), and the VCO simultaneously. In most contemporary synthesizers, modulation routings are less flexible. Patch cords are no longer an option, and CV signals are often limited to a single destination. For instance, on the SubTractor synthesizer front panel, the LFO 1 signal can be routed to modulate only one parameter at a time, but this only applies to the front panel. On the rear of the rack, Reason CV signals can target multiple destinations, and by using a Combinator, CV signals can modulate almost every front panel parameter. In essence, a Reason rack is a modular synthesizer with an endless number of modules and patch cords.

Reason CV Connections

In a CV cable routing, there is a source, a destination, and an amount (also known as scale or sensitivity) control. On the rear view of the Reason virtual rack, most devices have CV modulation sockets, graphically depicted as minijacks similar to those on modular analog synthesizers. These sockets provide access points for CV connections. "Out" or "Mod Output" sockets indicate sources, while most CV destinations are labeled with "CV In" or "Modulation Input." Modulation routings within Reason devices and CV signals available on output jacks are the same type of data. The LFO 1 signal operating within a SubTractor is the same signal available from the LFO 1 modulation output.

CV Values

Within the software, Reason CV signals are floating point numbers, but these values are best understood in terms of MIDI continuous controller values, which range from 0 to 127. Certain control voltage signals are strictly integer values, while others are truly floating point. The difference is that integer values create artifacts called *zipper noise*, where each value change causes a noticeable, stepped sound. The resolution of floating point CV values allow for smooth modulations free of zipper noise.

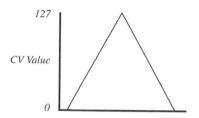 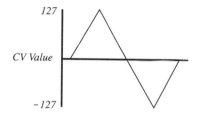

Figure 3-2
Unipolar CV curves have a range between 0 and 127. Bipolar CV curve values range between −127 and 127.

There are two varieties of control voltages, unipolar and bipolar. Unipolar control voltages are positive values that range from 0 to127. Bipolar control voltages have both positive and negative values that range between −127 and 127. Control voltages can be inverted in order to impose a negative modulation, so a unipolar CV signal inverted has a range of −127 to 0.

Reason's CV signals fall into three categories: Note CV, Gate CV, and Curve CV. Curve signals are general-purpose modulation sources that take advantage of the high-resolution floating-point arithmetic, and have fractional values between 0 and 127 (or between −127 and 127). Note CV signals are unipolar values that increase at integer steps associated with MIDI note numbers. Gate CV signals are related to MIDI velocity messages, which are typically integer values between 1 and 127.

Reason CV Sources

The number of CV patching permutations is virtually limitless depending on the Reason device configuration in a song file, but there are only a few specific types of sources: the note, gate, and curve outputs from the Matrix, plus LFOs, envelopes, Malström modulators, the Scream 4 envelope follower, the BV512 Vocoder band levels, MClass Gain Reduction, and the Spider CV. The following sections detail the particular behavior of the different CV sources. Understanding how the sources operate will illustrate the types of modulations you can establish with CV connections.

Note CV

Note CV signals correspond to the MIDI note numbers in the chromatic scale (where Middle C has a value of 60). These control voltages send note values to the different sound modules, and are generated by the Matrix Pattern Sequencer. The CV value is determined by the note programmed in the key edit view of the Matrix. The lowest value is at C1, which has the numeric equivalent of 36, and the highest value is C6, which has the numeric value of 96. The Matrix Note CV is limited to a

60 value range, but for most musical applications, this is adequate. Note CV values are stepped at integer intervals, so increasing the Note CV from C1 to D1 jumps in value from 36 to 38.

Gate CV/Velocity

Gate CV signals are pulses that trigger events. Normally the signal on a gate connection is zero. When an event occurs, the gate value jumps to a value between 1 and 127, then returns back to zero. The unipolar gate value is also called *velocity* and indicates the intensity of an event. Gate control voltages can modulate the loudness of a sound, and higher gate CV values will translate to louder notes. A zero value or *zero velocity* indicates that the note/trigger is off.

The Redrum, Dr.REX, and Matrix have gate CV outputs, which generate gate impulses that can trigger other devices. Each of the Redrum channels has a gate CV output, and when the channel is triggered, a gate impulse appears at this socket. The Dr.REX has only one gate CV output. Each time a slice is triggered, a gate impulse appears on this socket. The Matrix gate CV signals follow the values of the gate events programmed in the pattern.

Matrix gate impulses are paired with note control voltages, and typically, these connect to sequencer control inputs on sound modules. The gate CV triggers a note event, and the note CV specifies the pitch. The gate CV provides a velocity value, which can be used to modulate the note event dynamics. Normal Matrix gate events are half the duration of the step resolution. If the Matrix Sequencer is set with a resolution of sixteenth-notes, the gate event duration is a 32nd-note. The duration of *tied* gate events equals the step resolution, and adjacent steps can be tied together to form a longer gate event.

Redrum gate CV impulses vary depending on the module's decay/gate and length settings. If the Redrum channel is set to decay mode, the gate duration is very short. In gate mode, the duration is longer, being determined by the length setting. Dr.REX gate signals are very short and are very similar to those coming from the Redrum channels in decay mode.

Matrix Curve CV

Matrix curve CV signals are general-purpose modulation sources that are either unipolar or bipolar, selected by a polarity switch on the rear of the unit. The Matrix curve display changes depending on the polarity. In bipolar mode, the display shows a zero-crossing line across the middle. Events above the line are positive values, and events below the line are negative.

The Matrix curve CV can modulate any parameter in Reason for which there is a rear-panel CV input jack. A common use of the curve CV is to modulate the cutoff frequency of an ECF-42 Filter module. Different values for each pattern step generate a CV signal that modulates the filter, repeating each time the pattern cycles.

Low-Frequency Oscillator CV

Low-frequency oscillators (LFOs) are curve CV generators. LFO CV signals are found on almost all synthesizers. LFOs cycle continuously and don't require an external trigger source. They can run freely or synchronize to the song tempo, and the rate parameter controls the frequency of the cycle. The LFO Sync button enables tempo synchronization, in which the waveform locks to the start of the sequence and provides a consistent curve signal. Several Reason devices have LFO features, but only the SubTractor, NN19, and Dr.REX have LFO CV output sockets. The functions are the same for all three devices.

LFO CV signals are bipolar, and generate a curve determined by the waveform shape parameter. A SubTractor LFO set to a triangle wave generates a CV signal that behaves as follows: The signal starts at zero, rises to 127, falls back to zero, dips to −127, and then rises back up to zero. The ramp waveforms generate CV curves that rise from −127 to 127 or fall from 127 to −127. The square wave is an impulse signal that starts at 127, drops to −127, and jumps back up to 127. The last two waveforms are random signal generators. The first random waveform is stepped; a stepped random CV value is often known as *sample-and-hold*—a random control voltage is sampled (that is, its value is determined) and then held briefly before a new random value is sampled. The other random waveform is smooth: the CV signal randomly sweeps between values.

Envelope CV

Envelope generators create curve CV signals with specific time characteristics. Envelopes are crucial for modulating the volume of synthesizer or sampler note events, but this time-controlled CV can be used in a variety of applications like changing pitch or filter cutoff frequency, which is why devices like SubTractor have three envelope generators. Every sound module in Reason has some form of envelope generator, but envelope CV sources are found only on the SubTractor, Dr.REX, NN19, and Malström.

Envelope CV signals are unipolar, and rely on a gate trigger to initiate the envelope. When triggered, the envelope CV rises and falls, but until then, the CV value is zero. Two factors determine the rate of change—the envelope's attack, decay, sustain, and release parameters, and the duration of the gate event triggering the envelope.

The attack, decay, and release values control the length (time) stages of the envelope. The sustain value controls a CV level value. When a trigger is received from either gate CV or MIDI note-on events, the envelope CV value increases from 0 to 127 at the rate determined by the attack setting. Once the envelope peaks at 127, the CV value decreases at the rate set the by the decay setting. The destination CV value of the envelope decay is set by the sustain parameter. The envelope CV maintains the sustain value until the gate CV or MIDI note-on event switches off. When the gate is switched off, the envelope CV decreases from the sustain level back to zero. The time it takes to fall back to zero is determined by the release setting.

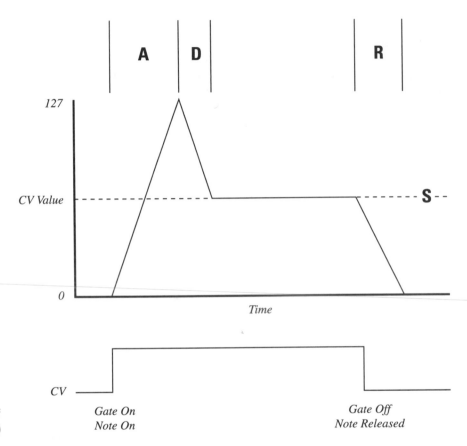

Figure 3-3
An ADSR envelope CV signal rises to a level of 127, and falls back to 0 when the gate ends.

The release stage works independently of the gate duration. If the gate stops at a point in the middle of the attack phase, the CV value stops rising and decreases back to zero. This also applies if the trigger stops in the middle of the decay stage of the envelope. If the attack and decay rates are set to zero, the envelope CV signal instantly rises from zero to the sustain level when the envelope is triggered. When the gate ends, the envelope CV signal decreases to zero at the release rate (see Figure 3-4).

Malström Modulator CV
Each Malström Graintable Synthesizer has two modulation sources, which are labeled Mod A and Mod B. Both have the same basic functions, but they have different modulation routings within the synthesizer. On the rear of the Malström, a CV modulation output socket is provided for each modulator.

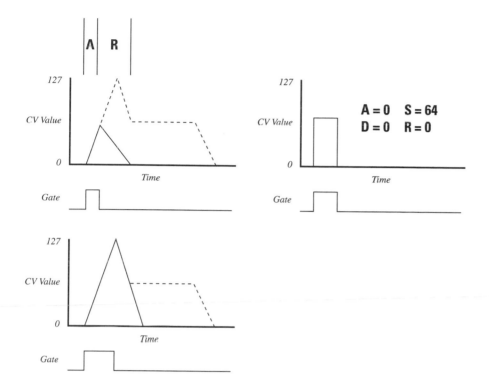

Figure 3-4
The gate duration changes the ADSR's output curve.

Modulators are curve CV generators, and are similar to LFOs, but they feature 32 waveforms. Some waveforms are unipolar, while others are bipolar. The waveform icons indicate the polarity of each modulator curve. Icons seated in the upper half of the waveform display are unipolar. Icons that use the entire display are bipolar. Modulator curves reset each time the Malström receives note or gate events; otherwise the output behaves like an LFO, cycling at a frequency controlled by the rate and sync parameters. The one-shot feature alters the modulator so that it behaves like an envelope. With the 1 shot button enabled, the Modulator waits for a gate event. Once triggered, the modulator cycles through the waveform and stops after one period. The rate and sync parameters control the duration of the modulator cycle.

Scream 4 Envelope Follower CV

The Scream 4 Sound Destruction Unit has a unique CV output labeled "Auto CV Output." The Scream 4 has an internal envelope follower. An envelope follower creates a CV signal based on the loudness of the audio signal received by the Scream 4. The auto CV output values are unipolar, and when the input audio signal is silent, the CV value is zero. When the input audio signal peaks to maximum, the CV value is 127.

The envelope follower establishes a variety of modulation possibilities, because it links audio signals with CV signals. The Scream's auto CV output can be connected to the pitch modulation of a SubTractor, for instance, while a Dr.REX loop feeds a signal into the Scream 4. The pitch of the SubTractor is then determined by the loudness of the drum hits: Louder hits drive the pitch higher.

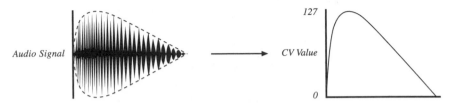

Figure 3-5
The Scream 4 envelope follower's CV output.

Vocoder Band Level CV

The BV512 Vocoder device has another unique CV source similar that of the Scream 4. Each of the 16 band level CV outputs acts as a frequency-dependent envelope follower. When the vocoder is set to four-, eight-, or 16-band mode, the band level outputs correspond to the band levels on the analyzer. In 32-band or FFT mode, the CV outputs reflect the levels of adjacent pairs of bands. The Band Level CV signals are unipolar. When the analyzer detects frequencies in the range associated with a vocoder band, a CV signal is generated depending on the intensity of the frequencies in that range.

The attack and decay parameters on the BV512 contour the envelope follower's response. The attack parameter controls the rate at which a band level can increase, while the decay parameter controls how fast it decreases. When the attack and decay settings are at zero, the band levels and the corresponding CV values change rapidly. Higher decay settings can generate a lag effect, where the peak level briefly holds before the band level CV decays to zero.

MClass Compressor Gain Reduction CV

The MClass Compressor Module features a unipolar CV signal that reflects the amount of gain reduction applied in the dynamics processor. This is similar to an envelope follower in the Scream 4 or BV512, but instead of corresponding to the levels of input signals, this CV follows the amount of compression determined by the MClass parameters and the level of the input audio signal.

The Compressor generates CV signals only when an audio signal is greater than the threshold setting, and it can be set to respond to only very loud audio signals. The threshold feature makes the device useful as a transient gate source. The ratio parameter controls the intensity of the gain reduction, and this parameter should always be set to a value of 1.2:1 or greater when using the Compressor as a CV source. A setting of 1.00:1 does not impose any gain reduction, and subsequently CV values remain at zero. The attack and release parameters alter the gain reduction behavior and thus affect the gain reduction CV value. These function like BV512 envelope parameters, controlling the rate of increase and decrease. Minimum settings will respond quickly to the natural envelope of incoming audio signals.

Spider CV

The Spider CV Merger and Splitter module does not generate CV signals, but it includes a signal inverter, which modifies control voltages. The inverted signal becomes a new modulation source, and an inverted unipolar curve imposes negative modulation on a parameter.

A control voltage connected to a splitter input is inverted on the fourth splitter out socket. This means that a CV signal with a value of 32 going into the splitter has a value of –32 on the inv jack. Because the Spider will split and invert control voltages, symmetrical inverted signals can impose a mirror image modulation. One device is connected to the normal splitter output (Out 1, Out 2, or Out 3), and the other device is connected to the inverted Out 4. The pitch modulation is opposite for the two devices (see Figure 3-6).

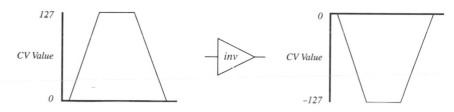

Figure 3-6
A CV inverted by the
Spider CV Splitter.

Modulation Amount

On the front panels of Reason devices, modulation sources have *amount* parameters that control the intensity of the modulation. For example, a filter envelope generates a unipolar signal that starts at 0 and rises to a value of 127. If the filter envelope amount is set to 64, then the modulation is scaled to 50%, and the peak modulation value is 64. Modulation amount varies on different sources, and when the amount is set to 127, the internal routing of the SubTractor LFO has a range of ± 64. The amount parameter does not affect the LFO CV value on the rear socket, which has a range of ±127.

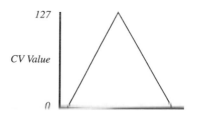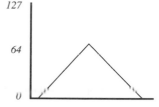

Figure 3-7
The trim knob scales
CV values.

Both internal modulation routings and incoming control voltages are added to current parameter settings. If a filter cutoff parameter is 80, the value from the Filter Envelope generator is added to 80. When the sum of the parameter value and modulation reaches 127, the modulation peaks at the maximum value until the combined value decreases below 127. Carefully setting the amount parameter prevents this modulation clipping, and for external CV inputs, the CV Trim knobs provide a means to scale input signals.

The CV trim knobs located next to the modulation input sockets on various Reason devices attenuate incoming CV signals. These controls function like the LFO amount, mod amount, and envelope amount knobs located on the front panels. The default setting is 64, which scales the range 50% from 0 to 64 for unipolar signals or ± 64 for bipolar signals.When the trim is set to 0, no modulation is applied from incoming CV. Turning the trim knob to 127 allows the full modulation range. For example, a bipolar LFO curve connected to a Combinator rotary CV input will modulate the rotary value ±127 when the input trim is set to 127. If the rotary control is set to 0, the positive phase of the LFO modulates the rotary from 0 to 127, while the negative phase clips at 0.

CV Signals Are Universal

CV outputs must be connected to CV inputs, and any of the three types of CV signals can be used as a source (output). Typically, the Matrix gate CV and note CV outputs are connected to the corresponding gate and CV inputs on the sound modules, but you can switch these, or use the curve CV output as the source of gate signals, or use gate signals to modulate note CV inputs. The result of mismatching CV source types and destination types is not always predictable. Trial-and-error patching often leads to something unusually interesting. The next few examples demonstrate that these signals are interchangeable.

Figure 3-8
SubTractor LFO
connected to Redrum
gate CV input.

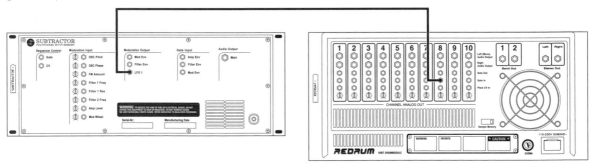

LFO Triggering Gate Events

A square/pulse waveform from an LFO can be used to generate gate CV signals that trigger events on the sound modules or the ECF-42 Envelope Controlled Filter. Since the SubTractor LFO is free-running, note events occur as soon as the connection is made. Enabling the Sync feature on the LFO will trigger these events in time with the master tempo of the track.

1. In an empty rack, create a reMix mixer.
2. Create a Redrum Drum Computer and load the patch "Abstract Kit 01.drp" from the Reason Factory Soundbank\Redrum Drum Kits\Abstract HipHop Kits directory.
3. Create a SubTractor Synthesizer Module.
4. Connect the SubTractor Modulation Output LFO 1 output to the Redrum channel 8 gate input.
5. Set LFO 1 to a square wave. (Some of the other waves will offset the LFO wave in relation to the beat.)
6. Adjust the LFO 1 rate knob lower for regular hi-hat hits, adjust the rate higher for some unique rapid hi-hat sample smearing, or adjust it to 16/4 so the hi-hat channel triggers only once every four measures.

Matrix Curve as a Gate CV Source

The Matrix curve CV can be used as a gate CV source. Since the duration of a curve CV event is a full pattern step, it behaves like a tied gate event. In fact, there is one application of this configuration that works better than gate events. The maximum value of a Matrix gate event is 126. If the Matrix is used to trigger an NN-XT sample zone mapped to a velocity of 127, the Matrix gate does not trigger the zone.

Figure 3-9
Matrix curve CV connected to Malström gate CV input.

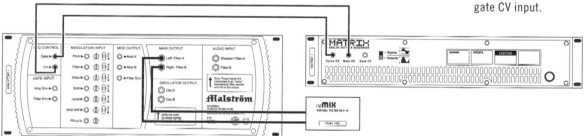

1. In an empty rack, create a reMix mixer.
2. Create a Malström Graintable Synthesizer.
3. On the Malström, set the LVL:A velocity setting to 41
4. Bypass auto-routing by holding down the Shift key, and create a Matrix Pattern Sequencer.
5. Connect the Matrix curve CV output to the Malström seq control gate input.
6. Connect the Matrix note CV socket to the Malström seq control CV input.

7. Program the following pattern on the Matrix. The curve values shown are approximate:

Matrix 1 (Steps 1–16)

Step	1	2	3	4	5	6	7	8	9	10	11	12	13	14	15	16
Curve	64	0	32	0	96	0	10	0	80	0	64	0	96	0	24	0
Note	C4	C4	C4	C3	C3	C3	C4	C4	C4	C3	C3	C3	C4	C4	C4	C3
Gate																

▸ Press Run on the Matrix to hear the curve events gate the Malström.

Using a Gate to Control a Note CV Input

The Matrix in the preceding example isn't doing anything you couldn't do with its gate CV output. The point of the experiment is simply to show that the curve CV can be used as a gate. This example demonstrates that note and gate CV signals are interchangeable. The only specific difference is the behavior of the source signals. Gate CV signals last for half of the time value of a Matrix step, and then fall back to zero. Note CV outputs from the Matrix are fixed for the duration of the step, as are curve CV outputs. The resolution of curve CV values is not as precise as that of the note CV, because the note values correspond to MIDI note numbers. The note CV will always be between 36 and 96, while the curve value has a wider range.

1. In an empty rack, create a reMix mixer.
2. Create a SubTractor Synthesizer Module.
3. Connect the SubTractor modulation output from LFO 1 back to the sequencer control gate input of the SubTractor. The SubTractor will start to beep.
4. Bypass auto-routing and create a Matrix Pattern Sequencer.
5. Connect the Matrix gate CV to the SubTractor sequencer control CV input. The beeping will drop to a low pitch.
6. Program gate events from steps 1 through 16 on the Matrix.
▸ Press Run on the Matrix.

+ play with Subtractor knobs etc.

Envelope CV Gate Source

Envelope curves with short durations behave like gate CV impulses. The SubTractor envelope modulation output can trigger a Redrum channel, for instance. A chain of gate CV events can be created to trigger several different sources simultaneously.

1. Start with an empty rack and create a reMix mixer.
2. Create a SubTractor Synthesizer.

PROGRAMMING TABLE ABBREVIATIONS. Throughout this book, the letters H, M, and L are used in programming tables for Matrix and Redrum patterns. H refers to a high-velocity event, M to a medium-velocity event, and L to a low-velocity event. In the Matrix, the values are approximations as shown here. The letter T is used in Matrix tables to refer to a tied gate event.

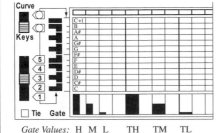

Gate Values: H M L   TH   TM   TL

3. Set the mod envelope attack and decay to 0, sustain to 127, and release to 0.
4. Create a Matrix Pattern Sequencer.
5. Program the following Matrix pattern (note: the letter 'H' in the Gate row indicates that you're to put a normal gate event on that step):

Matrix 1 (Steps 1–16)

Step	1	2	3	4	5	6	7	8	9	10	11	12	13	14	15	16
Curve																
Note	C3	C3	C3	C3	C3	C3	C3	C3	C3	C3	C3	C3	C3	C3	C3	C3
Gate	H				H				H		H		H			

6. Create a Redrum Drum Computer.
7. Load the Redrum patch "Electronic Kit 1.drp" from the Reason Factory Sound Bank\Redrum Drum Kits\Electronic Kits directory.
8. Connect the SubTractor mod envelope modulation output to the Redrum channel 3 gate in socket.
▸ Run the Matrix pattern.

The Matrix sequence triggers note events on the SubTractor Synthesizer. As each note event occurs, the modulation envelope is triggered, sending a gate-like CV signal to the Redrum.

Modulator as a Note CV Source

This example should eliminate any question about the nature of control voltage signals. Instead of using a Matrix note CV to control the pitch of a SubTractor synthesizer, a ramp signal from a Malström modulation source sends note CV data to the SubTractor (see Figure 3-10).

1. Start with an empty rack and create a reMix mixer.
2. Create a SubTractor Synthesizer.
3. Set the SubTractor Polyphony to 1, and Filter 1 Freq to 127.
4. Create a Matrix Pattern Sequencer.
5. Set the Matrix pattern to one step and program a tied gate event on Step 1.
6. Disconnect the cable connected to the Matrix sequencer control CV output.
7. Bypass auto-routing and create a Malström Graintable Synthesizer.
8. Connect the Malström mod A output to the SubTractor sequencer control CV input.
9. Set the Malström mod A rate to 1 and modulator curve to 12 (ramp).
▸ Run the Matrix.   *Try ramp down for bass drop*

As the ramp signal from the Malström increases, the SubTractor note pitch also increases. Each value of the control voltage signal is equal to a half-step.

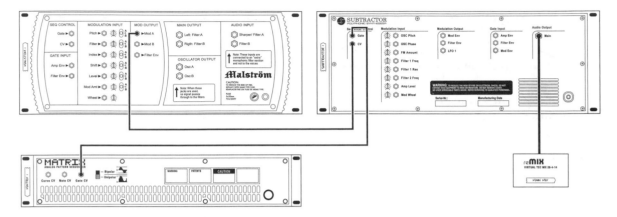

Figure 3-10
Malström modulator
CV sending note CV
events.

Merging & Splitting CV Signals

The Spider CV Merger & Splitter performs the simple functions of merging CV signals and splitting CV signals so you can distribute a control voltage to several inputs. This section illustrates a few common uses of merging, splitting, and inverting CV signals.

Matrix CV/Gate Splitting

This is a method for creating polyphonic tracks from a single Matrix pattern. Although the intervals are fixed to the oscillator tuning, splitting the Matrix CV/gate signals can be used to layer or stack oscillators for thicker sounds.

1. Start with an empty rack, and create a reMix mixer.
2. Create three SubTractor Synthesizers.
3. Bypass auto-routing and create a Matrix Pattern Sequencer.
4. Bypass auto-routing and create a Spider CV.
5. Connect the Matrix note CV output to the Spider CV split A input.
6. Connect the Matrix gate CV output to the Spider CV split B input.
7. Connect the split A outputs to each of the SubTractors' sequencer control CV inputs.
8. Connect the split B outputs to each of the SubTractors' sequencer control gate inputs.
9. Program the following Matrix pattern:

Matrix 1 (Steps 1–16)															
Step	1	2	3	4	5	6	7	8	9	10	11	12	13	14	15	16
Curve																
Note	C3	C2	C3	C3	C2	C3	C3	C2	C3	C2	C3	C3	C2	C3	C3	C2
Gate	H	H	H	H	H	H	H	H	H	H	H	H	H	H	H	H

10. On all three SubTractors, load the patch "Acid Saw 2" from the Reason Factory Sound Bank\SubTractor Patches\MonoSynth directory.
11. On SubTractor 1, adjust osc 1 and osc 2 semitone settings to 7.
12. On SubTractor 2, adjust osc 1 cent setting to 0 and osc 2 cent setting to –8.
13. On SubTractor 3, adjust osc 1 and osc 2 octave settings to 4.
14. Pan mixer channel 1 to –63.
15. Pan mixer channel 2 to 64.
▶ Run the Matrix.

Adjust the values of the Matrix gate events to produce an accent pattern.

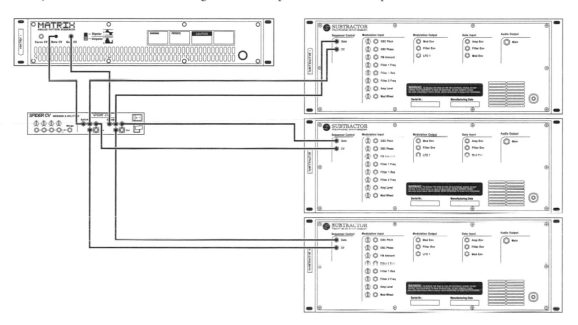

Figure 3-11
Splitting the Matrix note CV and gate CV to three SubTractors.

Merged Modulator CV Signals

Complex modulation patterns can be created by merging several CV sources together. This examples uses modulators A and B from a Malström, merges them, and modulates the pitch of the oscillator.

1. In an empty rack, create a reMix mixer.
2. Create a Malström Graintable Synthesizer.
3. Enable sync on mod A and mod B.
4. Set the mod A rate to 1/8.
5. Set the mod B rate to 4/4.
6. Set the mod B waveform to curve 9.
7. Create a Spider CV while disabling auto-routing.

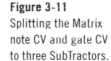

8. Connect the Malström mod A and mod B outputs to the Spider CV merger input 1 and input 2.

9. Connect the Spider CV merge output to the Malström pitch modulation input

▸ Play a note from a MIDI controller directed to the Malström to hear the effect of the combined modulation signals on the pitch of the note.

Figure 3-12
Merging two Malström modulator CV signals.

Try play chords + hold sequences to stagger starts... try adjusting these

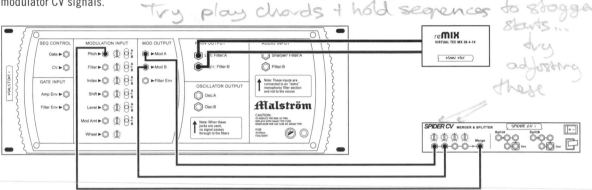

also mess with the Malström settings.

Matrix-Controlled Cross-Pan

This example demonstrates using the Spider CV inverter to modulate panning. Using the Spider CV signal inverter and splitter, the Matrix curve CV modulates panning on two mixer channels. The reversed modulations result in the two channels panning in opposite directions.

1. In an empty rack, create a reMix mixer.
2. Create two Dr.REX Loop Players.
3. On Dr.REX 1, load the Recycle file "125_Moogerized2_mLp_eLAB.rx2" from the Factory Sound Bank from the Music Loops\Variable Tempo (rex2)\ Uptempo Loops directory.
4. Copy the REX data to the Dr.REX 1 sequencer track.
5. From the Same directory, load the file "130_Circle_mLp_eLAB.rx2" into Dr.REX 2.
6. Copy the REX data to the Dr.REX 2 sequencer track.
7. Create a Spider CV Merger & Splitter.
8. Bypass auto-routing and create a Matrix Pattern Sequencer.
9. On the rear panel, set the Matrix to bipolar mode.
10. Connect the Matrix curve CV output to the Spider CV split A input socket.
11. Connect a Spider CV split A output to the pan CV in socket on channel 1 of the mixer.
12. Connect the Spider CV split A inv output socket to the mixer's channel 2 pan CV input.
13. Set the mixer's rear-panel pan CV trim to 64 on input channels 1 and 2.

nice subtle effect

14. Set the Matrix pattern to 32 steps.
15. On the Matrix, draw a curve ramp from −127 to 127 starting at step 1 and ending at step 32.
▸ Run the sequence.

As the sequence runs, the Matrix curve CV modulates the panning on channels 1 and 2. The inverted curve CV signal causes channel 1 to pan left while channel 2 pans right, and vice-versa. Although the pan parameter ranges from −64 to 63, the Pan CV inputs require a full bipolar signal (±127) to modulate a hard left to hard right pan, so the input trim should be set to 127.

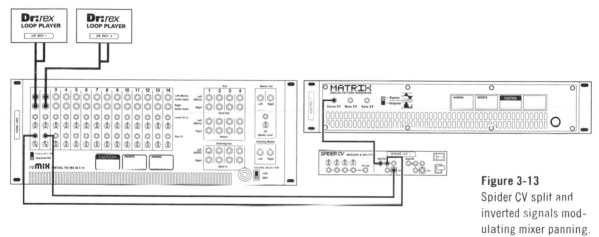

Figure 3-13
Spider CV split and inverted signals modulating mixer panning.

Matrix CV Examples

The Matrix Pattern Sequencer is the most versatile source for control voltages in Reason. Its primary function is to generate monophonic music patterns that trigger note events in the sound modules, but it has many applications beyond note sequencing. The following examples demonstrate a variety of uses, and others are described throughout this book.

Matrix Curve LFO

This technique creates an LFO modulation curve that is synchronized to the tempo. This is an obsolete method since the LFO sources in all Reason devices feature tempo sync, but you can't control the phase (waveform starting point) of these LFO sources. The Matrix curve can be offset by shifting the pattern using the edit menu or keyboard commands, thus altering the phase of the modulation shape.

1. In an empty rack, create a reMix mixer.
2. Create a SubTractor Synthesizer.
3. Create a Matrix Pattern Sequencer.
4. In the Matrix, program tied gate events from step 1 through step 16.

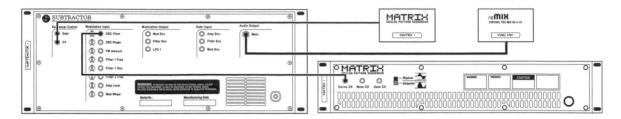

Figure 3-14
Patching two Matrix
Sequencers with offset
patterns.

5. Bypass auto-routing and create another Matrix.
6. On Matrix 2, pattern A1, set the pattern length to 32 steps and the resolution to 1/128.
7. Hit the Tab key to flip the rack to the rear view and switch Matrix 2 to bipolar mode.
8. Cable the Matrix 2 Curve CV output to the SubTractor osc pitch mod input socket.
9. Set the SubTractor osc pitch mod trim to 12.
10. Switch Matrix 2 into curve edit mode.
11. Enable the line tool and draw a triangle wave starting at the zero crossing on step 1 with a peak on step 9 and a trough at step 25.
12. Select the two Matrixes and the SubTractor. Hold down the Alt/Option key and drag the duplicate group of devices to the bottom of the rack.
13. Connect the SubTractor 1 Copy to mixer input channel 2.
14. Select Matrix 2 Copy.
15. From the Edit menu, select the item Shift Pattern Right, or type Ctrl-K. Repeat this 15 more times until the triangle wave trough is in the first half of the pattern and the peak in the second half.
16. Pan mixer channel 1 hard left and mixer channel 2 hard right.
   ▸ Run the sequence.

experiment with some steps 'tied'

Matrix Arpeggiator Effect
An arpeggio is a musical chord where the notes are played in a sequence rather than simultaneously. Some electronic instruments have built-in arpeggiators that perform this musical task. Typically, when a chord is played on the synthesizer keyboard, the arpeggiator plays a sequence starting with the lowest key and moving up to the highest key, then back down to the lowest key. Reason does not have an arpeggiator, but this effect can be simulated. The configuration below is a polyphonic arpeggiator and requires note events from a MIDI keyboard or from the sequencer.

experiment

1. In an empty rack, create a reMix mixer.
2. Create a SubTractor.
3. Load the SubTractor patch "Sweeping Strings" from the Reason Factory Sound bank\SubTractor Patches\Pads directory.

4. Edit the SubTractor patch by changing the osc 1 and osc 2 octave setting to 2.
5. Bypass auto-routing and create a Matrix.
6. Cable the Matrix note CV output to the SubTractor osc pitch modulation input.
7. Set the SubTractor osc pitch modulation trim to 127.
8. Switch the Matrix Keys view to Octave 1.
9. Set the Matrix pattern length to 6 steps.
10. Edit the pattern to create a C minor arpeggio:

Matrix C Minor Arpeggio (Steps 1–6)						
Step	1	2	3	4	5	6
Curve						
Note	C1	E♭1	G1	C2	G1	E♭1
Gate	H	H	H	H	H	H

11. Press Run on the Matrix, and enable MIDI on the SubTractor sequencer track.
12. Play octaves or open fifths on the keyboard to hear the Matrix pitch modulation of the SubTractor oscillators.

This effect is handy for creating arpeggio chord effects since the Matrix is used to transpose rather than send note values. Because the Matrix output value of the note CV starts at 32, the oscillators must be transposed down to compensate for the increase in pitch value. With the osc pitch CV input trim set to 127, the note CV value modulates the pitch in chromatic steps.

Dual Matrix Arpeggiator
This example demonstrates how two Matrix note control voltages can be merged in a Spider CV merger to create an arpeggio pattern sequence. One Matrix pattern controls the root note of the chord, while the second Matrix pattern generates the cascading chord notes in C minor. The second Matrix can easily be programmed to other chord variations such as major or dominant seventh, but the root note must be C1. The actual root value is set by the first Matrix. The pitch value is the sum of these two control voltages merged in a Spider CV Merger.

1. Start with an empty rack, and create a reMix mixer.
2. Create a SubTractor Synthesizer.
3. Set the polyphony to 1 and osc 1 octave transposition to 0.
4. Bypass auto-routing and create a Spider CV Merger & Splitter and two Matrix Pattern Sequencers.
5. Matrix 1 controls the gate events and the root note of the arpeggio, so connect the Matrix 1 gate CV output to the SubTractor gate sequencer control input.
6. Connect the Matrix 1 note CV output to the Spider CV merge input 1.
7. Set the Spider CV Merge input 1 trim to 127.

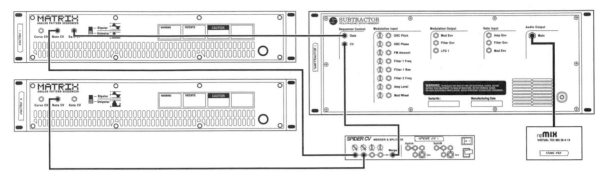

Figure 3-15

Matrix note CV signals merged to create a summed note CV for the SubTractor.

8. Set Matrix 1 pattern length to 32 steps, and program the following on Matrix 1 pattern A1:

Matrix 1 Root Note and Gate Events (Steps 1–16)

Step	1	2	3	4	5	6	7	8	9	10	11	12	13	14	15	16
Curve																
Note	C3	C3	C3	C3	C3	C3	C3	C3	G3	G3	G3	G3	G3	G3	G3	G3
Gate	H	H	H	H	H	H	H	H	H	H	H	H	H	H	H	H

Matrix 1 Root Note and Gate Events (Steps 17–32)

Step	17	18	19	20	21	22	23	24	25	26	27	28	29	30	31	32
Curve																
Note	B♭3	B♭3	B♭3	B♭3	F3	F3	F3	F3	E♭3	E♭3	E♭3	E♭3	C♯3	C♯3	C♯3	C♯3
Gate	H	H	H	H	H	H	H	H	H	H	H	H	H	H	H	H

9. Connect the Matrix 2 note CV output to the Spider CV merge input 2. Matrix 2 generates the chord sequence of the arpeggio. Only the note CV values are used, and the chord structure is based on C minor.
10. Set the Spider CV merge input 2 trim to 127.
11. Set Matrix 2 pattern length to 8 steps.
12. Program the following on Matrix 2 pattern A1:

Matrix 2 Arpeggio Chord

Step	1	2	3	4	5	6	7	8
Curve								
Note	C1	E♭1	G1	C2	E♭2	C2	G1	E♭1
Gate								

13. Connect the Spider CV merger output to the SubTractor CV sequencer control input.
   ▸ Press Play on the sequencer.

experiment !

The numeric value of C1 is 36 and the value of C3 is 60. The resulting sum is 96, which is the equivalent of C6. In order to compensate for the high pitch, the Sub-Tractor's oscillator has to be transposed down to octave 0. Because the maximum CV value is 127, the root note is limited in range between octave 1 and octave 3 on Matrix 1. Notes higher than octave 3 create note values that clip at 127.

CV Examples

CV routing is one of the features that make Reason so versatile. The following examples illustrate a few other ways CVs can be used. "Real-Time CV Control" is a particularly important example, since this configuration is a control voltage source that changes with manual adjustments from a slider.

Envelope-Controlled Panning

The SubTractor has two envelope generator outputs, making it the most useful source of a general-purpose envelope CV. Since the SubTractor won't be used to generate a sound in this type of patch, the polyphony should be set to 1, low bandwidth (BW) should be enabled, and the audio output should be disconnected. These steps economize CPU resources.

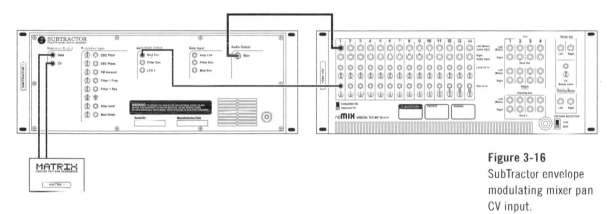

Figure 3-16
SubTractor envelope modulating mixer pan CV input.

1. Start with an empty rack, and create a reMix mixer.
2. Create a SubTractor, and set its polyphony to 1.
3. Set the filter 1 frequency to 62 and resonance to 63.
4. Set the mod envelope attack to 65, decay to 0, sustain to 127, and release to 72.
5. Set the filter envelope attack to 0, decay to 57, sustain to 07, release to 75, and amount to 63.
6. Set the amp envelope attack to 0, decay to 0, sustain to 120, and release to 72.
7. Set the velocity filter envelope modulation level to 0.
8. Connect the SubTractor mod envelope modulation output to the mixer channel 1 pan CV in.

9. Set the mixer channel 1 pan CV trim to 127.
10. Set the mixer channel 1 front-panel pan to about –28.
11. Create a Matrix Pattern Sequencer.
12. Program the following in Matrix pattern A1:

Matrix 1 (Steps 1–16)

Step	1	2	3	4	5	6	7	8	9	10	11	12	13	14	15	16
Curve																
Note	C3	C3	C3	C3	C3	C3	C3	C3	C3	C3	C3	C3	C3	C3	C3	C3
Gate	TH	TH	TH	TH	TH											

▸ Press Run on the Matrix. You should hear each note start in the left speaker, pan across to the right speaker, and then pan back to the left.

Envelope generator CV outputs are always positive unipolar values. The inverter option next to the ADSR settings only applies to modulation routings within Sub-Tractor, but routing the envelope curve through a Spider CV can invert the control voltage. By using the Spider CV to split and invert the envelope CV, this configuration can be modified to cross-pan two signals.

Real-Time CV Control

This example illustrates a method of changing an envelope generator CV value from a slider, making it possible to change CV signals in real time.

The Matrix Pattern Sequencer sends a constant note-on message to the SubTractor. A one-step pattern with a tied gate event on step 1 ensures that whenever the song is running, the SubTractor constantly plays a single note. When the envelope sustain level is changed, the envelope generator CV value changes accordingly, but when the Matrix stops, the envelope CV returns to zero.

1. Bypass auto-routing and create a SubTractor.
2. Enable the Low BW (bandwidth) button.
3. Set the SubTractor's polyphony to 1.
4. Set the Mod Envelope ADSR settings all to 0.
5. Set the Filter Envelope ADSR settings all to 0.
6. Create a Matrix.
7. Program the following Matrix pattern:

Matrix 1—Pattern Length = 1 Step

Step	1
Curve	
Note	C3
Gate	TH

This pattern holds a note while the Matrix or Sequencer is running. This is like a single note that plays for the entire length of a song.

8. Bypass auto-routing and create a Spider CV Merger & Splitter.

9. Connect the SubTractor mod env output to the Spider CV split A input.

10. Connect the SubTractor filter env output to the Spider CV split B input.

The sustain sliders on the mod envelope and filter envelope now control the CV signal sent out the modulation outputs. These signals are split by the Spider CV, and they can be routed to any CV destination for real-time control. Automation of these controls can be recorded on a sequencer track, and can be assigned to an external knob or slider controller. (When sending MIDI controller data from external hardware, you can either use the controller assignments listed in Reason's MIDI Implementation Chart, or choose Options/Enable MIDI Remote Mapping and then select the controllers of your choice in each slider's pop-up mapping window.)

Chapter 4
Audio Signal Routing and Busses

The number of different cable routings that can be set up in Reason is nearly infinite, and connecting modules together without some kind of plan can easily become confusing. By simplifying the process and looking at some basic circuit configurations, we can outline a framework in a way that's easy to grasp. Not only does this framework help in making the proper connections among devices, it allows one to understand how to make variations in existing connections.

This chapter introduces the terminology and concepts of audio electronics as applied in Reason. The key issues discussed are routing audio devices in series, splitting signals in parallel connections, audio busses, merging and mixing signals, attenuation, and feedback. Having a grasp of the terms and concepts will make it much easier to understand some of the more complex configurations described later in the book.

Devices in Series

A *series* connection describes a group of devices in which outputs from each device are wired into the inputs of the next device in a chain or "series." If there are more than two devices, the inputs of each device in the chain are connected to the outputs of the previous device. In traditional mixers, effects that are connected to a channel in series are said to be *insert* effects. Adding an effect is commonly described as "inserting an effect" into the signal path. For instance, let's say the output of an ECF-42 Envelope Controlled Filter module has too much bass. Inserting a PEQ-2 Parametric Equalizer to contour the low frequencies will solve the problem. The resulting signal could have very drastic changes in loudness, so a Comp-01 Compressor could then be inserted after the

PEQ-2 to control the dynamic changes. Almost limitless numbers of devices can be connected in series, especially in Reason, where adding a device to the signal chain is as easy as a mouse-click.

Many modern keyboards have effects built into each patch—essentially, several signal processing effects connected in series to create lush and rich timbres. Removing these effects reduces the sound to a simple tone. With the variety of effects available in Reason, and the ability to connect these effects in any order, it's quite easy to create similar sounds from the output signals of a single SubTractor or Malström synthesizer module.

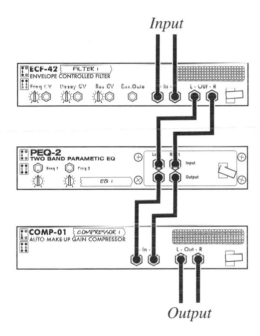

Figure 4-1
Three effects devices connected in series.

There is a limit beyond which adding more effects yields no significant benefit, especially when economizing CPU usage becomes an issue. Every computer has a limit in terms of the number of modules, processors, and effects devices you can add. The CPU usage meter on the Reason Transport Bar indicates when the processor is reaching its limit. In the example described above, a bass shelf equalizer could be used instead of adding a PEQ-2 to roll off the bass frequencies, thus saving a few CPU cycles.

Parallel Circuits

In a *parallel* circuit, a signal is split into branches, each carrying the original source signal. At a later point in the signal path (often the main mixer or output), the parallel signals will be joined back together. When it's necessary to route the same audio signal to different devices, a signal is split and a parallel circuit is created.

An example of a parallel circuit is where the mono output of a SubTractor is required to connect into the stereo inputs on a mixer. In the hardware realm, you would use a Y-cable. The SubTractor audio output is split into two parallel signals that connect into the left and right inputs of a mixer channel. There are several methods of splitting audio signals in Reason.

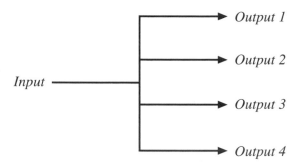

Figure 4-2
A four-way splitter splits the incoming signal into four parallel paths.

Each Spider Audio Splitter can distribute a mono input signal to seven outputs at once. To do this, patch the input to splitter A, and then patch one of the A outputs into the B input. When stereo connections are made with input connections on both inputs A and B, the stereo signal can be split four ways.

A pair of outputs from one splitter can be chained to the splitter inputs of a second Spider Audio module, creating a series of stereo "taps." Because these signals are running in parallel, each effect patched to the Spider outputs receives the original signal. For instance, six split signals can be directed to six DDL-1 Digital Delay Lines, each with a different delay time, to create a multi-tap delay. This chain of splitters can continue to create as many taps as necessary.

Other Methods of Splitting Audio Signals

Prior to Reason 2.5, audio signals could be split using the mixer. The pre-2.5 mixer has two master outputs and four effects sends. A mono signal can be routed through an input channel. When the fader and aux send levels are set to 100, the input signal is distributed to each of these outputs, providing a six-way splitter. In version 2.5, the mixer is modified so that each aux send bus is stereo, thus expanding the aux bus with four more outputs. A mono input signal can be split to as many as ten outputs through the mixer. The microMix can split a mono signal four ways.

For a simple Y-cable, or two-way splitter, a mono signal can be routed through a CF-101 Chorus/Flanger effect with the device set on bypass. The mono input signal is split to the CF-101's left and right outputs. These techniques can still be applied in newer versions of Reason, but the Spider Audio module is designed specifically for this purpose.

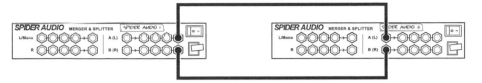

Figure 4-3
Two Spider Audio
splitters chained.

Audio Signal Busses

A bus (sometimes spelled "buss") is an electronic circuit along which a signal moves from one place to another. In hardware mix desks, wires connect each input channel to the master output bus. The level of the signal on the master output bus is then controlled by the master fader. Since most mixers function in stereo, they employ a stereo bus, which is actually two individual busses, left and right, that carry the signals on the left and right audio output channels. Busses can be used to split signals into parallel circuits, or they be used to merge (mix) parallel signals together. Reason employs virtual busses in the reMix, microMix, and Spider Audio modules. These devices are used for routing and combining audio signals from various sources in the Reason rack.

Of the three, the Spider Audio Merger is the most limited, being simply a bus that combines signals without other controls. The Spider Audio Merger has two busses, and each bus combines up to four incoming signals. In any situation where you simply need to merge signals without requiring panning or faders, the Spider Audio Merger is an adequate solution.

The microMix (Line Mixer 6:2) has four internal signal busses. There is a stereo master bus for combining signals from the mixer input channels, and also a stereo auxiliary (Aux Send) bus. Like the master mix bus, the aux send bus is stereo and combines the signals coming from the individual channels' aux sends. Including its stereo aux return, the microMix can combine a total of fourteen mono or seven stereo inputs.

The reMix (Mixer 14:2) has ten busses. Of the three signal combining devices, the reMix is best suited as the main mixer in a song rack. There is a stereo master mix bus. Each mixer channel routes to the master mix bus, where the signals are combined. The chaining master inputs are also connected to the mix bus. The combined signal on the mix bus goes through the master fader, and the combined signal output is available at the master output. The four aux sends are stereo busses that combine signals from the channel aux sends. The aux send busses also have direct inputs through the mixer chaining aux send In sockets. The combined signals on the aux send busses appear on the aux send out sockets, and the aux return busses eventually connect to the master mix bus. In total, 46 input signals can be combined, but the typical configuration uses 14 stereo inputs.

Spider Audio Merger

The Merger combines the signals from four input signals to one output signal. There are two sets of mergers, which provide either a stereo bus with four inputs or two mono busses with four inputs each. The two mergers can be connected in series for a seven-input monophonic bus on one Spider Audio Merger. Likewise, several mergers can be connected in series to combine as many stereo signals as necessary.

The Spider Audio Merger can be used to group signals being sent to a mixer channel. Connect signals from different sound modules into a Spider Audio Merger, then route the Merger outputs into the mixer channel. This creates a bus for the mixer input channel, with the sum of the signals controlled by one fader. Individual levels are then controlled from the output levels of the various sound modules. With the exception of the Scream 4, Reason's effects devices don't have output level controls, so a mixer is usually more suited for combining signals coming from the effects.

Bussed Redrum Sends

The Spider Audio Merger can also be used to expand the inputs on a mixer's chaining aux busses. A Redrum module has two effects send outputs, which are automatically routed to the mixer's chaining aux input 1 and input 2. If more than one Redrum module is used, the second Redrum effect send can't be routed to the mixer send bus. Using a Spider Audio Merger, effects sends from several Redrum modules can be merged, then routed into the chaining aux connections on the mixer module. The chaining aux inputs are inputs to the mixer's aux busses, so any signal received at these inputs will be passed on to the corresponding aux send sockets.

1. Start with an empty rack, and create a reMix mixer.
2. Create a Spider Audio Merger & Splitter.
3. Connect the Spider merger output A to splitter input A.
4. Connect the Spider merger output B to splitter input B.
5. Connect the Spider splitter A out 1 and out 2 to the mixer chaining aux 1 inputs L and R.
6. Connect the Spider splitter B out 1 and out 2 to the mixer chaining aux 2 inputs L and R.
7. Create three Redrum Drum Computers.
8. Connect the send out 1 from each Redrum to the Spider merger inputs L/mono 1, 2, and 3.
9. Connect the send out 2 from each Redrum to the Spider merger inputs R 1, 2, and 3.

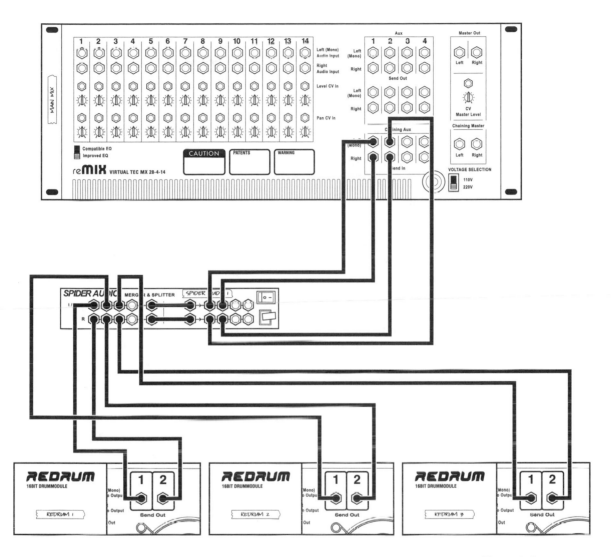

With this patch, the Redrum channel sends share effects with the main mixer's aux 1 and aux 2 sends, which is useful for sending several snare drum sounds to the same reverb, for example. The Redrum send 1 outputs are combined on the merger A strip and the Redrum send 2 outputs are combined on the merger B strip. The output of each merger is then split to connect to both the left and right inputs of the mixer chaining aux inputs, which feed directly to the mixer's aux sends. This Y-cable connection is necessary, especially if you are using the RV-7000 Reverb module on the mixer's effect send bus. If the aux send uses a mono signal, then splitting the merger outputs is not necessary.

Figure 4-4
Redrum sends merged signals in a Spider Audio Merger. The merged signals are connected to the mixer's chaining aux inputs.

Rack configurations in Reason can become very intricate. Sometimes several mixer devices must be chained together. In such circumstances, the merged sends from the Redrums should be disconnected before adding the second mixer to the rack. Once the second mixer is chained into the first mixer, the merged Redrum sends can be connected to the chaining aux send inputs on the second (or last) mixer with free inputs available.

A signal on an Aux Send is equivalent at any point in the path, so an alternative method of bussing send signals would be to merge the mixer aux send outputs with the Redrum effect sends, and bus the result to the effect.

Attenuation

The main difference between the mixers and a Spider merger is that the mixers attenuate signals. "Attenuate" means to decrease the signal level. This is the primary function of a mixer input channel. Combined signals sometimes need to be balanced so that they don't overload or overshadow other signals. The mixer's master output bus combines incoming signals, and the mixer input channels attenuate the signal before they reach the bus.

The fader on a mixer channel controls the input signal attenuation to the stereo mix bus. A fader setting of 0 is the same as −∞ dB, or silence. Unity gain refers to 0dB of attenuation where the input signal is passed through without any increase or decrease of level. A fader setting of 100 is unity gain on the mixer 14:2. Settings above 100 will add gain to the incoming signals, making them louder. A fader setting of 127 amplifies the incoming signal about 6dB. These parameter settings also apply to the aux send controls, since they attenuate the signal levels going to the aux send busses.

Panning

Panning is another form of attenuation. It affects simultaneously the levels of two output signals coming from the stereo mix bus. When an input signal is panned center, an equal amount of attenuation is applied to the left and right input signals. When the input signal is panned all the way to the left, the left channel signal increases while the right signal is attenuated to silence (−∞ dB). When the input is panned all the way to the right (*hard* right), the left signal decreases to silence while the right signal increases to unity gain. The shift in levels is perceived as a change in the location in the stereo field.

Panning in most contemporary mixers follows this convention called Constant-Power panning. The combined level between the left and right channels is the same regardless of the pan position. There is about 3dB of attenuation when pan is at center, and panning toward either the left or right channel will increase the loudness of the signal on that channel. If the Mixer outputs are combined together to a mono signal, there is no change in loudness as pan is adjusted from hard left to hard right. This rule applies to both the reMix and microMix devices.

If different signals are received on the left and right inputs of a single reMix channel, turning the pan knob away from center attenuates either the left or the right channel. The location of the signals in the stereo field is not actually affected by panning, as it would be if a mono signal were received in the left channel input.

Dual Mono vs. Stereo Mixer Channels

Stereo input signals on the left and right input sockets of a single mixer channel sound different from connecting the stereo inputs to two mono mixer channels panned hard left and hard right, because the levels are slightly louder when two mixer channels are used. Connecting stereo signals to two mixer channels offers more panning flexibility, as the separation can be decreased to fit in a narrow space in the stereo field instead of occupying the full range between left and right.

Several signals from effect outputs can be panned to different locations between the left and right speakers to create rich stereophonic effects. From the example mentioned earlier, in which four delay units are running in parallel, the outputs of the four delays can be combined in a mixer with different pan positions and levels. One possible result would be a multi-tap delay with echoes starting from one speaker and moving toward the other speaker, gradually becoming louder as the echo is heard from each delay unit.

Because of the constant-power law governing panning, signals connected in dual mono mode are louder than those connected to stereo inputs. Panning the incoming signals hard left and hard right on discrete input channels adds 3dB to each of the incoming signals. This is one method of increasing the loudness of signals, but loud signals should be trimmed back either with the mixer faders, or simply by adjusting the output volume on the sound module.

Aux Send Busses

Digital signal processing effects such as reverb units are typically connected to the aux send and return sockets of a mixer. Four different effects can be connected to a reMix in this way, and one effect can be connected to the microMix. These effects are shared by the sends on all of the input channels. Signals routed to the reMix aux send bus are tapped after the channel fader, so both the channel fader and aux send knob attenuate the signal. This is called a post-fader send, because the relative loudness of the send and the channel signal itself remains constant.

Effects connected in aux send/return loops typically return a 100% wet signal, so the aux send knob works like a dry/wet balance control. When the aux send is set at unity gain, the incoming signal is split equally between both the mix bus and the aux send bus. The aux return from the effect processor is then combined with the dry signal on the mix bus. A parallel circuit is created after the fader: One branch is processed through the effect, then combined with the dry signal. When the aux send and aux returns are set to unity gain, the result is a 50% dry/wet balance. With post-fader effect sends, the dry/wet balance cannot exceed 50% by more than a small margin. (If the send is raised past unity gain, more wet than dry signal will be heard.) The range of 60% to 99% wet signals can be achieved either by using the effect as an insert or by using a pre-fader send.

Pre-Fader Effects

The microMix and reMix aux send bus 4 have a pre-fader option. When the pre-fader option is selected, the signal bypasses the fader and is attenuated only by the aux send knob. When the pre-fade option is enabed, the aux send taps directly to the input signal rather than after the fader attenuation.

The microMix pre-fade option is a switch on the rear of the unit to the left of the Aux Send/Return jacks. When this is enabled, pre-fade applies globally to all six input channels.

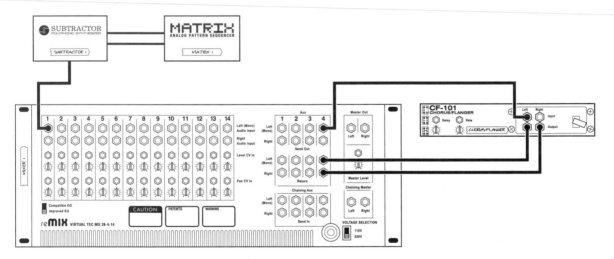

Figure 4-5
Pre-fader effects are routed through the mixer's aux 4 send and return.

The reMix has a pre-fade enable button to the left of the Aux 4 send control on each channel, allowing the option to be selected for the desired input channels. Sometimes a signal may need to have more effect processing without an increase of the dry signal to the mix. In this situation, the dry signal from the fader can be mixed low and the effect level, controlled independently with the aux send 4 knob, can be set higher.

Mute FX on Solo

When the Solo button is enabled, signals are still routed to the aux send busses, and the effects signals are still heard in the mix. Instead of using the aux return inputs, effect returns can be connected to mixer input channels. If you do this, when the Solo button is enabled for a channel, the channel's effects will be muted. If you use this option, be careful not to create feedback loops! Keep the aux send amount to 0 on any mixer channel being used as an aux return bus, except when sending the return from one effect to another effect. It's best to avoid feedback loops, so return signals from the aux 1 effect should not be added back to the aux 1 send bus. There are special cases where audio feedback can be used constructively, but it usually causes problems.

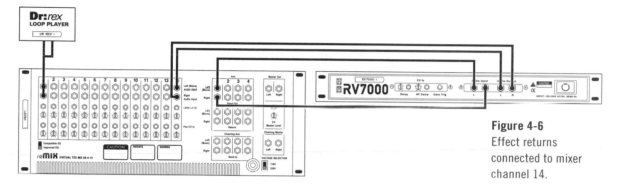

Figure 4-6
Effect returns connected to mixer channel 14.

1. Start with an empty rack, and create a reMix mixer, an RV-7000 Reverb, and a Dr.REX Loop Player.
2. Load the ReCycle loop "Elc16_Sequential_110_eLAB.rx2" from Reason Factory Sound Bank\Dr Rex Drum Loops\Electronic directory.
3. Copy the REX slice data to the Dr.REX 1 sequencer track.
4. Set the mixer channel 1 aux send 1 level to 79.
5. Run the sequence and click on the channel 1 Solo button to verify that the Dr.REX loop is soloed with the reverb aux send/return.
6. Disconnect the RV7000 outputs from the aux return 1 inputs, and reconnect them to the mixer channel 14 inputs.

▶ Run the sequence.

While running the sequence, click on the channel 1 Solo button to solo the signal and hear the signal without the aux return from the reverb module.

Panning Effects

There are some other benefits to routing effects returns into mixer channels. The effect returns can be quickly muted, or processed with some equalization. For some extra processing, effect returns can be sent to other aux send busses. Instead of routing pairs of effects into one mixer channel, effect returns can be routed to the mono inputs of two mixer channels. The individual returns can then be panned to different locations in the mix. For example, the RV7000 returns could be panned just a little off center to create a hollow cave reverb effect.

Another example is panning PH-90 Phaser inputs to −18 and 19. The stereo separation is not as wide as panning the effect hard left and hard right. Too many effects connected to aux returns can fill the stereo field, cluttering the mix. Routing and panning effects to different locations in the mix is an effective means of controlling the balance of the mix.

Submixers

Any number of mixer modules can be created in the Reason rack. Multiple mixers can be bussed together using the chaining aux and chaining master inputs. This is useful when more input channels are required to accommodate more than 14 sound modules. When extra mixers are created, auto-routing is set to make the proper connections to chain the series of mixers.

Secondary mixers can also be used as submixers for grouping inputs. A common type of submix would have input signals from Redrum channels and Dr.REX drum loops. The relative levels between the drum sounds can be balanced in the submixer, and the submixer can then be connected to the input channel of the primary mixer. When creating a submixer, bypass auto-routing to avoid chaining the secondary mixer to the primary.

Submixer Shortcut

A submixer that groups drum signals is usually an afterthought, needed after a considerable amount of the song is done. In the process of creating the track, fader, EQ, and effect send settings have been set, and duplicating them on a submixer can be tedious. Instead of creating a new submixer, simply duplicate the primary mixer. The cables from the primary mixer can then be manually moved to the submixer, and the parameters will not need adjustment. The submixer outputs can be chained to the primary mixer, or grouped to a primary mixer input channel.

If the submixer is specifically a drum group mixer, you might want to copy effects like reverb along with the mixer. Select the mixer and the effects, and then duplicate them below the main mixer. The drag-and-drop duplicate shortcut works really well in this situation. Select the mixer and appropriate effects and drag-duplicate them. Connect the duplicate mixer master outputs to a free input channel on the primary mixer. An MClass Compressor can be inserted on the master output of the submixer to control the dynamics of the entire drum submix.

Once the input channels have been connected to the submixer, collapse the device to conserve user interface space. The submixer should be moved to a position above the primary mixer. This will prevent auto-routing from cabling new devices into the submixer.

Aux Send 4 Submix Bus

The aux send 4 bus can also be used to group input signals when the pre-fader button is enabled. The aux send 4 outputs are then connected to mixer channel 14 audio inputs, so all signals routed to the aux 4 bus will be routed into mixer channel 14. Channels routed to the aux 4 submix bus should have faders set to zero.

1. Start with an empty rack, and create a reMix mixer.
2. Create a Dr.REX Loop Player.
3. Load the ReCycle loop "Rnb14_Original_100_eLAB.rx2" from the Dr Rex Drum Loops\RnB HipHop directory in the Reason Factory Sound Bank.
4. Copy the REX slice data to the Dr.REX 1 sequencer track.
5. On the mixer, connect the aux send 4 left and right sockets to the channel 14 input sockets.
6. Set the mixer channel 1 fader level to 0.
7. Enable the pre-fader option on mixer channel 1 and set the aux 4 knob to 100.
▶ Run the sequence.

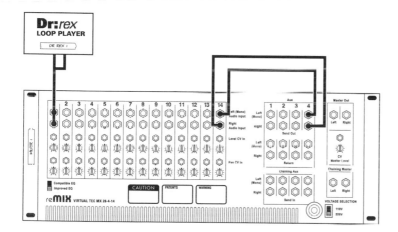

The signal from mixer channel 1 is routed through the aux send 4 bus, which leads back into mixer channel 14. This creates a submix group controlled on mixer channel 14. (At the moment the submix group contains only one mixer channel, but you can add more channels to it as needed.) The individual levels are attenuated using the aux 4 knobs, and the mixer channels must be set to zero; otherwise the signal will be routed through both the aux bus and the master mix bus. The aux 4 knob on mixer channel 14 should be set to zero; otherwise a feedback loop will occur.

Figure 4-7
Aux 4 send outputs connected to mixer channel 14 inputs.

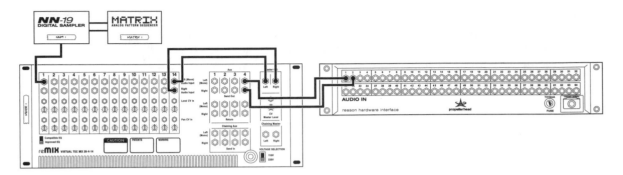

Figure 4-8

Master outputs connected to mixer channel 14 inputs. Aux 4 send outputs connected to Reason Hardware Interface inputs 1 and 2.

Devices like a Comp-01 Compressor/Limiter or PEQ-2 Equalizer can be inserted between the aux 4 send outputs and the mixer channel 14 inputs. This must be manually cabled. Since the input channels from the grouped signal will not direct signals to aux sends 1, 2, or 3, aux effects can be applied on mixer channel 14 for the entire submix. An RV7000 Advanced Reverb can be inserted, for instance, to add reverb to the submix signal.

CV Control of the Mixer

Each mixer channel has CV inputs to modulate the level and pan parameters. By using different CV sources, a variety of panning and dynamics control effects can be created. The level CV is unipolar and matches the fader level range from 0 to 127. Pan is bipolar and has a range of –64 (hard left) through 0 (center) to 63 (hard right). The incoming CV signals are added to the current fader and pan settings, and the sum of the two will not exceed the value range. An envelope CV signal will go from 0 to 127, so if the fader is set to 100, the modulation will only have an effect when the envelope CV value is between 1 and 27.

This section contains several examples of modulating the mixer parameters. More examples of modulating level CV are described in the chapter on dynamics processing.

Modulated Mixer Level

In this example, the Malström Modulator CV is used to control the level of a mixer channel. The Malström Graintable Synthesizer Modulator is Reason's only source of a sine wave CV LFO. There is a slight difference between a sine and a triangle wave, but in this example, the sine wave sounds better because the peak duration is longer than with a triangle wave.

1. In an empty rack, create a reMix mixer.
2. Create a Dr.REX Loop Player.
3. On Dr.REX, load the ReCycle file "Hhp_Ephit_095_Chronic.rx2" from the Factory Sound Bank\Music Loops\Variable Tempo (rex2)\Downtempo Loops directory.

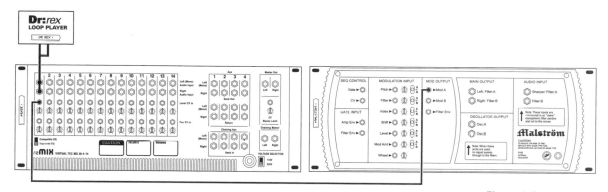

Figure 4-9
Malström modulator
connected to mixer
level CV input.

4. Copy the REX data to the Dr.REX 1 sequencer track.
5. Bypass auto-routing and create a Malström Graintable Synthesizer.
6. Set the Malström polyphony to 1 and disable OSC A, filter A, filter B, and Mod B.
7. On the Malström Mod A, enable sync and set the rate to 1/16.
8. Connect the Malström output mod A socket to the mixer channel 1 level CV in socket.
9. Set the mixer channel 1 level CV trim to 120.
10. Set the mixer channel 1 fader level to 0.
▶ Run the sequence.

experiment with Rex settings.

The sine wave modulation creates the effect of a smooth fader increase and decrease synchronized to the tempo of the track. This configuration is sometimes more appropriate than gating effects because the transitions are smoothed by the curve of the sine wave.

Matrix-Controlled Crossfader

A crossfader is a type of attenuator commonly used on DJ mixers to mix between the input signals from two turntables. When the crossfader is centered, the two sources are mixed equally. When the crossfader is set to the extreme left or right, only one of the two sources is heard. The following two examples show methods of simulating the crossfader effect by using split and inverted CV signals modulating mixer levels.

1. In an empty rack, create a reMix mixer.
2. Create two Dr.REX Loop Players.
3. Create a Spider CV Merger & Splitter.
4. Bypass auto-routing and create a Matrix Pattern Sequencer.
5. Connect the Matrix curve CV socket to the Spider CV split A input.
6. Connect a Spider split A output to the mixer channel 1 level CV input.
7. Connect the Spider split A inverted output to the mixer channel 2 level CV input.
8. Set the mixer channel 1 and 2 level CV trim to 127.

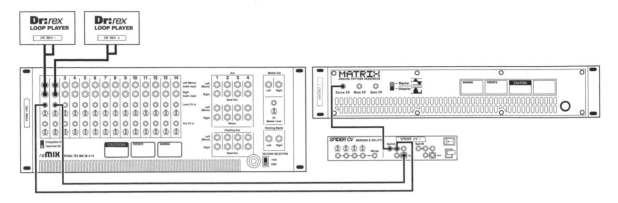

Figure 4-10
Spider CV Splitter and Inverter routed to two mixer level CV inputs.

9. Set mixer channel 1 fader level to 0.

10. Set mixer channel 2 fader level to 127.

11. On Dr.REX 1, load the Recycle File "125_DaftChord_mLp_eLAB.rx2" from the Factory Sound Bank from the Music Loops\Variable Tempo (rex2)\Uptempo Loops directory.

12. Copy the REX data to the Dr.REX 1 sequencer track.

13. From the same directory, load the file "130_Looped_mLp_eLAB.rx2" into Dr.REX 2.

14. Copy the REX data to the Dr.REX 2 sequencer track.

15. On the Matrix, select curve edit mode.

16. Set the Matrix pattern length to 32 steps.

17. Draw a ramp curve on the Matrix from step 1 to 32 from 0 to 127. (Hold down the Shift key to enable the line tool.)

▸ Run the sequence to hear the crossfade between mixer channels 1 and 2.

While you might normally want to experiment with this configuration, you should refrain until the next chapter where a better crossfader solution is presented using the Combinator.

Feedback Loops

One normally associates the term "feedback" with the howling noise heard when a P.A. microphone picks up a signal from the loudspeaker. The audio signal from the loudspeaker loops back through the microphone, causing an unpleasant oscillation that increases in amplitude. In other cases, feedback is used in a musical way, such as when an electric guitar pickup is placed near the amplified speaker cabinet. Both types of feedback can be applied in Reason, and when applied carefully, audio feedback loops can create interesting effects.

In Figure 4-11, the feedback loop schematic, the audio input signal is merged with the output signal, creating a direct feedback loop. This circuit is unpleasant to listen to, but it shows the basic method with which feedback loops are established. This effect is more practical when used in conjunction with an effect like a digital delay, which is why there is a feedback control on the DDL-1 Digital Delay Line. The feedback control attenuates the processed delay signal being combined with the input signal. With the DDL-1 feedback setting at zero, there is no feedback within the device, so any amount of external feedback signal, when combined with the incoming signal, will result in an echo effect with the delayed signals repeating at the rate set on the DDL-1.

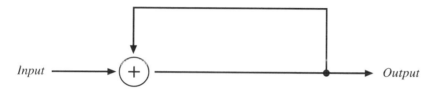

Figure 4-11
Feedback loop schematic. (Don't try this without turning down your speakers!)

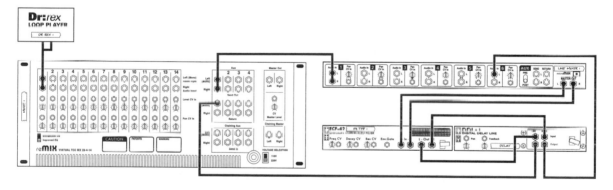

Figure 4-12
Delay and Filter feedback loop wired through a microMix Mixer.

Hardwired Feedback Delay

Instead of using the built-in feedback control of a DDL-1, a feedback loop can be created in Reason using a mixer. The input signal combines with the feedback audio signal in the mixer, and the channel fader attenuates the feedback signal going into the digital delay module.

1. In an empty rack, create a reMix mixer, and set the tempo to 85 BPM.
2. Create a Dr.REX Loop Player.
3. On Dr.REX 1, load the Recycle File "Dub24_Dread_070 eLAB.rx2" from the Factory Sound Bank\Dr Rex Drum Loops\Dub directory.
4. Copy the REX data to the Dr.REX 1 sequencer track.

[handwritten: Line Mixer 6:2 ↗]

5. Bypass auto-routing and create a microMix.
6. Connect the main mixer 1 aux send 1 to the microMix channel 1 inputs.
7. Set the microMix channel 6 level to 55.
8. Bypass auto-routing and create an ECF-42 Envelope Controlled Filter.
9. Set the ECF-42 Freq to 74, Res to 32, and Mode to BP.
10. Connect the microMix master outs to the ECF-42 inputs.
11. Bypass auto-routing and create a DDL-1 Digital Delay Line.
12. Set the DDL-1 feedback to zero.
13. Connect the ECF-42 outs to the DDL-1 inputs
14. Bypass auto-routing and connect the DDL-1 left output to the Mixer 1 aux return 1 left input.
15. Connect the DDL-1 right output to the microMix channel 6 left input.
16. Turn up aux send 1 on channel 1 of the main mixer to 100.

  ▸ While running the sequence, mute and unmute channel 1 on the main mixer. When it's muted, only the bandpass-filtered and delayed feedback will be heard.

The advantage of using a wired loop is that feedback can be processed through an equalizer or filter to create a frequency damping effect. The echoes filter during each cycle, making them sound duller. High feedback levels, regardless of devices processing the signal, will cause the circuit to self-oscillate and overload. Also, note that if you patch a PEQ-2 equalizer into the feedback signal path, increasing the gain on an EQ band will add to the amount of feedback, so levels should be compensated to prevent overloads.

[handwritten: V. quickly overloads – how is the effect controlled?!]

Chapter 5
The Combinator

The Combinator is a Reason rack device that serves as a powerful tool for synthesis and signal processing. It's a programming environment that adds flexibility and real-time control previously unavailable in Reason. It's not simply one device in Reason 3.0, but the foundation for an entire range of new devices that can be saved as patches with custom graphic user interfaces or "skins."

The Combinator contains a nested sub-rack within a Reason Song File. Within the sub-rack, you create and connect devices as you would normally. There are four rotary controllers and four button controllers, which are assignable to almost any parameter of any device nested in the sub-rack. Each button and rotary control can modulate a parameter on every device nested in the Combinator Rack. A single button or rotary control can modulate a maximum of three parameters per device. As mentioned in Chapter 3, the Combinator rotary controls respond to CV inputs, allowing modulation of any parameter of any device using the CV sources in Reason.

The Combinator is open-ended, lacking a preconceived framework like a synthesizer or even a reverb algorithm. One must first create the framework, then assign the controls and define settings for a particular purpose. This chapter introduces basic Combinator structures, employed in examples found throughout the book. The examples work through the basic steps, but the later examples will assume that you understand these procedures, especially modulation routing and handling devices in the Combinator sub-rack.

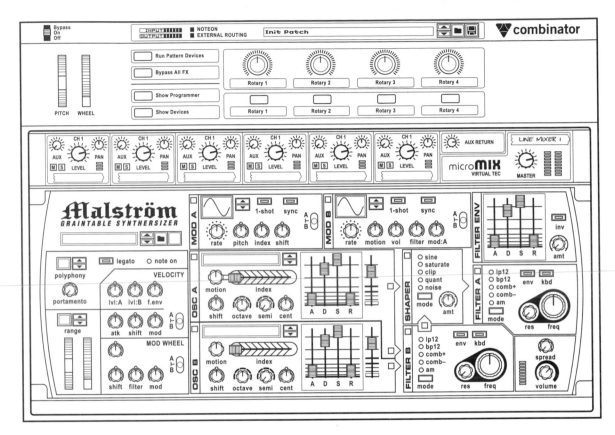

Figure 5-1
Combinator front
panel and sub-rack
with a microMix and
Malström.

Combinator Modulation Routing

The Combinator programmer is the section where modulation routing assignments are established. Combinator rotary control assignments have a maximum and minimum range setting. The 128 steps of a rotary control can be truncated to modulate only a small range of the full depth. For example, a Combinator rotary control can be assigned to a filter cutoff frequency knob on an ECF-42 filter, and the range can be adjusted so that the filter frequency parameter is only adjusted between the values 38 and 100. The modulation routing allows you to reverse the range as well, so that a setting of 128 will adjust a parameter to zero and vice-versa.

1. In an empty rack, create a reMix and a Combinator.
2. In the Combinator, create an ECF-42 Envelope Controlled Filter.
3. Click on the Show Programmer button to expand the programmer interface.
4. Click on the Filter 1 item in the programmer interface.
5. In the modulation routing list, set the rotary 1 target to Frequency and set rotary 1 Min to 38 and Max to 100.

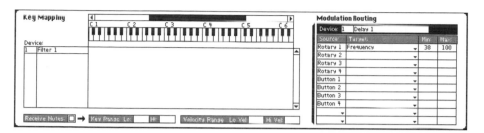

Figure 5-2
The Combinator pro-grammer interface. Filter 1 frequency is assigned to rotary 1 with a limited range.

6. Adjust the rotary 1 control fully clockwise and counterclockwise and watch the ECF-42 frequency knob. You will observe that when you set the rotary 1 control to zero, the ECF-42 filter cutoff is down to 38, and when the rotary 1 control is adjusted to 128, the frequency goes up to 100.
7. In the modulation routing list, set the Filter 1 rotary 1 Min to 100 and Max to 38.
8. Adjust the rotary 1 control on the Combinator and observe the ECF-42 frequency knob. The new minimum and maximum settings have inverted the modulation behavior while limiting the range, so that turning the rotary 1 control clockwise moves the ECF-42 filter cutoff from 100 down to 38.

Now that you have the basic idea of how control modulations are assigned using the Combinator rotaries and buttons, it should become apparent that completely new control configurations can be created. Once you have the controls assigned, it's a good idea to label the control appropriately. Double-click on the Rotary 1 label to enable the edit field, and change the name to Inverted Filter.

Button Controls

The four button controls on a Combinator are programmed in the same manner as the rotary controllers, but the modulations are fixed values assigned to either the on or off state of the button. The minimum value is the off state and the maximum value is the on state.

Modulation Routing

Device: 1	Delay 1			
Source	Target		Min	Max
Rotary 1		▾		
Rotary 2		▾		
Rotary 3		▾		
Rotary 4		▾		
Button 1	Enabled	▾	2	1
Button 2		▾		
Button 3		▾		
Button 4		▾		
		▾		
		▾		

Figure 5-3
Button modulation routing to switch effect into bypass mode.

A common use of the button control would be to assign it to the off/on/bypass parameter of an effect device. Another example would be to assign the button to mixer mute or solo buttons. Any configuration where parameter modulation is limited to an on or off state is ideally suited for a button control. Because the Matrix and Redrum Pattern Select controls can be modulated by the Combinator controls, the button control can be assigned to switch between two patterns: one pattern that plays a rhythmic part, and one that is silent.

Multiple Modulation Routing

This example demonstrates using a single Combinator rotary control to create a custom modulation control of three Malström parameters simultaneously. This example illustrates how to set multiple destinations on a single device. There is a limitation where only one rotary controller or one button can be assigned to three parameters within a given device; the other controls will be limited to one destination per control in that device.

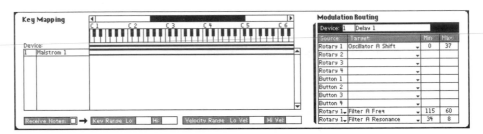

Figure 5-4
The assignable modulation sources set to rotary 1.

1. Start with an empty rack, and create a reMix mixer.
2. Create a Combinator.
3. In the Combinator rack, add a Malström synthesizer.
4. Set the Malström OSC A graintable to Wave:Sawtooth and Enable the OSC A to Shaper routing.
5. Click on the Combinator Show Programmer button to open the programmer.
6. In the Combinator programmer, Click on Malstrom 1 in the device list.
7. In the modulation routing list, set the rotary 1 target to Oscillator A Shift.
8. Set Rotary 1 Min to 0 and Max to 36.
9. Beneath the button 4 source field, set the empty source field to Rotary 1.
10. Set the target to Filter A Freq, Min: 127, Max: 60.
11. On the bottom empty source field, set the source to Rotary 1.
12. Set the target to Filter A Resonance, Min 34, Max: 8.
▸ Play a few notes and adjust the rotary 1 knob to hear the effect.

Having the single rotary control modulate the shift, filter cutoff, and resonance parameters simultaneously creates a new frequency response control. Because the cutoff and resonance parameters are using inverted modulation, the filter tapers off the high frequencies as the oscillator shift generates higher harmonics.

Crossfader

In Chapter 4, an example demonstrated a technique of using a CV signal and an inverted CV signal to modulate two fader levels simultaneously in order to create a crossfader. A more elegant solution to this effect can be created using a Combinator.

1. In an empty rack, create a reMix mixer.
2. Create a Combinator.
3. In the Combinator sub-rack, create a microMix mixer.
4. Click on the Show Programmer button, and click on Line Mixer 1 in the device list.
5. In the modulation routing list, set the rotary 1 target to Channel 1 Level. Set the rotary 1 Min to 127 and Max to 0.
6. Beneath the button 4 source field, set the empty source field to Rotary 1. Set the target to Channel 2 Level, Min 0, Max 127.
7. Double-click on the rotary 1 label and change the name to "X-Fade."
8. Click on the disk icon in the Combinator and save the patch as "Basic Crossfader.cmb."

This configuration fades between the microMix channel 1 and 2 inputs, and now that it is saved as a patch, you can recall it at anytime in the future for use in other projects. The next section illustrates how to implement the crossfader with sound sources.

9. Click on the empty rack area beneath the Combinator.
10. Bypass auto-routing and create a Dr.REX Loop Player.
11. On the Dr.REX, load the ReCycle file "Hhp11_Chronic_093_Chrnc.rx2" from the Factory Sound Bank\Dr Rex Drum Loops\Hip Hop directory.
12. Copy the REX data to the Dr.REX 1 sequencer track.
13. Connect the Dr.REX 1 audio outputs to the microMix channel 1 inputs.
14. Click on the empty rack area beneath the Dr.REX.
15. Bypass auto-routing and create another Dr.REX Loop Player.
16. On the second Dr.REX, load the ReCycle file "Glt09_MangledSwing_112.rx2" from the Factory Sound Bank\Dr Rex Drum Loops\Glitch directory.
17. Copy the REX data to the Dr.REX 2 sequencer track.
18. Connect the Dr.REX 2 audio outputs to the MicroMix Channel 2 inputs.
▶ Run the sequence to play the loops, then adjust the Combinator's X-Fade rotary control to crossfade between the two loops.

Cables from outside of the Combinator can connect directly into devices in the sub-rack, but these connections are not saved with the patches. The Combinator will indicate "external routing" when such connections are present. The two Dr.REX loops provide two different sound sources. This example does not create an equal-power crossfade. To do that, a mixer's panpots have to be used. (The file Constant Power Crossfade.rns, on the CD, shows how to do it.)

Combinator Synthesis

There are several basic structures for creating new synthesis systems in Reason using the Combinator. Incoming MIDI note data is directed to all devices in the sub-rack, which allows the creation of synthesizer and sampler stacks. These Combinator stacks can be tailored in a variety of ways, giving rise to sonically rich workstation-style patches, split performance keyboard patches, and expressive velocity-mapped sounds. The following projects will demonstrate how stacks, splits, and velocity-switching frameworks are created using the Combinator. This section will also touch on some more elaborate methods of synthesis that mimic modular synthesizers.

Synthesizer Stack
The first structure involves stacking several synthesizers nested in a Combinator, a configuration often referred to as a "synth stack." The stack is derived from the concept of a MIDI stack, which involves chaining several MIDI synthesizers and samplers together to respond to the same keyboard in order to create a massive sound. Common types of stacks layer string samples with grand piano, brass with woodwinds for a full wind section, or female vocal samples with an analog synthesizer pad. Having the ability to layer sounds adds enormously to the flexibility of Reason in terms of sound design.

Lush SubTractor Synth Stack
A single synthesizer is usually adequate to fill a specific musical need in a track, but stacking synths allows you to create more versatile and complex timbres. The following example uses six duplicate SubTractor Synthesizers, each slightly detuned. The mixed outputs, panned to different positions, create a big stereo synthesizer patch.

1. In an empty rack, create a reMix mixer.
2. Create a Combinator, and in the sub-rack create a microMix Line Mixer.
3. Create a SubTractor Synthesizer within the Combinator sub-rack.
4. Load the patch "Analog Replicant.zyp" from the Factory Sound Bank\Subtractor Patches\Polysynths directory.
5. Drag-duplicate the SubTractor five times within the Combinator for six SubTractor synths.
6. Connect each of the duplicated SubTractor audio outputs to the left inputs of the remaining free channels of the microMix
7. Adjust the microMix master level to 80.
8. On each of the duplicate SubTractor synths, change the OSC1 detune to different settings in the range of 1 to 6. Make certain that no two have the same detune setting.
9. Change the OSC2 detune settings in a similar manner in the range of –1 to –6.

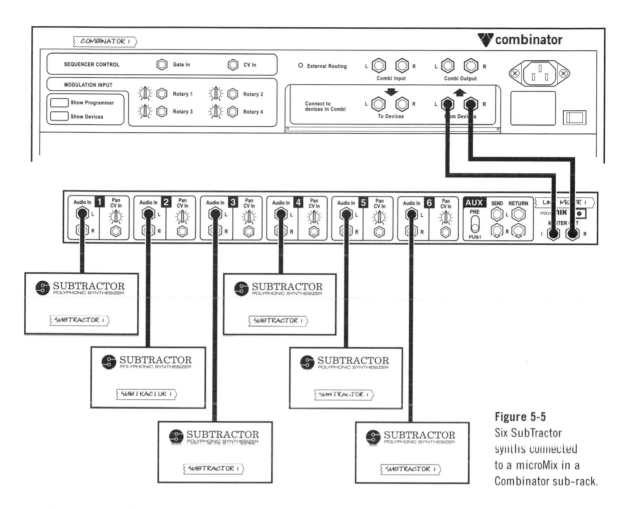

Figure 5-5
Six SubTractor
synths connected
to a microMix in a
Combinator sub-rack.

10. On the microMix, adjust panning as follows:
    Channel 1 pan –64
    Channel 2 pan –48
    Channel 3 pan –16
    Channel 4 pan 15
    Channel 5 pan 47
    Channel 6 pan 63

Save the patch as "Six Sub Stack.cmb," and play some notes to hear a big analog-style synth patch. To fully realize the power of the Combinator, edit the modulation routing assignments. On all six SubTractors, Rotary 1 should be assigned to the Filter 1 Cutoff Frequency; Rotary 2 should be assigned to the Filter 1 Resonance parameter. Pitch bend and modulation globally affect all sound modules nested in the Combinator.

This patch uses a lot of CPU power, so playing thick polyphonic passages with it will be impractical on all but the fastest computers. You can achieve a similar (though not identical) sonic result by routing a single SubTractor through a UN-16 Unison effect.

Split Key Zones

Reason users who are familiar with mapping samples on the NN-XT or NN-19 sampler will recognize the mapping features in the Combinator. A sound module can be assigned to play from a specific region of the keyboard. For example, the legendary Hammond B-3 organ has two keyboards and foot pedals. Each keyboard has its own tone controls so that the organist can play a different timbre with each hand. In a split patch, one timbre is mapped to the left half of the keyboard and another to the right half of the keyboard. This allows players to perform two different sounds without switching patches or relying on multiple keyboards.

Bass & Polysynth Split

Using the Combinator to create a split patch allows you to use a different module for each side of the split. While this example only describes a two-timbre patch, you can map many sounds across the keyboard within the Combinator.

Figure 5-6
Combinator key range map split at C3. NN-XT mapped to left of C3 and Malström mapped to the right of C3. The region can be altered by dragging the small square handles. Clicking and dragging any part shifts the entire region.

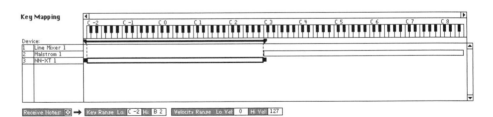

1. In an empty rack, create a reMix mixer.
2. Create a Combinator, and in the sub-rack create a microMix line mixer.
3. In the sub-rack, create a Malström synthesizer.
4. Load the patch "Mt. Juliet.zyp" from the Factory Sound Bank\Malström Patches\Polysynths directory.
5. Beneath the Malström, create a NN-XT Sampler.
6. Load the patch "Hofner Pick.sxt" from the Factory Sound Bank\NN-XT Sampler Patches\Bass\ directory.

7. Click on the Combinator's Show Programmer button.
8. In the programmer device list, click on Malström1.
9. Find the key range settings at the bottom of the programmer. To change the setting, click on the Lo: C-2 setting and drag upwards.
10. Change the key range lo to C3.
11. Click on the NN-XT 1 item in the Device List.
12. Change the key range high setting to B2.
13. Save the Combinator patch as "Bass & Poly Split.cmb."
   ▸ Play a few notes (using both hands) to hear the bass and polysynth split.

Notice that the user interface region blocks decrease as the settings change. These regions define what MIDI notes will pass through the Combinator to the device. Keys not covered by the map are filtered out and will not be played on a particular device. Keys are filtered out from note B2 downward for the polysynth Malström patch, and notes from C3 upward are filtered out for the NN-XT bass patch.

Velocity Layers
Gate messages and MIDI note on events also include velocity information. Velocity is a unipolar value of the gate/note on message in the range of 1 through 127; while a velocity message of zero indicates no event. The Combinator features velocity mapping, a system commonly found in samplers like the NN-XT. This system sorts incoming gate/note on messages. Different sounds are layered and triggered when incoming note on velocity messages or gate values match the range of the velocity message.

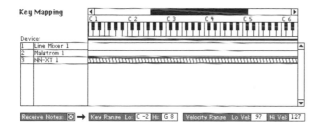

Figure 5-7
The velocity map sorts incoming gate/note on events to different devices in the sub-rack.

1. In an empty rack, create a reMix mixer.
2. Create a Combinator, and in the sub-rack create a microMix line mixer.
3. In the sub-rack, create a Malström synthesizer.
4. Load the patch "FollowMe.xwv" from the Factory Sound Bank\Malström Patches\Pads directory.
5. Beneath the Malström, create an NN-XT Sampler.
6. Load the patch "Metalogue S&H.sxt" from the Factory Sound Bank\NN-XT Sampler Patches\Textures and Musical FX directory.

7. Click on the Show Device List button.
8. Click on the NN-XT 1 item in the device list.
9. Change the velocity range low velocity to 97.
   ‣ Play a few notes on your keyboard. Start with soft (low-velocity) notes, then play harder until velocity triggers the NN-XT.

Workstation-Style "Instrument" Patch

Most popular synthesizers, especially the expensive workstation types, follow a fundamental architecture that can be easily recreated with a Combinator. The signal path follows a basic chain of devices starting with a sound generation module followed by a series of effects that embellish the dry signal. If you disable the effects, the original sounds basic, so to create a larger sound, the patch contains both the synth tone and effects. The following example uses a SubTractor Synthesizer with a Unison and an RV-7000 to create a lush stereo pad sound.

1. In an empty rack, create a reMix mixer.
2. Create a Combinator, and in the sub-rack, add a SubTractor Synthesizer.
3. Load the patch "Boards Pad.zyp" from the Factory Sound Bank\Subtractor Patches\Pads directory.
4. Adjust the SubTractor level to 118.
5. In the sub-rack, create a UN-16 Unison module. Verify that it's cabled between the SubTractor output and the Combinator's From Devices input.
6. Set the UN-16 dry/wet value to 96.
7. In the sub-rack, create an RV-7000 reverb.
8. Set the reverb's decay to 116 and dry/wet to 63.
9. Save the Combinator patch as "Boards Pad FX.cmb."
   ‣ Play some slow chords and octaves to hear this workstation-style pad sound.

Some users bypass the effects to get the original tone to use in conjunction with their outboard reverbs and signal processors to help the synth part fit with the rest of the mix. If you find that you want to compare the dry signal against the processed signal, simply click on the Bypass All FX button on the Combinator.

Modular Patching

Almost every parameter on the Reason rack devices can be assigned to a Combinator rotary control, allowing CV sources to be used to control them, just as on a modular synthesizer system. This feature opens up an entirely new range of sound design and synthesis possibilities, and the following projects present a handful of interesting approaches.

Random-LFO-Controlled Waveform

Random LFO modulation is normally associated with oscillator pitch or filter cut-off frequency, but using the Combinator, a random LFO source can modulate other parameters. This project demonstrates a method of generating timbres using a random LFO to modulate a SubTractor oscillator waveform.

1. Start with an empty rack, and create a reMix mixer.
2. Create a Combinator.
3. In the Combinator sub-rack, create a microMix Line Mixer and a SubTractor.
4. Set the SubTractor LFO 1 Rate to 38 and waveform to the Smooth Random Curve.
5. Connect the SubTractor LFO 1 output to the Combinator rotary 1 CV input.
6. Open the Combinator programmer and click on SubTractor 1.
7. Set the rotary 1 target to OSC1 wave.
▸ Play a few notes on a keyboard to hear the LFO modulation of the SubTractor waveform.

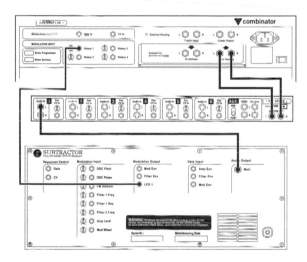
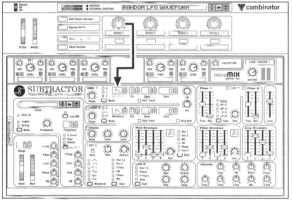

Figure 5-8
LFO connected to rotary CV input. Rotary modulation routing set to waveform.

Sweeping LFO Rate

Sweeping the LFO rate is not a new trick, but the following project illustrates a method of automating this task that allows for a rate sweep that triggers with each incoming note event.

1. Start with an empty rack, and create a reMix mixer.
2. Create a Combinator.
3. In the Combinator sub-rack, create a Malström.

4. Set the Malström OSC A graintable to Wave: PWM.
5. Set the Mod A pitch modulation to 22.
6. Set the Mod B curve to12, rate to 40, and switch on the 1-Shot button.
7. Connect the Malström Mod B CV output to the Combinator rotary 1 input.
8. Open the Combinator programmer and assign rotary 1 to the Malström Mod A rate.
9. Set the Combinator rotary 1 to 44.

▸ Play a single note on a keyboard and observe the Mod A rate knob.

The Mod B curve is modulating the rotary 1 value, which in turn controls the Mod A rate knob. The LFO pitch modulation is still a sine wave, but the rate slows down as the note is held.

Non-Retriggering Malström Modulator

When the Malström Graintable Synthesizer receives either a gate or note-on event, the Modulators are forced to cycle from the start of the waveform. In some instances, a free-running modulator waveform is desired rather than the constantly retriggered wave. The following example describes how to use a secondary Malström modulator to generate free-running CV signals without being retriggered by incoming note events.

1. Start with an empty rack, and create a reMix mixer.
2. Create a Combinator.
3. In the Combinator sub-rack, create two Malström synthesizers.
4. Connect the Malström 2 Mod A CV output to the Malström 1 pitch input.
5. Adjust the Malström 1 Pitch Mod rear-panel trim to 38.
6. Set the Malström 2 Mod A rate to 34.
7. On the Combinator programmer, Click on the Malstrom 2 item and disable the Receive Notes checkbox.

▸ Play a few notes to hear the continuous pitch sweep.

The Receive Notes checkbox controls whether a device will receive note or gate CV information from outside sources. In this example, disabling the box on the second Malström bypasses note reception so the modulators continue to cycle freely.

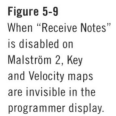

Figure 5-9
When "Receive Notes" is disabled on Malström 2, Key and Velocity maps are invisible in the programmer display.

Pattern Devices in the Combinator

Matrix Pattern Sequencers and Redrum Drum Machine devices can also be included in a Combinator patch. The pattern selection can be assigned to a Rotary control so that patterns can be changed by a twist of the knob. A useful trick is to nest Matrix Pattern sequencers in a Combinator and then save them as patches. When you need to recall that pattern, simply load the patch and connect the Note CV, Gate CV, and Curve CV outputs to the desired destination.

Auto Bass Riff

Anyone who has played with a consumer electronic keyboard has probably played with the built-in accompaniment features. These are the preset bass line and rhythm sections that can be played with one-finger ease and instantly make you sound quite talented on the keyboard. Using a Matrix pattern sequencer in a Combinator, a bass line accompaniment patch is quite easy to create. The following project demonstrates how to create an auto-bass riff system that is performed with one finger (not that finger).

1. In an empty rack, create a reMix mixer.
2. Create a Combinator, and in the sub-rack, create a SubTractor Synthesizer.
3. Load the patch "Triangle Sub.zyp" from the Factory Sound Bank\Subtractor Patches\Bass directory.
4. Bypass auto-routing and create a Matrix pattern sequencer in the sub-rack.
5. Connect the Matrix Gate CV output to the Subtractor Amp Env input.
6. Program the following pattern on the Matrix:

Pattern Length 8 Steps

H	TH	H	TH	H	H	H	

▸ Click on Run Pattern Devices or run the sequence, and play a note on your MIDI keyboard.

The Matrix Pattern nested in the Combinator is saved within the patch, so when the patch is recalled, the bass line pattern will remain intact.

Filterverb

The Combinator provides audio inputs so that chains of effects processing can be nested and saved as patches. The following example is a send effect with a reverb in series with a pattern-controlled filter. The Dr.REX drum loop provides a sound source, and the steps following the insertion of the Combinator should be performed entirely within the sub-rack. The auto-routing rules do not automatically route a new Combinator to effect send return jacks, so these must be connected manually.

1. In an empty rack, create a reMix mixer, and set the tempo to 94 BPM.

Filterverb Combinator Patch

2. Bypass auto-routing and create a Combinator.
3. Connect the Mixer Aux 1 send outs to the Combinator inputs, and the aux 1 returns to the Combi outputs.
4. In the Combinator sub-rack, create a RV-7000 reverb.
5. Insert an ECF-42 filter, and adjust the frequency to 58, resonance to 40, envelope amount to 52, and decay to 44.
6. Create a Matrix Pattern Sequencer, and zero out the gate events on all even-numbered steps.
7. In the Matrix curve edit window, on steps 2, 9, 12, and 16, set curve segments to 64.
8. Save the Combinator patch as "FilterVerb.cmb."

Sound Source

9. Create another Combinator.
10. Load the patch, "5 – Ahp10 90BPM Source.cmb" from the *Power Tools for Reason* CD \ Combinator Patches directory.
11. Adjust the mixer channel 1 aux send to 100.
   ‣ Run the sequence to hear the effect.

Combine

Several examples in following chapters make use of the Combinator, while some remain unchanged as legacy examples from the previous edition of *Power Tools for Reason 2.5*. The legacy examples can be converted into Combinator patches by using the Combine item in the Edit menu. First, use the multiple selection shortcut (shift-click on devices), then use the Combine command. Strategically selecting devices in the middle of a signal chain will automatically create a Combinator effect device or sound module. Once the modules are combined, apply modulation routings and controls to complete the device.

Reason Drum Kits

Owners of the Propellerhead Software ReFill Sample Library called Reason Drum Kits can take their favorite drum configurations and convert them into Combinator Patches. Whether you frequently use the same kit or rely upon a customized mix kit, having the mixer and equalizer configurations saved as Combinator patches will improve your workflow efficiency.

1. From the Reason File menu, select Open.
2. Using the Song Browser, navigate to the Reason Drum Kits ReFill.
3. Open the MULTI OUT NN-XT.rns file in the NN-XT Patches directory.
4. On the NN-XT, click on the patch browser button and load the very popular set "IdrisB 7D7 55 ALL.sxt" from the Reason Drum Kits\-NN-XT Patches\Preset Kits\Multi Out\All Mics (ALL)\Vintage Soul – Funk Directory.

5. Once samples are loaded, click on any device in the rack.

6. From the edit menu, choose Select All Devices.

7. From the edit menu, select Combine. This will automatically wrap the RDK setup into a Combinator.

8. Save the Combinator Patch as "IdrisB7D7 RDK.cmb."

Each time you use the IdrisB kit, your mix and EQ settings can be saved as customized configurations. Save the default "MULTI OUT NN-XT.rns" configuration as a Combinator as well. This alone will save time when you need to add RDK drums. Because auto-routing rules apply in the sub-rack, inserting a reverb into the configuration is quite easy, and the custom reverb settings can be included in the patch. If you want to insert a compressor on the stereo mix of the configuration, this will require manual cabling, so add the compressor with auto-routing disabled and manually cable the compressor as an insert between the mixer master outputs and the Combinator From Devices inputs.

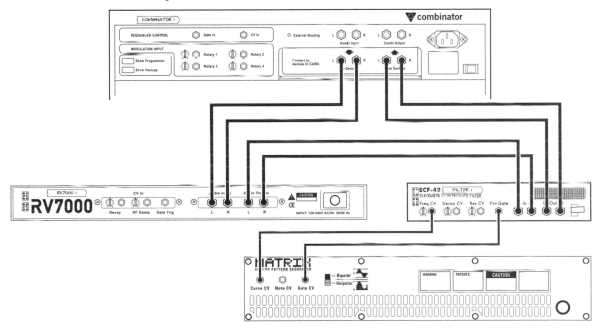

Figure 5-10
Combinator effects signal path starts from the To Devices outputs, goes through the reverb and filter, and then returns to the From Devices inputs.

Combinator Skins

The Combinator GUI (graphic user interface) is customizable, so users can develop their own synths and effects and add the final touch of a visual modification. The Combinator backdrop is a standard JPEG image file with the dimensions of 754 pixels wide by 138 pixels high.

1.In an empty rack, create a Combinator.

2. On the Edit menu, choose Select Backdrop.
3. Navigate to the Reason Application \ Template Documents \ Combi Backdrops directory.
4. Load the image file "Template Backdrop.jpg." The new image will replace the default interface. To restore the default interface, simply select the Remove Backdrop item from the Edit menu.

Several Combinator patches included in the Reason Factory Soundbank have customized backdrops. Use the Combinator Patch Search feature to locate patches like "Rhumbatronic," "Strumming Bridges," "Electro Do Brazil," "Guitar Strummer," and "Cyan Monday."

Chapter 6
Dynamics Effects

Loudness is determined primarily by the amplitude of an audio signal, and can be measured by VU meters or viewed in a display of a waveform in editing software. Visual references are not always reliable, however, because perceived loudness is determined both by amplitude and by the frequency content. Generally, tones with midrange and moderately high frequencies (up to 3kHz or so) sound subjectively louder than low-frequency timbres that have the same amplitude. It's important to keep this difference in mind as we discuss the topic of dynamics. In some cases, what you hear may not reflect what you see in the meters. When choosing between the two, assuming you have a decent monitoring setup, you should always trust your ears rather than the meters.

Dynamics are variations in loudness, and devices that control loudness are called dynamics processors. Included within this category are attenuators, compressors, limiters, and gates. These names reflect the processes the devices perform. A compressor squeezes down the dynamic range of a signal. Limiters prevent signals from exceeding a specified level. Gates, also called noise gates, allow signals above a certain level to pass through, while signals below the threshold are muted.

Reason features several dynamics effects, including the MClass Compressor, the MClass Maximizer, and the Comp-01 Compressor/Limiter. The Scream 4 tape algorithm also serves as a compressor. The modulation of mixer channels with CVs provides for "keyed" as well as traditional gating effects.

Headroom

Loudness is measured in decibels (dB), and the dynamic range of digital audio spans between the maximum of 0dB full-scale (0dBFS) and silence ($-\infty$ dB). Signals exceeding 0dBFS are called "overs" and cause clipping, a form of digital distortion. To prevent clipping, individual signals are attenuated so that when the signals are mixed (added together), the combined level does not exceed 0dB. When overs occur, the Audio Out Clipping lamp glows on the Reason transport.

Most digital audio systems, including Reason, are designed so that normal signal levels average below 0dB. Some dynamic range is left over so that occasional peaks can be handled without clipping. This extra space is called *headroom*. As noted in Chapter 4, a setting of 100 on the reMix mixer produces an output of unity gain; that is, the output of the mixer will be at the same level as its input. But in this case, unity gain is not the same as 0dB, because the latter is referenced to Reason's audio as a whole, not to individual mixer channels.

Compressors and limiters reduce the level of the highest peaks in the signal. A compressor can be inserted to tame a drum track with aggressive peaks, or an MClass Maximizer can be patched to the output of the main mixer to limit the entire mix and prevent clipping.

VU Meters

The MClass Maximizer features a multi-segment VU meter designed for critical measurement of signals. VU stands for *volume unit*, a unit that is more or less equivalent to a decibel. The Maximizer meter has two modes, Peak and VU. Peak mode measures the loudest portions of a signal while VU mode measures an average level between the peak and the RMS (root-mean-squared) level. Peak measurements help prevent overload and clipping, but the VU meter provides a better idea of the signal's subjective loudness.

Although they measure the same signal, Peak and VU modes behave differently. VU levels will generally be lower, because the VU meter shows an average of the signal level. Another difference is due to the meter movement or *ballistics*. Peak meters are fast and respond to quick dynamic changes. VU ballistics are slower because they require time to measure the average level. The fast ballistics of the peak meter help determine available headroom. When the meters register into the red (over) range, then there is no headroom—the signal is exceeding the 0dBFS limit.

Peak and VU Meter Comparison

This example illustrates how VU meters differ from peak level meters. Two Maximizer units are connected in series with the limiting features disabled, so signals pass unaffected but are still measured by the VU meters. This configuration is useful when mixing or mastering to help monitor problem signals and gauge loudness.

1. In an empty rack, create two MClass Maximizer Limiters. If your empty rack already contains a mixer or a Combinator functioning as a mastering suite, begin by deleting them.
2. Disable the limiter on both Maximizer units.
3. Set the Maximizer 2 meter mode to VU.

4. Create a Combinator and load the patch "6 – HHP09 Source.cmb" from the *Power Tools for Reason* CD \ Combinator Patches directory.

▸ Run the sequence.

As the sequence plays, observe the differences between Peak and VU modes. The Peak meter has faster ballistics that measure the loud clap sound from the drum loop, while the VU meter movement is slower and does not clearly indicate the loudness spike.

Gain Structure

Adjusting the gain structure of a song is a way of balancing mix levels to prevent overs. The principle involves adjusting the output volume controls of the sound modules so that the levels coming into the mixer don't clip. Once this gain structure is set, make small fader adjustments to balance the signals relative to each other. The following procedure can be applied to a Reason song that is ready for final mix:

Try this

1. Start with a song that is ready to mix.
2. Set the mixer master fader to 127.
3. Solo a mixer channel and set its fader to 127.
4. Run the sequence and watch the clipping indicator for overs.
5. Adjust the sound module's master level control downward, if necessary, until no clipping occurs.
6. Disable solo and decrease the mixer channel fader to 100.
7. Repeat this for each mixer input channel.
8. After adjusting all incoming levels, decrease the master fader level to 100. The master levels should peak near unity gain, leaving about 6dB to 14dB of headroom.

Adjusting the maximum input signals from sound modules is one method of overload prevention, but this can lead to other signals being too low in the mix. A solution is to constantly change the fader levels to keep the signals balanced, but certain signals require fast changes. This is where compressors become necessary, because they automatically control dynamics and thereby stabilize erratic levels.

The MClass Compressor

Producers commonly rely upon compressors in their projects, because they are said to make a mix sound better. Some might argue that compressors are magic devices that dramatically improve a mix. Compressors can prevent low levels from dropping too low and becoming inaudible, or restrain loud peaks from getting too high and dominating a mix. This added measure of dynamic stability often helps engineers balance a mix quickly.

When a signal passes through a compressor, portions of the signal that lie below the *threshold* level pass uncompressed. When the signal rises above the threshold, the compressor initiates gain reduction. The amount of reduction depends on the *ratio* parameter. If the ratio is to 2:1, the output signal above the threshold increases by 1dB for every 2dB of increase at the input. When the ratio is 10:1, the output level increases 1dB above the threshold for every 10dB that the input rises above the threshold. The output level still increases above the threshold value, but doesn't rise as high as it would without compression.

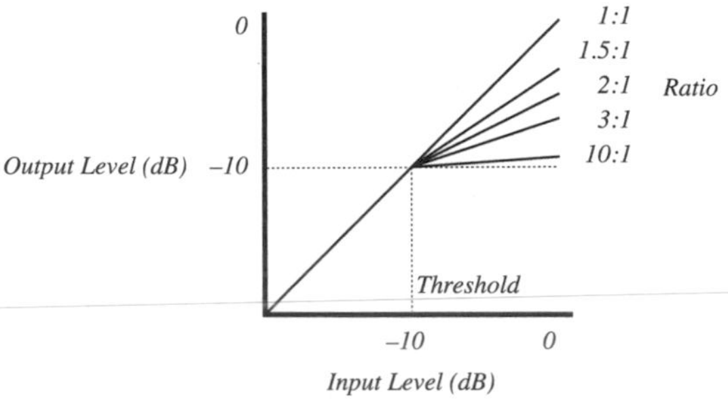

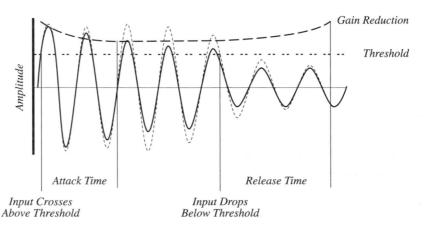

Figure 6-1
Transfer function graph of input signal levels vs. output levels at different ratio settings.

The *input gain* control boosts and attenuates incoming signals on the MClass Compressor. The lowest compression threshold is −36dB. This is normally adequate as a minimum threshold setting, but in some instances such as dialog where there are silent parts between words and phrases, it's useful to increase the input signal to establish more sensitive compression settings.

Figure 6-2
Gain reduction effects through the different stages.

When the input signal crosses the threshold level, gain reduction starts over the timeframe set by the *attack* parameter. Short attack times quickly compress signals, which is useful for taming unexpected peaks or instantly compressing incoming signals. Once the level drops, compression eases back at the rate set by the *release* parameter. Release time has a minimum setting of 50ms and ranges to 600ms. The Adaptive Release feature shapes the release time to reflect the incoming signals.

The output gain parameter controls the amount of make-up gain. Compression can significantly reduce the level of the incoming signal, and make-up gain compensates for the loss. The net result of using make-up gain can be that lower-level signals are brought up, making the compressed signal sound subjectively louder even though its peaks are no higher than before the compressor was applied.

MClass Compressor in the Mix

Using compressors in a real-world situation is a subjective task because compression is not a consistent process. The output of the MClass (or any) Compressor behaves differently depending on the input signal. Compressing a sustained synth pad, for instance, sounds different from compressing a drum loop. Percussive impulses cause the compressor to change its compression amount frequently, so the compressor is behaving differently than it would if it were processing a synth pad with no peaks. But while using a compressor is a subjective task, there are guidelines that lead to useful settings.

Most instrument, drum, and vocal recordings benefit from the use of compressors, and techniques normally associated with studio recordings apply within Reason songs. The general rule is to keep dynamics processing *transparent*—a signal is compressed without sounding compressed. When the ratio is too great or the threshold is too low and the amount of compression exceeds 12dB, signals lose liveliness and sound over-compressed.

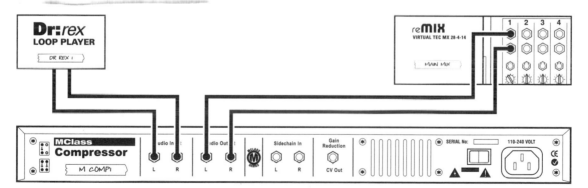

Figure 6-3
MClass Compressor inserted between Dr.REX and Mixer inputs.

General Rule?.

ESSENTIAL
LEARNING!

Compressing Drums

When compressing drums, use a ratio of 1.5:1 to 4:1, and adjust the input gain and threshold to limit compression to no more than 10dB with moderate attack time and moderate release time. The following example demonstrates how to use the MClass Compressor to increase the general loudness of a Dr.REX loop.

1. Start with an empty rack, and create a microMix Line Mixer.
2. Create a Dr.REX Loop Player, and set the level to 127.
3. Load the ReCycle Loop "Ahp06_Live_087_Chronic.rx2" from the Factory Sound Bank\Dr Rex Drum Loops\Acoustic\Hip Hop directory.
4. Copy the REX slice data to the Dr.REX 1 sequencer track.
5. Insert an MClass Compressor between the Dr.REX and the microMix.
6. Run the sequence and listen to the loop processed by the default compressor settings.
7. Switch the compressor between On and Bypass. Notice that the loudness is about the same. Before proceeding, switch the Compressor to On.
8. Decrease the threshold setting to –32.6 dB. The loudness of the drum loop decreases as compression initiates.
9. As the drum loop plays, sweep the ratio setting from 1:1 to ∞:1. The ratio setting controls the intensity of gain reduction. 1:1 means no gain reduction, so the output level matches the input level. As the ratio increases, the levels become more uniform between the loud kicks, rim shots, and hi-hats. Also, notice how loudness decreases as the ratio increases—the increased ratio value intensifies gain reduction.
10. Set the MClass Compressor Ratio to 2.95:1.
11. Watch the gain reduction meter. It should occasionally peak around –6dB. To compensate for this attenuation, increase the output gain setting to 4.5dB.
▸ Run the sequence, and as the loop cycles, compare the uncompressed signal with the compressed signal by switching the Compressor between On and Bypass modes. The loudness of the kick is about the same between the two, but the hi-hats and rim shot are louder on the compressed signal.

Finding the right compressor settings is a balancing act. Changing the ratio or threshold will alter the output level, making it necessary to compensate with the output gain control. The threshold setting determines the level where compression initiates; when the input signal is too low, compression occurs on only the loudest peaks. The input gain control allows you to boost the incoming signals, which allows more flexibility in setting the threshold value.

Pumping & Breathing

The attack and release parameters of a compressor can drastically change the character of the output. This example demonstrates the phenomenon of breathing, in which the decreased dynamic range increases the loudness of low-level noise, making it more noticeable.

1. Start with an empty rack, and create a microMix Line Mixer.
2. Create a Dr.REX Loop Player
3. Load the ReCycle loop "Hhp_Gtrstrm_092_eLAB.rx2" from the Factory Sound Bank\Dr Rex Instrument Loops\Various Hip Hop Loops directory.
4. Copy the REX slice data to the Dr.REX 1 sequencer track.
5. Insert an MClass Compressor between the Dr.REX and the microMix.
6. Set the Compressor input gain to 10.3dB, threshold to –32.6dB, ratio to ∞:1, attack to 30ms, and release to 331ms.
▸ Run the sequence.

As the loop plays, you'll hear unnatural changes in dynamics. The release stage slowly reverts to the normal loudness characteristics, which creates the breathing effect, and the high ratio setting and short attack time cause pumping during the attack stage.

experiment with other elements / samples / beats

Sharp Transients

A *transient* is a sharp change in dynamics, and the most common type of transient is the attack of a drum hit. The initial strike of a drum head is louder than the rest of the sound, so by compressing the transients, a compressor can change the dynamic character of drums and drum loops. Longer attack times allow sharp transients to pass through the compressor without compression. The initial hit is loud, and as compression gradually takes effect the level is brought down. The following example demonstrates how the MClass Compressor shapes the transient hits of a drum loop.

1. Start with an empty rack, and set the song tempo to 98.
2. Create a microMix Line Mixer.
3. Create a Dr.REX Loop Player.
4. Load the ReCycle loop "Ahp04_Live_085_Chronic.rx2" from the Factory Sound Bank\Dr Rex Drum Loops\Acoustic\Hip Hop directory.
5. Copy the REX slice data to the Dr.REX 1 sequencer track.
6. Set the Dr.REX master level to 127.
7. Insert an MClass Compressor between the Dr.REX and the microMix.
8. Set the compressor's input gain to 8.8dB, threshold to –27.8dB, ratio to 6.72:1, attack to 32ms, and release to 600ms.
▸ Run the sequence.

As the sequence is running, toggle the Compressor between On and Bypass to compare the uncompressed loop. The compressed drum loop emphasizes the attacks of the kick drum and snare drum hits, and the high compression ratio and input gain increases the reverb tail. The original loop sounds rather plain, like a drummer playing in a room, but compressed it has more power with more tonal character. The emphasized transients result from the 32ms attack time. This time span leaves enough space for the loud strikes to pass before the signal is compressed. Adjust the attack time to 1ms and listen as the transients become compressed.

Compressing Sound Modules

To help shape the mixdown, sounds from Reason synthesizers and samplers can be processed through an MClass compressor. Sounds like strings, guitars, bass, and synths can benefit from compression. Instrument compression is usually transparent, and the *soft knee* feature changes the gain reduction ratio to produce a smoother gain reduction. A normal compression ratio is a linear function, and the soft knee changes the function to a non-linear curve. Compression near the threshold is less noticeable, while compression near maximum gain reduction values is more noticeable.

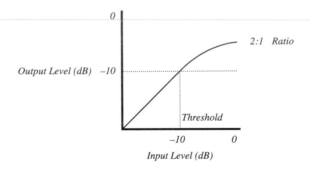

Figure 6-4
Transfer function with
Soft Knee enabled.

Compressing Instruments

Try starting with a ratio between 2:1 and 3:1, and adjust the threshold and input gain controls to limit the gain reduction to less than 10dB.

1. In an empty rack, create a reMix mixer.
2. Create a Combinator.
3. Load the patch "6 - Rhodes Source.cmb" from the *Power Tools for Reason* CD \ Combinator Patches directory. This patch loads the source audio for the example.
4. On the Combinator, click on Run Pattern Devices to initiate audio playback. Listen and observe the VU meters to see the levels jump in range.
5. Insert an MClass Compressor between the Combinator outputs and the mixer inputs.
6. Set the compressor's threshold to –20.1 dB, enable the soft knee function, set ratio to 3.03:1 and release to 379ms, and enable the adaptive release button.

You should immediately notice the levels are more stable than in the uncompressed signal. The compressed levels are not as loud because no make-up gain is applied. Adjust the compressor output gain to about 3 dB to make the signal louder.

Compressing Vocals

Vocals follow a similar rule. With a ratio of 1.5:1 to 3:1, short attack, and long release, compression should not normally exceed more than 10dB. It's generally a good idea to compress vocals to help them sit well in a mix, but it's also a good idea to compress vocal and dialog parts used as modulation sources.

1. In an empty rack, create a reMix mixer.
2. Create a Combinator.
3. Load the patch "6 – Vocal Source.cmb" from the *Power Tools for Reason* CD \ Combinator Patches directory. This patch loads the source audio for the example.
4. On the Combinator, click on Run Pattern Devices to initiate audio playback.
5. Insert an MClass Compressor between the Combinator outputs and the Mixer inputs.
6. Set the compressor's threshold to –27.5 dB, soft knee enabled, ratio to 2.13:1, attack to 36ms, release to 296ms, and adapt release enabled.

Compare the uncompressed signal and observe the VU meter to see how much the vocals fluctuate. The compressor tightens up the dynamic range and makes the levels less erratic. When compression is used on vocals within a mix, it helps keep the vocal track balanced with instrument and drum tracks.

MClass Compressor Sidechain

The MClass Compressor has a sidechain input, which can be used for processing techniques like ducking and de-essing. Inside the compressor, the signal splits with one path leading to the dynamics processor and the other to the sidechain. The compressor measures the sidechain signal, senses the threshold level, and adjusts the gain reduction accordingly. When cables connect to the sidechain inputs, the compressor uses the secondary signals to control the processing instead of the signal being processed. The following examples illustrate two common uses of the sidechain inputs on the MClass Compressor.

MClass Compressor Ducking

Ducking is a process in which an external sidechain signal controls the compression of a different signal. The following project demonstrates how to configure the compressor to receive two sound sources, where one signal modulates the compression applied to the other signal.

experiment

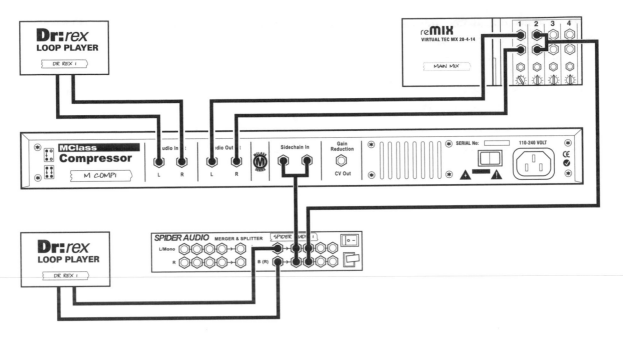

Figure 6-5

MClass Compressor
Sidechain inputs
receiving audio sig-
nals from a split out-
put from the second
Dr.REX Loop player.

1. In an empty rack, create a reMix mixer.
2. Create a Dr.REX Loop Player.
3. Load the ReCycle loop "125_ClubCraze_mLp_eLAB.rx2" from the Factory Sound Bank\Music Loops\Variable Tempo (rex2)\Uptempo directory.
4. Copy the REX slice data to the Dr.REX 1 sequencer track.
5. Insert an MClass Compressor between Dr.REX 1 and the mixer.
6. Set the threshold to –32dB, ratio to about 10:1, and enable soft knee.
7. Bypass auto-routing and create a Dr.REX Loop Player.
8. Load the ReCycle loop "Hse04_Plump_130_eLAB.rx2" from the Factory Sound Bank\Dr Rex Drum Loops\House directory.
9. Copy the REX slice data to the Dr.REX 2 sequencer track.
10. Bypass auto-routing and create a Spider Audio Merger & Splitter.
11. Connect the Dr.REX 2 audio outputs to the Spider Audio Split A & B inputs.
12. Connect the Spider Audio Split A1 & B1 outputs to the MClass Compressor sidechain in.
13. Connect the Spider Audio Split A2 & B2 outputs to the Mixer channel 2 inputs.

Run the sequence to hear the ducking effect. As the sequence plays, switch the MClass Compressor into Bypass to hear the difference between the compressed and uncompressed music loop. You'll hear the distinct difference when the signal ducks with the peak of each kick drum.

Frequency-Dependent Compressor

De-essing is a form of frequency-dependent compression in which a bandpass filter processes the sidechain signal. The filter allows a certain range of frequencies to pass into the sidechain. When signals pass through the filter and enter the sidechain, the signal triggers the threshold and clamps down on the unfiltered signal. The following project is a Spectral Compressor Combinator patch that is useful for de-essing or other forms of selective compression.

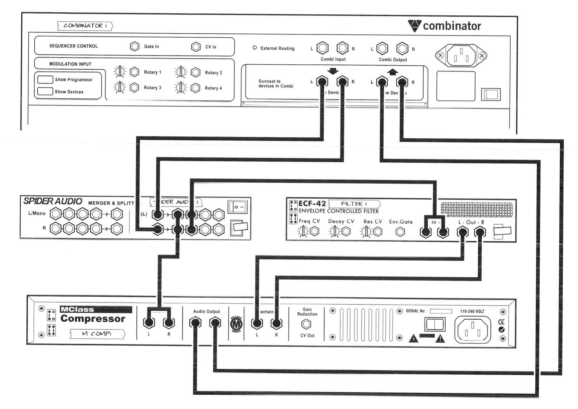

Figure 6-6
MClass De-esser using a bandpass filter.

1. Start with an empty rack and create a reMix mixer.
2. Create a Combinator.

Spectral Compressor Combinator

3. In the Combinator sub-rack, bypass auto-routing and create a Spider Audio Merger & Splitter.
4. Connect the Combinator's To Devices outputs to the Spider split L&R inputs.
5. Bypass auto-routing and create an MClass Compressor.

6. Connect the Spider Audio split output 1 L&R to the compressor's audio inputs.
7. Connect the compressor's audio outputs to the Combinator's From Devices inputs.
8. On the compressor, enable soft knee and set the attack to 4ms.
9. Bypass auto-routing and create an ECF-42 Envelope Controlled Filter.
10. Connect the Spider Audio split output 2 L&R to the ECF-42 inputs.
11. Connect the ECF-42 outputs to the compressor's sidechain inputs.
12. Set the ECF-42 mode to BP12.
13. Open the second Combinator's programmer and set the following modulation routings:

Device	Source	Target	Min	Max
Filter 1	Rotary 1	Frequency	0	127
Filter 1	Rotary 2	Resonance	0	127
Filter 1	Button 2	Enabled	1	2
MComp 1	Rotary 3	Threshold	0	127
MComp 1	Rotary 4	Ratio	0	127
MComp 1	Button 1	Sidechain Solo	0	1

14. Rename the Combinator controls and set the parameters as follows:

Control	Name	Default Value
Rotary 1	Sidechain Freq	117
Rotary 2	Sidechain Q	119
Rotary 3	Threshold	0
Rotary 4	Ratio	84
Button 1	Monitor	Off
Button 2	Bypass Filter	Off

15. Close the programmer and rack, and then save the Combinator patch as "Spectral Compressor.cmb."

Sound Source

16. Click in the main rack below the Combinator and create a second Combinator. Verify that the second Combinator's outputs are connected to the Spectral Compressor Combi's inputs.
17. On the second Combinator, load the patch "6 - Essess Source.cmb" from the *Power Tools for Reason* CD \ Combinator Patches directory.

▸ Run the sequence to hear the de-essing process. Click on the Monitor button to solo the sidechain signal, then switch back and toggle the Bypass Filter button to hear the difference between the filtered sidechain and the normal signal.

This is an example of perceived loudness, in which human hearing is more sensitive to certain frequencies. Compression is greater when "esses" are spoken, and this reduces the level to a comfortable listening range. Equalization can be applied without de-essing, but this changes the harmonic content of the signal and makes it sound artificial. De-essing simply ducks the signal level instead of changing the frequency response.

Comp-01 Auto Make-Up Gain

The auto make-up gain feature of the Comp-01 Compressor/Limiter is useful for controlling the levels of non-percussive synthesizer and sampler signals. Each sound module voice (polyphony) increases the output level, and performances that require six to ten voices can become very loud and require level balancing. Simply inserting a Comp-01 between the sound module and the mixer input provides a quick solution to maintain a stable level. The default settings on the Comp-01 are generally most effective for this application.

The ratio and threshold settings on the Comp-01 determine the amount of make-up gain. There are three rules to remember about the auto make-up gain. First, the ratio parameter determines the amount of gain added. Second, the threshold parameter decreases the gain added by the ratio setting. Third, the amount of gain will not drop below zero.

The maximum amount of make-up gain added occurs when ratio is 127 and threshold is zero. Because make-up gain changes when threshold and ratio are adjusted, the output signal level is sometimes unpredictable, and some settings increase the output level because of the auto make-up gain feature.

A threshold of 64 and ratio of 80 are the optimal settings for attenuating the output level from a high incoming signal. This has nothing to do with the amount of compression or make-up gain, only amplitude reduction. The output levels start to increase as the threshold parameter nears the far extremes of 0 or 127. A similar pattern of behavior occurs when adjusting ratio toward 0 or 127. When the output levels start to increase, reduce the fader level of the channel receiving signals from the compressor.

"Pumping" Drum Loops

Pumping is one of the dynamic artifacts that are normally discouraged when using compressors, but this effect setting sometimes leads to interesting results with drum loops and Redrum drum patterns. These settings take advantage of the auto gain make-up feature and add a significant amount of level to the softer hits in ReCycle drum sounds. It's an odd effect, because the Comp-01 behaves like a limiter on the louder drum hits and like an expander on the softer hits. The quick envelope stages induce the pumping effect, which makes the softer hi hats sound louder.

1. In an empty rack, create a reMix mixer.
2. Create a Dr.REX Loop Player.
3. Load the ReCycle loop "Hse06_Strictly_130_eLAB.rx2" from the Reason Factory Sound Bank\Dr Rex Drum Loops\House directory.

4. Copy the REX slice data to the Dr.REX 1 sequencer track.
5. Set the Dr.REX output level to 127.
6. Insert a Comp-01 Compressor/Limiter between the Dr.REX and the mixer input.
7. Set the Comp-01 ratio to 107, threshold to 22, attack to 0, and release to 24.

▸ Run the sequence.

MClass Maximizer

Limiting is a standard feature of compressors because the two processes are essentially the same. Compressor with ratio settings of 10:1 or greater are considered limiters because the output level barely exceeds the threshold value, no matter how high the input level gets. The high compression ratio protects against sudden spikes in audio levels that may clip, and limits the dynamic range to a specified maximum. Intended as a mastering device, the Maximizer can prevent any signal from exceeding 0dB full scale. It's similar to a compressor with a high ratio setting and a fixed threshold set around −2dB.

The MClass Maximizer has fixed attack time settings of 4ms, 16ms, and 64ms, and release times of 150ms, 400ms, and automatic. The auto-release time is similar to the compressor's adaptive release feature: Release time changes according to the duration and level of the incoming signal. As with the compressor, the short 4ms attack time is better suited for catching transients before they clip.

Brick Wall Limiter

The Maximizer is a peak limiter intended to process a complete mixdown. The 4ms Look Ahead and Soft Clip features establish the brick wall settings to prevent clipping and distortion. This establishes an absolute output maximum.

The first method is by enabling 4ms Look Ahead and setting the attack to 4ms (Fast). The look-ahead feature delays the signal processing in order to scan for unexpected transient spikes. When used with a 4ms attack time, it compresses the signal enough to prevent transients from exceeding the 0dB level, and the input signal can be driven to a high level without clipping. Attack times longer than 4ms won't detect fast transient spikes and the output may exceed 0dB full scale. Because of the time delay, this method of limiting is not recommended for inserts on sound modules.

1. Start with an empty rack, and create a reMix Mixer.
2. Create a Dr. REX Loop Player.
3. Load the ReCycle loop "Hhp05_Puffin_092_Chrnc.rx2" from the Reason Factory Sound Bank\Dr Rex Drum Loops\Hip Hop directory.
4. Copy the REX slice data to the Dr.REX 1 sequencer track.
5. Set the Dr.REX output level to 127, and Velocity AMP to −64.
6. Insert an MClass Maximizer between the Dr.REX and the mixer.

7. Enable the 4ms Look Ahead.

▶ Run the sequence.

As the loop plays, observe the VU meter. It will show that the output level does not exceed the 0dBFS level. Disable the 4ms look-ahead, and notice that the transients are not limited and cause overs in which the VU meter moves into the red range.

Longer attack times, which allow transients to pass unchecked by the limiter, add punch to the signal passing through. The signals will most likely clip, but the Soft Clip feature contours the signal and prevents overs. Using the limiter with the soft clip feature enabled provides brick wall limiting without the 4ms delay, making this configuration suitable as an insert device. Continuing from the previous example:

8. On the Maximizer, disable the 4ms look-ahead.

9. Set the Maximizer attack to slow (64ms) and enable soft clip.

▶ Run the sequence.

As the sequence plays, you can see that brick wall limiting working, because the VU meter and the audio out clipping meter do not indicate overs. Try changing the Maximizer attack times to MID and FAST to hear the changes in the amplitude envelope. Also, try changing the soft clip amount feature to hear how it affects the drum loop.

Bass Limiter

Bass is often the cornerstone of a mixdown. It is sometimes difficult to mix because the spectrum of frequencies can range from the very low sub-audible range to the difficult-to-harness, low-mid range. One method of harnessing the dynamics of the bass is to insert a Maximizer into the signal path.

1. Start with an empty rack and create a reMix mixer.

2. Create a Combinator.

3. Load the patch "6 - Bass Pattern.cmb" from the *Power Tools for Reason* CD \ Combinator Patches directory.

4. Insert an MClass Maximizer between the Combinator and the Mixer.

5. Adjust the Maximizer input gain to 4.1dB, set release to auto, soft clip enabled, soft clip amount 85.

6. Adjust the mixer channel 1 fader to 66.

▶ Run the sequence.

This example uses the soft clip feature to provide brick wall limiting. The incoming signal is increased in order to cross the limiter threshold setting, and the soft clip adds the brick wall limiting so that the output does not exceed 0dB. This sound is loud and powerful, and by comparing the Peak and VU ballistics, it is apparent that the loudness and the peak are both near maximum. To compensate for the loud Maximizer output, the mixer attenuates the level.

Scream 4 Tape Compression Effect

The Scream 4 tape compression algorithm is quite useful for adding "colored" compression to an audio signal. The algorithm simulates a type of compression of audio signals recorded to analog tape. The Scream 4 tape compression algorithm is simple: The main parameters are Damage Control, which adds input gain; P2, which controls compression ratio; and the master level output, which controls make-up gain. P1 emulates a tape speed control by changing a lowpass filter. Setting P1 to 127 opens the filter.

1. Start with an empty rack and create a reMix mixer.
2. Set the song tempo to 140.
3. Bypass auto-routing and create a Dr.REX.
4. Load the ReCycle loop "Chm25_Winditup_140_eLAB.rx2" from the Reason Factory Sound Bank\Dr Rex Drum Loops\Chemical Beats directory.
5. Copy the REX slice data to the Dr.REX 1 sequencer track.
6. Insert a Scream 4 Distortion unit between the Dr.REX and the mixer.
7. Program the following settings on the Scream 4: Damage on, Cut off, Body off, Damage control 88, algorithm Tape, P1 60, P2 88, Master level 65.

▸ Run the sequence.

CV-Based Dynamics Effects

All dynamics effects are based on circuitry that senses the levels of incoming audio signals. The sensing aspect of a compressor is, in essence, an envelope follower. The CV signal from the envelope follower is scaled by the ratio setting, and then modulates an amplifier circuit to control the output level. The MClass Compressor features a dedicated CV output whose value depends on the amount of gain reduction, and the Scream 4 Distortion and BV512 Digital Vocoder envelope followers can modulate mixer level CV inputs. The following examples illustrate using this combination of devices to create dynamics effects.

Envelope Follower Limiter

Ideally, this example results in silence. The control voltage signal generated from the Scream 4 Auto CV output corresponds to the loudness of the audio signal input. Using a Spider CV to invert the envelope follower CV value, the mixer level changes based on the loudness of the source signal.

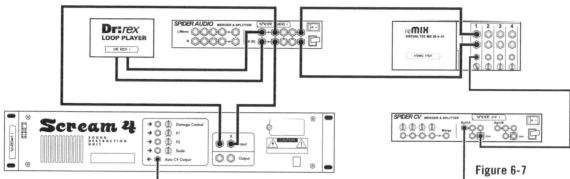

Figure 6-7
Scream Auto CV con-
nected to Spider CV.
The inverted output
modulates the mixer
channel level.

1. In an empty rack, create a reMix mixer.
2. Bypass auto-routing and create a Dr.REX Loop Player.
3. Load the ReCycle Loop "Chm22_Compress_135_eLAB.rx2" from the Dr Rex Drum Loops\Chemical Beats directory from the Reason Factory Sound Bank.
4. Copy the REX slice data to the Dr.REX 1 sequencer track.
5. Set the Dr.REX output level to 127.
6. Split the audio output from the Dr.REX Loop Player using a Spider Audio Splitter.
7. Connect one split signal from the Spider back into mixer channel 1.
8. Bypass auto-routing and create a Scream 4 Distortion unit.
9. Connect a second pair of signals from the Spider to the Scream 4 inputs. The distortion effect is not used to process audio, so the outputs are disconnected.
10. Create a Spider CV Merger & Splitter.
11. Connect the Scream 4 auto CV output to the Spider CV split A input.
12. Connect the Spider CV split A inverted output to the mixer channel 1 level CV input.
13. Set the mixer channel 1 level CV trim to a value of 2 or 3 for limiting. A value of 6 or 8 produces a severe pumping effect.
▶ Run the sequence.

When the audio signal is silent, there is no modulation of the mixer level. When the audio signal is loudest, the inverted CV signal value is –127, which modulates the mixer level down to zero. Decreasing the mixer level CV trim scales the modulation. Because the envelope follower tracks the changes quickly, this effect is not as effective as a compressor with controllable attack and release settings. The envelope follower on the BV512 may be more suited for this purpose.

Envelope Follower Ducking
This example builds on the inverted envelope follower configuration to modulate a different mixer input channel. The gain reduction induced by the envelope follower decreases the level of another signal, creating a ducking effect.

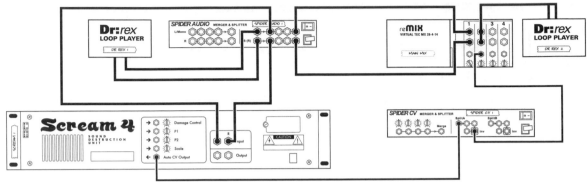

Figure 6-8
Inverted envelope fol-
lower modulating a
different mixer chan-
nel's level for ducking.

1. Start with the song file you created in the previous example.
2. At the bottom of the rack, add another Dr.REX Loop Player.
3. Load the ReCycle Loop "125_OrganRiff_mLp_eLAB.rx2" from Music Loops\
   Variable Tempo (rex2)\Uptempo Loops directory from the Reason Factory
   Sound Bank.
4. Copy the REX slice data to the Dr.REX 2 sequencer track.
5. Set the Dr.REX 2 output level to 127.
6. Re-route the Spider CV Splitter inverted output from mixer channel 1 to the
   channel 2 level CV input socket.
7. Set the mixer channel 2 level CV trim to 11.

Run the sequence and listen as the Dr.REX 2 signal is ducked by the inverted
modulation signal from the envelope follower receiving the Dr.REX 1 audio signal.
Adjusting the mixer channel 2 level CV trim to 0 disables the modulation from the
envelope follower.

This configuration is rather extreme, and acts more like a gate rather than a
ducker in the true sense of the word. Using low trim settings and adjusting the fader
level to 127 works best when this technique is used for ducking.

Noise Gate

Noise gates are used to automatically silence signals that fall below a threshold setting. These are typically used to prevent unwanted noise entering a mix, but
noise is not usually a factor in Reason, so noise gates are unnecessary. The noise gate
can be used as a sound shaping tool that forces silence in rhythmic parts.

1. In an empty rack, create a ReMix mixer.
2. Bypass auto-routing and create a Combinator. This device is the sound source.
3. Load the patch "6 -Break Source.cmb" from the *Power Tools for Reason* CD \
   Combinator Patches directory.

4. Create another Combinator. This will be used for the noise gate.
5. Connect the Combinator 1 outputs to the Combinator 2 inputs.

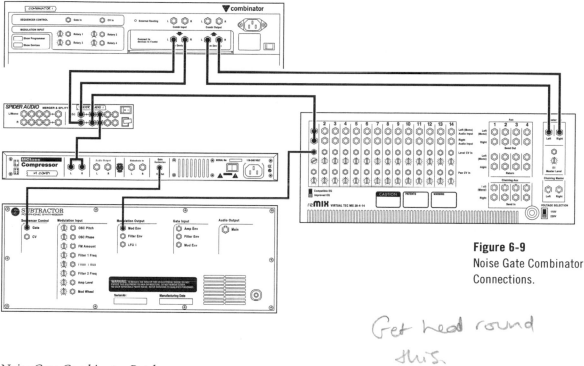

Figure 6-9
Noise Gate Combinator
Connections.

Noise Gate Combinator Patch

Proceed with the following in the Combinator 2 Sub Rack:

6. Create a Spider Audio Splitter.
7. Connect the Combinator's To Devices outputs to the Spider Audio A & B inputs.
8. Create a reMix Mixer, and set the Channel 1 fader level to zero.
9. Connect the Spider split output 1 L & R to the inputs of mixer 2 channel 1.
10. Bypass auto-routing and create an MClass Compressor.
11. Set the Compressor ratio to 33.3:1.
12. Connect the Spider Audio split output 2 L&R to the inputs of Compressor.
13. Bypass auto-routing and create a SubTractor synthesizer.
14. Set the SubTractor polyphony to 1 and mod envelope sustain to 127.
15. Connect the Compressor gain reduction CV Out to the SubTractor sequencer control gate input.
16. Connect the SubTractor Mod Env CV output to the mixer 2 channel 1 level CV input.
17. Set the Mixer 2 channel 1 CV trim to 82.

18. On the Combinator Programmer set the following modulation routings:

Device	Source	Target	Min	Max
MComp 1	Rotary 1	Threshold	127	0
MComp 1	Rotary 2	Input Gain	63	127
MComp 1	Rotary 3	Attack	0	127
MComp 1	Rotary 4	Release	0	127
SubTractor 1	Rotary 3	Mod Env Attack	0	26
SubTractor 1	Rotary 4	Mod Env Release	0	127

19. Rename the Combinator controls and set the parameters as follows:

Control	Name	Default Value
Rotary 1	Threshold	40
Rotary 2	Input Gain Trim	0
Rotary 3	Attack	13
Rotary 4	Release	44

20. Save the patch as "Noise Gate.cmb."

▶ Run the sequence.

As the sequence is playing, you can hear just a few peaks of the snare loops triggering the gate to open and pass the signal. The Compressor CV is used as a sensor to trigger the Subtractor Envelope. This envelope CV in turn opens and closes the mixer channel to create the gate effect. Adjusting the threshold and input gain trim parameters allows changes to the sensitivity of the sensor, while the attack and release parameters shape the gate behavior.

Gated Mixer Channel

A variation on the noise gate idea is called "keyed gating," which functions like a sidechain that opens and closes the gate. Keyed gating can be used as a production technique that chops a signal into a rhythmic pattern. This example uses a Matrix curve CV signal to modulate a mixer channel between open and silence.

1. In an empty rack, create a ReMix mixer.
2. Create an NN19 Digital Sampler.
3. Load the sample "BurstAway_eLAB.aif" from the Reason Factory Sound Bank\ Other Samples\FX-Vox directory.

Not available! →

4. Edit the NN19 sequencer track, drawing note events on C3 that are two measures long.
5. Bypass auto-routing and create a Matrix Pattern Sequencer.
6. Connect the Matrix curve CV output to the mixer channel 1 level CV input.
7. Set the mixer channel 1 level CV trim to 100.
8. Set the mixer channel 1 fader level to 0.
9. Set the Matrix pattern to 32 steps and the resolution to 1/32.
10. Draw maximum curve events on steps 1 through 17, 19, 21, 23, 25, 27, 29, and 31.

▶ Press Play and listen to the sample break up as the Matrix curve CV modulates the mixer level like a keyed gate.

Chapter 7
Filter and Equalizer Effects

Filters and equalizers are devices that alter the frequency content of an audio signal, and anything that changes frequency response is considered a filter. In acoustic instruments, a guitar body is a filter system that changes the frequency response of vibrating strings and produces the specific sonic character or *timbre* of a guitar. Filters found in Reason synthesizers and samplers shape the timbre by removing harmonics. Almost every electronic music track has drum loops, sweeping synth pads, or elastic acid leads created with filter effects.

Similar to the way dynamics processors control the loudness of different signals, filters and equalizers control the frequency or *harmonic content*. Filters remove harmonics (or, to be more technical, partials) from audio signals in order to deemphasize certain frequency ranges. An equalizer is a device that uses filters and amplifiers to boost and cut frequency ranges. Equalizers can shape the harmonic content much the way filters do, but they are more commonly used to balance the frequency response.

The SubTractor Synthesizer, Dr.REX, NN19, and NN-XT have dedicated filters, and the RV7000 has a dedicated equalizer section, as does the Scream 4. Other devices in Reason designed specifically to filter and equalize signals include the ECF-42 Filter, the BV512 Digital Vocoder, the MClass Equalizer, the MClass Spatializer, and the PEQ-2 Parametric Equalizer. The Malström filters can process external signals connected to the audio inputs as well as the tones generated by the oscillators. This chapter discusses a variety of applications for filters and equalizers, and covers a few key issues about using equalizers to balance frequencies in a mix.

Frequency Ranges

The frequency of a sound is measured in Hertz (Hz)—the number of oscillations that occur in one second. A person with normal hearing is sensitive to sound frequencies between 20Hz and 20kHz. This is considered the audible spectrum of sound. Human hearing is more sensitive in certain frequency ranges, and perceived loudness varies depending on the frequency.

The audible frequency spectrum is typically divided into five regions: bass, low-mids, mids (middle), high-mids, and highs. These ranges have generally accepted values in audio engineering, and many equalizers have fixed parameters based on these ranges. The chromatic scale is a subset of pitches used as the standard for composition in Western music. Musical pitch is not quite the same thing as frequency, but for most purposes we can use the words "pitch" and "frequency" interchangeably. It's important to understand the relationship between pitches and frequencies. Equalizers use Hertz as a measurement increment, while musical pitch is measured in notes and octaves.

In the table below, Middle C (MIDI note 60, a pitch whose frequency is about 270Hz) is referred to as C3.

Frequency Range	Range Value (Hertz)	MIDI Notes	BV512 Bands (FFT)
Highs	8,000Hz–22,000Hz	C8–G8 and up	31–32
High mids	2,000Hz–8,000Hz	C6–B7	22–30
Mids	500Hz–2,000Hz	C4–B5	13–21
Low mids	100Hz–500Hz	G#1–B3	5–13
Bass	20Hz–100Hz	E-1–G1	1–5

Filters

The filters on Reason devices have different modes, each mode corresponding to a specific type of filter. The standard filter types are lowpass, highpass, bandpass, and notch (band-reject). Filters generally have two parameters, governing frequency (cutoff frequency) and resonance amount. On the Reason devices, there is a mode selector to choose the filter type.

The *frequency* parameter tunes the filter cutoff frequency—the point in the audio spectrum where filtering is applied. A low parameter value corresponds to a low frequency setting, while a high value sets the cutoff frequency in the high range. A lowpass filter rejects signals above the cutoff frequency while allowing frequencies below the cutoff to pass through. A highpass filter allows frequencies above the cutoff setting to pass. A bandpass filter allows frequencies at or near the cutoff frequency to pass through, while rejecting frequencies that are above or below the cutoff. A notch filter allows all frequencies to pass except for a range around the cutoff frequency. In the case of bandpass and notch filters, the term "center frequency" is more correct than "cutoff frequency."

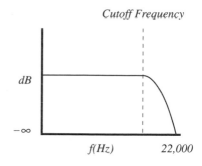

Lowpass Filter

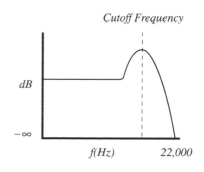

Resonant Lowpass Filter

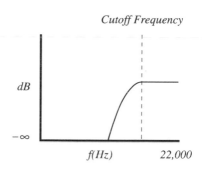

Highpass Filter

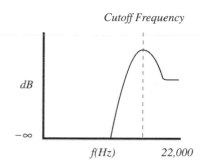

Resonant Highpass Filter

Figure 7-1
Four filter response curves.

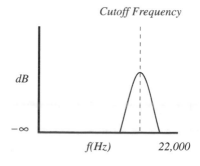

Bandpass Filter

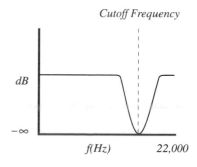

Notch Filter (Band Reject)

Figure 7-2
The response curves of bandpass and notch filters.

Filter resonance is a form of feedback, and the *resonance* parameter controls the amount of feedback in the region around the cutoff frequency. Resonant lowpass, highpass, and bandpass filters can produce a significant amount of gain near the cutoff frequency. With many filters, a maximum resonance feedback setting will send the filter into self-oscillation causing a characteristic howling sound. With notch filtering, the resonance parameter controls the bandwidth of the notch: High resonance settings result in a narrow slice of the spectrum being notched out.

The ECF-42 Envelope Controlled Filter is a multimode lowpass and bandpass filter, and the Malström Graintable Synthesizer has audio input sockets for processing external signals through the filter section. Besides having the standard lowpass and bandpass types, the Malström has comb filter modes and an amplitude modulation (AM) mode. Modulating the frequency and resonance parameters on these devices creates exciting sounds. Other filter effects can be achieved through automation, the module's own envelope, LFOs, and CV modulation sources.

Wah-Wah Effect

The following wah-wah effect uses two filters, a resonant 24dB lowpass filter connected in series with a 12dB resonant bandpass filter. The resonant lowpass filter adds a little extra body to the original tone and cuts off extraneous high frequencies that the bandpass filter does not cut. The wah-wah effect is only evident when the cutoff frequency is swept, so it's important to actively adjust the parameter.

1. Start with an empty rack, and create a reMix mixer.

Wah-Wah Combinator Patch

2. Create a Combinator.
3. In the Combinator sub-rack, create two ECF-42 filters, and verify they are connected in series to the input and outputs of the Combinator.
4. Set the Filter 1 Res to 48 and Mode to LP 24.
5. Set the Filter 2 Res to 72 and Mode to BP 12.
6. Open the Combinator Programmer and set the following modulation routings:

Device	Source	Target	Min	Max
Filter 1	Rotary 1	Frequency	36	101
Filter 2	Rotary 1	Frequency	26	110

7. Rename the Combinator controls and set the parameters as follows:

Control	Name	Default Value
Rotary 1	Wah Wah	40

8. Save the patch as "Wah-Wah.cmb."

Signal Source Section

9. Create a second Combinator.

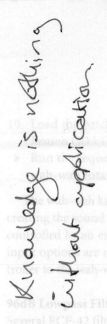

Knowledge is nothing without application

10. Load the patch "96 D! Guitar Chord Source.cmb" from the *Power Tools for Reason 4.0 Combinator Patches* directory.

» Run the sequence. As the guitar sample is being triggered, manually adjust the wah-wah rotary control.

The wah-wah knob opens and closes the filters, and changes to the cutoff frequency creating the sound made famous by the guitar pedal effect. Ideally the filters should be controlled by an expression pedal, but a knob or slider works as a substitute. If these input options are not available, assign the pitchbend wheel from your keyboard controller to the wah-wah control using Reason's MIDI Remote Mapping feature.

96dB Lowpass Filterbank

Several ECF-42 filters can be chained together to create an extreme 96dB-per-octave lowpass filter. A single filter provides 24dB of stop-band attenuation, and when another filter is added with the same cutoff frequency, another 24dB is cut. Using four filters will create a very sharp filtering effect that literally cuts out the entire dynamic range above the cutoff. This effect becomes very interesting when resonance is added, but the results are very loud and will distort. For your safety, a series of MClass dynamics processors are added to this effect—it can get really loud.

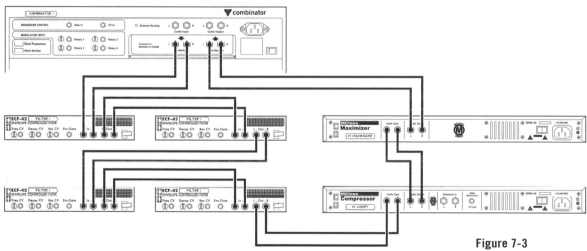

Figure 7-3
The 96dB lowpass filter includes four ECF-42 filters connected in series. The Combinator controls modulate the cutoff frequency and resonance on all of the devices.

1. Start with an empty rack, and create a reMix mixer.

96dB Lowpass Filterbank Combinator Patch

2. Create a Combinator.
3. In the Combinator sub-rack, create four ECF-42 filters, and verify they are connected in series to the input and outputs.
4. Click on Filter 4 and create an MClass Compressor. Enable soft knee.
5. Create an MClass Maximizer and enable soft clip.

6. Open the Combinator Programmer and set the following modulation routings:

Device	Source	Target	Min	Max
Filter 1	Rotary 1	Frequency	0	127
Filter 1	Rotary 2	Resonance	0	127
Filter 2	Rotary 1	Frequency	0	127
Filter 2	Rotary 2	Resonance	0	127
Filter 3	Rotary 1	Frequency	0	127
Filter 3	Rotary 2	Resonance	0	127
Filter 4	Rotary 1	Frequency	0	127
Filter 4	Rotary 2	Resonance	0	127

7. Rename the Combinator controls and set the parameters as follows:

Control	Name	Default Value
Rotary 1	Frequency	40
Rotary 2	Resonance	0

8. Save the patch as "96dB Filterbank.cmb."

Signal Source Section

9. Create a second Combinator.
10. Load the patch "7 – REX Loop Source.cmb" from the *Power Tools for Reason* CD \ Combinator Patches directory.
11. Turn down your monitors or headphones to a low level.
  ▸ Run the sequence.

Be very careful when tweaking the Resonance control of the 96dB filterbank patch. Even though dynamics processors reduce some of the output gain, this effect can still get extremely loud. Try setting the frequency to 30 and the Resonance to 110 for a wild, room-shaking bass.

Screamin' Filterbank (Version 2)

This effect was inspired by a hardware filter device called the Sherman Filterbank. The configuration is based on the 96dB lowpass filter described above, but it adds several other features, including a Scream 4 Distortion and a dry/wet crossfade control, and it uses dynamics processors to govern the extreme output levels of the resonant filters.

1. Start with an empty rack, and create a reMix mixer.

Screamin' Filterbank Combinator Patch

2. Create a Combinator. The following devices will all be created in the Combinator sub-rack:
3. Create a microMix Line Mixer.
4. Bypass auto-routing and create a Scream 4 Distortion unit.
5. Connect the Combinator To Devices outputs to the Scream 4 inputs.
6. Set the Scream 4 as follows: P1 83, P2 62, Master Level 100.

7. Create a Spider Audio Merger & Splitter.
8. Connect the Scream 4 outputs to the Spider splitter inputs.
9. Connect the Spider split 1 outputs to the microMix channel 1 inputs.
10. Bypass auto-routing and create an ECF-42 Filter.
11. Connect the Spider split 2 outputs to the ECF-42 inputs.
12. Create three more ECF-42 Filters, and verify the series connections with Filter 1.
13. For Filter 1 through Filter 4, set the Mode to LP 24.
14. Click on Filter 4 and create an MClass Compressor.
15. On the MClass Compressor, enable soft knee and adaptive release.
16. Create an MClass Maximizer and set the release to auto.
17. Connect the Maximizer outputs to the MicroMix channel 2 inputs.
18. Bypass auto-routing, create an MClass Compressor, and rename it "Follower."
19. Connect the Spider Audio split 3 outputs to the Follower audio inputs.
20. Connect the Follower gain reduction CV output to Combinator rotary 1 input.
21. Set the Follower threshold to −29.2dB, soft knee on, attack 1ms, release 426ms, adapt release on.
22. Open the Combinator Programmer and set the following modulation routings:

Device	Source	Target	Min	Max
Line Mixer 1	Rotary 4	Channel 1 Level	100	0
Line Mixer 1	Rotary 4	Channel 2 Level	0	100
Scream 1	Rotary 3	Damage Control	0	127
Scream 1	Button 3	Damage Type	0	1
Filter 1-4	Rotary 1	Frequency	0	110
Filter 1-4	Rotary 2	Resonance	0	80
Follower	Button 1	Enabled	0	1

23. Rename the Combinator controls and set the parameters as follows:

Control	Name	Default Value
Rotary 1	Frequency	40
Rotary 2	Resonance	0
Rotary 3	Drive	100
Rotary 4	Dry/Wet	100
Button 1	Env Follower	On
Button 3	Damage Type	Off

24. Save the Combinator patch as "Screamin Filterbank V2.cmb."

Signal Source

25. Create a second Combinator.
26. Load the patch "7 – REX Loop Source.cmb" from the *Power Tools for Reason* CD \ Combinator Patches directory.

▸ Run the sequence.

The limited filter parameter range prevents extreme settings in this patch, but very high output is possible with maximum resonance settings. The MClass dynamics processors are a means of protecting the output signal (and ears) from overloads. The gain reduction CV of the second MClass Compressor modulates the filter cutoff frequency, and with the right settings creates an interesting wobbling filter effect.

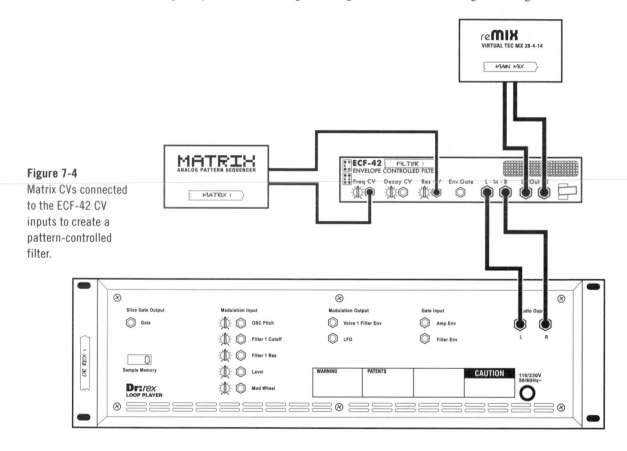

Figure 7-4
Matrix CVs connected to the ECF-42 CV inputs to create a pattern-controlled filter.

PCF: Pattern-Controlled Filter

Pattern-controlled filtering (PCF) is a technique unique to electronic music, in which a pattern of gate events causes filter envelope modulation. In Reason, the tools of choice are a Matrix to create the gate events and an ECF-42 Filter. The repeating pattern of opening and closing filters creates an interesting rhythmic effect similar to a feature in Propellerhead Software ReBirth RB-338.

1. In an empty rack, create a reMix mixer.
2. Bypass auto-routing and create a Dr.REX Loop Player.

3. Load the ReCycle loop "Chm04_Shag_125 eLAB.rx2" from the Factory Sound Bank\Dr Rex Drum Loops\Chemical Beats directory.
4. Copy the REX slice data to the Dr.REX 1 sequencer track.
5. Disable the filter on the Dr.REX.
6. Insert an ECF-42 Envelope Controlled Filter between Dr.REX 1 and the mixer input channel 1.
7. Set the ECF-42 cutoff frequency to 0, resonance to 30, envelope amount to 40, and velocity to 40, with envelope settings of A 10, D 0, S 127, R 70.
8. At the bottom of the rack, create a Matrix Pattern Sequencer.
9. Program the following in Matrix pattern A1:

Matrix Pattern

Step	1	2	3	4	5	6	7	8	9	10	11	12	13	14	15	16
Curve																
Note	C3	C3	C3	C3	C3	C3	C3	C3	C3	C3	C3	C3	C3	C3	C3	C3
Gate	H	M		M	TH	H	L	TM	M	L	L	M	H			

▸ Start the sequence to hear the pattern-controlled filtering of the drum loop.

Malström PCF

The independent filter section of the Malström synthesizer can also become a pattern-controlled filter. Matrix gate events trigger the Malström filter envelope. This PCF takes advantage of the inverted envelope modulation as well as the velocity to filter amount modulation. The traditional PCF created using the ECF-42 filter and a Matrix only has positive envelope modulation.

Figure 7-5
Dr.REX connected to the Malström audio inputs. A Matrix gate CV triggers the Malström filter envelope.

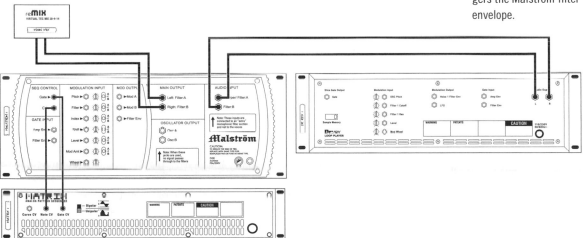

1. In an empty rack, create a reMix mixer.
2. Bypass auto-routing and create a Dr.REX Loop Player.
3. Load the ReCycle loop "Chm04_Shag_125_eLAB.rx2" from the Factory Sound Bank\Dr Rex Drum Loops\Chemical Beats directory.
4. Copy the REX slice data to the Dr.REX 1 sequencer track.
5. Disable the filter on the Dr.REX.
6. Create a Malström Synthesizer.
7. Connect the Dr.REX audio outputs to the Malström filter audio inputs.
8. On the Malström, disable osc A, osc B, mod A, and mod B.
9. Set the Malström velocity filter envelope setting to 39.
10. Set the Malström spread setting to 127.
11. Set the cutoff frequency to 127 and resonance to 30 on the Malström's filter A and filter B.
12. Enable the inverse setting on the Malström filter envelope and set the envelope as follows: A 18, D 36, S 127, R 42.
13. At the bottom of the rack, create a Matrix Pattern Sequencer.
14. Program the following on Matrix Pattern A1:

Matrix Pattern

Step	1	2	3	4	5	6	7	8	9	10	11	12	13	14	15	16
Curve																
Note	C3	C3	C3	C3	C3	C3	C3	C3	C3	C3	C3	C3	C3	C3	C3	C3
Gate	H	H			H	H	H		H		H	H	H		TH	H

15. Select the Malström and Matrix Pattern Sequencer.
16. Select the Combine command from the Edit menu and save the Combinator as "Malstrom PCF.cmb."

▶ Start the sequence to hear the pattern-controlled filtering of the drum loop. When the Malström spread parameter is set to zero, the outputs from Filter A and Filter B are combined into a mono output. Setting the spread parameter to 127 splits the two signals into discrete stereo channels.

Equalizers

Like many audio devices, equalizers are the byproduct of early telecommunications technology. They were first used to balance out the frequency response of telephone lines. Telephone lines would lose energy in certain frequency ranges, so special filters and amplifiers were applied to *equalize* the frequency response. The principles in these filters eventually evolved into audio equipment commonly found in broadcast studios, hi-fi equipment, recording studios, and Reason's virtual devices. The primary use of equalizers is to balance frequencies of sounds in a mix, but they can be used like filters to alter the timbre of a sound.

A common type of equalizer is the tone control on a stereo system. These controls, usually labeled treble and bass, boost or cut high frequencies and low frequencies. The tone controls balance the frequency of the response to suit the room acoustics and the listener's tastes. The similar principle applies to equalizers in Reason, which shape the tone of an instrument or the entire mix.

There are two general methods of using equalizers. The first method is similar to the use of the hi-fi tone control. A complete mix is processed, and the equalizer boosts the bass and high ranges to add some body and clarity to the mix. The second method is a corrective measure in which specific frequencies of specific sounds are attenuated to make the sound fit into a mix. For example, kick drums and electric bass guitars produce sounds whose frequencies overlap. Equalizers can be inserted on these sounds to contour overlapping frequencies so that a part of each sound is more audible in the mix. The same idea can be applied to other instruments, so that each sound fills a part of the spectrum to balance the frequencies in a mix.

The MClass Equalizer, the reMix Mixer 14:2, the PEQ-2, and the RV7000 Reverb have parametric equalizers, and the BV512 Digital Vocoder features a graphic equalizer option. Besides using equalizers with fixed settings to contour the frequency response, you can automate equalizer parameters or gang several equalizer parameters together within a Combinator patch. The equalizer parameters can be automated or modulated for some interesting time-varying effects.

Parametric Equalizers

The MClass Equalizer and the PEQ-2 Equalizer both have two parametric bands that alter two different frequency ranges to passing signals. The MClass Equalizer parametric controls are indicated as Param 1 and Param 2. The PEQ-2 controls are indicated as A and B. Each equalizer band has three controls: center frequency, bandwidth (Q), and gain/cut. The center frequency is the highest or lowest point of the equalization curve. The bandwidth control adjusts the width of the curve, and the gain control adjusts the height of the curve. The RV7000 Reverb has a parametric equalizer band similar to one band of the PEQ-2, as well as a low shelving band.

The MClass Parametric Equalizer is superior to the PEQ-2 because it has better specifications. The PEQ-2 has a frequency range of 31Hz to 16kHz controlled with the standard 128-position center frequency control, but the MClass Equalizer has a broader range from 39Hz to 20kHz, and the center frequency resolution is about 1,000 steps. The tooltip shows real-world center frequency and gain/cut values, while the PEQ-2 simply shows a parameter value. For general equalization, however, the PEQ-2 is still very useful unless you need to boost high frequencies or really want the tweakhead control of the MClass Equalizer.

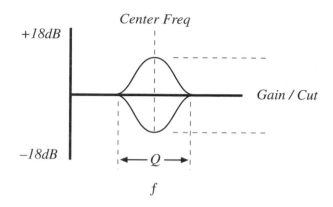

Figure 7-6
The frequency
response curve and
parameters of the
PEQ-2 and MClass
Equalizer parametric
sections.

The key to using any parametric equalizer is to find the ideal center frequency for the sound being equalized. This is the point where the gain change will be the greatest. Finding the ideal center frequency is quite easy. First, set the Q to a narrow bandwidth and set the gain to maximum. Adjust the frequency setting up or down until you hear the frequency levels suddenly spike. Then lower the Q to emphasize a broader range of frequencies and decrease the gain control as needed so that it will boost or cut the level of the desired frequency range.

Shelf EQ
Another parametric equalizer type is the shelf EQ. A shelf EQ has a response curve that looks like half of the bell curve produced by a parametric band. Shelf EQs resemble lowpass and highpass filters. The MClass Equalizer has two shelf EQ sections. A low shelf EQ designed to control the bass and low-mid ranges, while a high shelf EQ is designed for the high and high-mid ranges. The MClass shelf EQ has the same controls as the parametric bands, but because the response curve is different, the center frequency becomes a corner frequency. Signals above (high shelf) or below (low shelf) this corner frequency are boosted or cut. The Q parameter governs the sharpness of the curve.

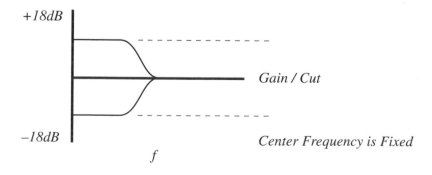

Figure 7-7
Shelf EQ response
curve for the mixer's
bass EQ.

The RV7000 EQ section has a low shelf EQ with two controls. This is sometimes called a *semi-parametric* equalizer because the Q parameter is fixed. The two controls adjust the frequency and gain/boost parameters.

The Mixer 14:2 has two limited shelf equalizers for bass and treble ranges. There is only one control, which adjusts the gain. The center frequency and Q are both fixed.

The Mixer 14:2 EQ has two modes controlled by a switch on the rear of the device. Compatible EQ is the same EQ found in early versions of Reason. The shelf EQ in compatible mode has a wide bandwidth (low Q shelf), and when both treble and bass are reduced, it sounds like attenuation. Improved EQ has a narrower bandwidth, and the bass control distinctly affects frequencies in the 20Hz to 80Hz range. The improved treble EQ also has a more distinct bandwidth as it affects frequencies in the 6kHz to 20kHz range.

Highpass Filter

Highpass filters are available in Reason only in certain sound modules, so there is no means of highpass-filtering sounds in a signal routing configuration. The following project is a Combinator effect that uses several MClass Equalizers to create an approximation of a highpass filter effect. The resonance control differs from that of a normal filter in that peak and bandwidth are controlled by separate rotary controllers. (The bandwidth control has no effect until resonance is turned up.)

1. Start with an empty rack, and create a reMix mixer.
2. Create a Combinator
3. In the Combinator sub-rack, create three MClass Equalizers. Auto-routing will connect them in series between the To Devices and From Devices input and output jacks.
4. On M EQ 1, set Lo Shelf On, Gain –18.3dB, Q: 2.0. Param 1: On, Gain: –1.7dB, Q: 2.8. Param 2: On, Gain: –17.1dB, Q:1.0.
5. On M EQ 2, set Hi Shelf On. Param 1: On, Freq: 224.1 Hz, Q: 1.0. Param 2: On, Freq: 2.354 Hz, Q: 1.0.   *should read 235.5 Hz*
6. On M EQ 3, set Low Shelf: On, Gain –18.3dB, Q: 0.92. Param 1: On.
7. Open the Combinator Programmer and set the following modulation routings:

Device	Source	Target	Min	Max
M EQ 1	Rotary 1	Low Shelf Frequency	0	1000
M EQ 1	Rotary 1	Parametric 1 Freq.	215	595
M EQ 1	Rotary 1	Parametric 2 Freq.	0	560
M EQ 2	Rotary 1	Parametric 2 Gain	0	–64
M EQ 2	Rotary 1	Hi Shelf Gain	0	14
M EQ 2	Rotary 1	Parametric 1 Gain	21	–64
M EQ 3	Rotary 1	Parametric 1 Freq.	0	1000
M EQ 3	Rotary 2	Parametric 1 Gain	0	63
M EQ 3	Rotary 3	Parametric 1 Q	0	127
M EQ 3	Rotary 1	Lo Shelf Frequency	0	1000

8. Rename the Combinator controls and set the parameters as follows:

Control	Name	Default Value
Rotary 1	Cutoff Freq	40
Rotary 2	Resonance	2
Rotary 3	Bandwidth	6

9. Save the patch as "Resonant High Pass Filter.cmb."

PEQ-2 Sweeping Bands

This effect uses two PEQ-2 parametric equalizers with very narrow bands. An LFO CV source modulates the center frequency parameters of the bands to create a sweeping EQ effect. The effect almost sounds like a phaser without the actual shift in signal phase.

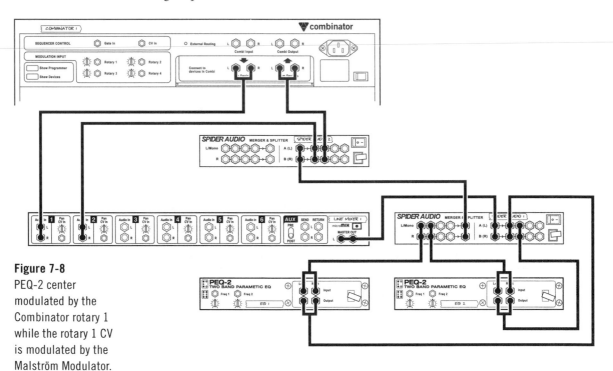

Figure 7-8
PEQ-2 center modulated by the Combinator rotary 1 while the rotary 1 CV is modulated by the Malström Modulator.

1. In an empty rack, create a reMix mixer.

The PEQ-2 Sweeping Band Combinator Patch

2. Create a Combinator.
3. In the Combinator sub-rack, bypass auto-routing and create a microMix Line Mixer.
4. Connect the Combinator's To Devices outputs to the microMix channel 1 inputs.

5. Set the MicroMix channel 2 fader to zero. Channel 2 will be wired as a feedback loop. To protect the system, this should be initially set to zero.
6. Still in the sub-rack, create a Spider Audio Merger & Splitter.
7. Connect the microMix master outputs to the Spider Audio split inputs.
8. Bypass auto-routing and create two PEQ-2 Parametric Equalizers. For both, switch the B band on.
9. In both EQ 1 and EQ 2, set Gain A and Gain B to 52.
10. Connect the Spider Audio split 1 outputs to the EQ 1 inputs.
11. Connect the Spider Audio split 2 outputs to the EQ 2 inputs.
12. Connect the EQ 1 outputs to the Spider Audio merge 1 inputs.
13. Connect the EQ 2 outputs to the Spider Audio merge 2 inputs.
14. Create a second Spider Audio Merger & Splitter. The second splitter will route the feedback loop. Before going on, make certain step 5 was completed.
15. Connect the Spider Audio 1 merger outputs to the Spider Audio 2 splitter inputs.
16. Connect the Spider Audio 2 split 1 outputs to the microMix channel 2 inputs.
17. Connect the Spider Audio 2 split 2 outputs to the Combinator's From Devices inputs.
18. Bypass auto-routing and create a Malström synthesizer.
19. Connect the Malström Mod A CV output to the Combinator rotary 1 CV input.
20. Open the Combinator Programmer and set the following modulation routings:

Device	Source	Target	Min	Max
Line Mixer 1	Rotary 3	Channel 2 Level	0	38
EQ 1	Rotary 1	Filter A Freq.	14	77
EQ 1	Rotary 1	Filter B Freq.	54	117
EQ 1	Rotary 2	Filter A Q	103	127
EQ 1	Rotary 2	Filter B Q	103	127
EQ 2	Rotary 1	Filter A Freq.	38	101
EQ 2	Rotary 1	Filter B Freq.	64	127
EQ 2	Rotary 2	Filter A Q	103	127
EQ 2	Rotary 2	Filter B Q	103	127
Malstrom 1	Rotary 4	Modulator A Rate	0	127
Malstrom 1	Button 3	Modulator A On/Off	0	1
Malstrom 1	Button 4	Modulator A Sync	0	1

21. Rename the Combinator controls and set the parameters as follows:

Control	Name	Default Value
Rotary 1	Freq	63
Rotary 2	Q	127
Rotary 3	Feedback	0
Rotary 4	Rate	46
Button 3	Mod On	On
Button 4	Sync	Off

22. Save the patch as "PEQ Sweeping Bands.cmb."
23. In the Reason Rack, create a second Combinator.
24. Load the Patch "7 – REX Loop Source 3.cmb" from the *Power Tools for Reason* CD \ Combinator Patches directory.

▸ Run the sequence.

Graphic Equalizer

A graphic equalizer is an array of bandpass filters whose center frequencies are spaced at regular intervals. The vertical sliders provide a visual, or graphic, representation of how the equalizer is changing the frequency response. The bands overlap, so that the entire frequency range is covered. Graphic equalizers are better suited for contouring frequency response rather than isolating precise frequencies, because the band values are fixed. The BV512 bandpass filters can be swept using the shift parameter. Graphic equalizers normally boost and cut frequencies bands about 15dB, but the BV512 graphic equalizer will cut frequencies to –∞ dB. These two features make the BV512 a useful device for dramatic filtering effects as well as for shaping the overall frequency response.

There are some idiosyncrasies about the BV512 graphic equalizer. The first issue is that the band count modes 4, 8, 16, and 32 *color* the signal—the tone of the signal is changed even if no filtering is applied. In some cases, this is obvious, because certain frequencies seem obscured when processed through the graphic equalizer. This is due to the filter band overlap. The coloration can sound like resonating filters. The effect is less noticeable in 4-band mode, but as the count is increased to 32, the number of overlapping filters doubles. The 512-band FFT mode should be used if coloration is not desired.

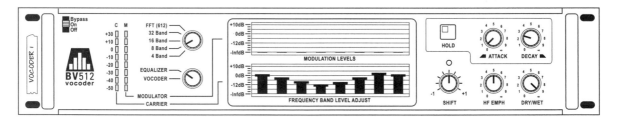

Figure 7-9
The BV512 in 8-band equalizer mode.

FFT mode has 512 bands and does not induce the same coloration as the lower band counts, but FFT requires time to process, and the time window used by the FFT process will induce a noticeable delay in the signal. If you use the graphic equalizer between the mixer master outputs and the Reason Hardware Interface to shape the overall mixdown, then the processing delay is relevant only if Reason is running in ReWire mode and needs to stay in sync with sound sources in other software. However, if the FFT graphic equalizer is used to process drums within a Reason song, the delay is long enough to influence timing. One solution to this is to run all of the instruments except the one to which you want to apply the FFT through a submixer, and then delay the output of the submixer using a DDL-1.

BV512 Filtering

The BV512 bandpass filters are useful if you want to completely strip a frequency range from a signal. This example demonstrates how the bass frequencies can be stripped from a drum loop. Using only four filter bands, the bass and low-mid frequency ranges are cut by setting the first two band levels to –InfdB (–∞ dB). The shift parameter is adjusted down to tune the filters with the signal.

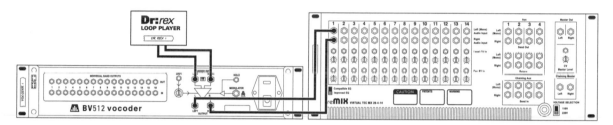

1. Start with an empty rack, and create a reMix mixer.
2. Create a Dr.REX Loop Player.
3. Load the ReCycle loop "Trh18_OlSchool_100_eLAB.rx2" from the Reason Factory Sound Bank\Dr Rex Drum Loops\Abstract HipHop directory.
4. Copy the REX slice data to the Dr.REX 1 sequencer track.
5. Insert a BV512 Digital Vocoder between the Dr.REX and the mixer.
6. Set the BV512 to these settings:

Figure 7-10
BV512 equalizer inserted between Dr.REX and the mixer input.

BV512 Settings

Mode	Equalizer	
Band count	4	
Hold	Off	
attack		
decay		
Shift	–14	
HF Emphasis		
Dry/wet		
Band levels	1	–InfdB
	2	–InfdB
	3	0dB
	4	0dB

Run the sequence and hear how the BV512 Graphic Equalizer filters out all of the low and low-mid frequencies. This is an effective way of filtering elements from drum loops to layer with kick drums from a Redrum or a different ReCycle loop.

Crossovers & Multi-Band Effects

Filters are commonly used in sound systems in devices called *crossovers*. Loudspeaker systems use crossovers to split incoming audio signals into different frequency regions, commonly separating the bass and treble. The outputs are then connected to a woofer and a tweeter. This concept of splitting signals and then filtering each of the splits to different frequency ranges can be applied to create spectral or multi-band effects.

The MClass Stereo Imager has a variable crossover control that functions like a highpass filter and a lowpass filter controlled by one cutoff frequency control. From a single input, parallel outputs are split, but each output carries the frequency from a different part of the spectrum. The split signals are routed through the stereo width effects and then merged back together at the output. Each of the split signals can be isolated using the solo buttons on the front panel, and there are separate output connections on the rear that are also selectable to either the Hi or Low bands. When you want to split these signals, the solo can be set to Solo Lo Band so that the low frequency range appears at the audio output; the separate output mode default is Hi Band, so the high frequency range appears at the separate outputs.

BV512 Multi-Band Crossover

An audio signal can be split and filtered through several graphic equalizers. One equalizer filters all except the low frequencies, another filters out everything except the highs, and a third only passes midrange frequencies. As a result, each frequency range can be isolated and sent down its own signal path. The split frequency signals can be processed with any effect device, then merged back together to create a multi-band effect. A typical example of multi-band processing is to use Comp-01 compressors with limiter settings for multi-band limiting, but you can use distortion units or delays to create some very interesting multi-band effects. This example demonstrates how to split a signal through three BV512 Graphic Equalizers in 8-band mode.

1. In an empty rack, create a reMix mixer.

BV512 Crossover Combinator

2. Create a Combinator.
3. In the Combinator sub-rack, create a microMix Line Mixer.
4. Still in the Combinator, create a Spider Audio Merger & Splitter.
5. Connect the Combinator To Devices outputs to the split A and split B inputs.
6. Bypass auto-routing and create three BV512 Digital Vocoders.
7. Connect a pair of Spider splitter outputs to each of the BV512 carrier inputs.
8. Connect the BV512 carrier outputs to mixer channel inputs 1, 2, and 3.

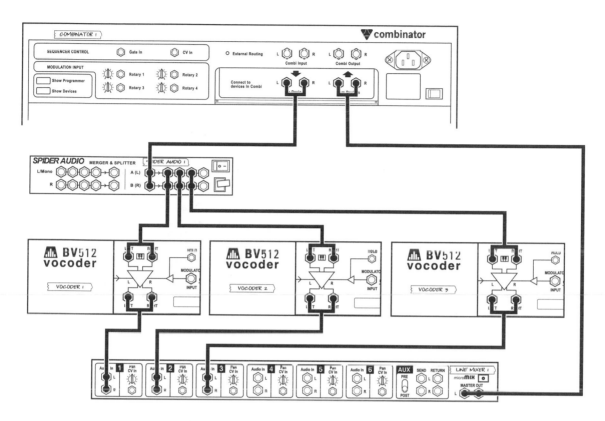

9. Set the BV512 Vocoders as follows:

BV512 Multi-Band Graphic Equalizer Settings

	Vocoder 1	Vocoder 2	Vocoder 3
Mode	Equalizer	Equalizer	Equalizer
Band count	8	8	8
Shift	−10	0	14
Band levels	1–2 0dB	1–2 –InfdB	1–6 –InfdB
	3–8 –InfdB	3–6 0dB	7–8 0dB
		7–8 –InfdB	

Figure 7-11
Three-way crossover Combinator patch using BV512 to split frequecy ranges.

10. Save the patch as "BV512 Crossover.cmb."

Sound Source

11. In the main rack, create a second Combinator.

12. Load the patch "7 – 120BPM Loop Source.cmb" from the *Power Tools for Reason* CD \ Combinator Patches directory.

Run the sequence and solo the submixer channels 1, 2, and 3 to hear how the original loop is divided into low, mid, and high frequency ranges. With the crossover circuits built, you can create multi-band effects by inserting effects after each graphic equalizer. Scream 4 Fuzz and Overdrive algorithms work well with this particular loop.

Phase-Shifting Graphic EQs

This example uses CV signals to modulate the shift parameters of two BV512 Graphic Equalizers to create a stereo phase-shifting effect. The band filters' settings are offset between the two equalizers. Modulating the shift parameter creates movement in the stereo field.

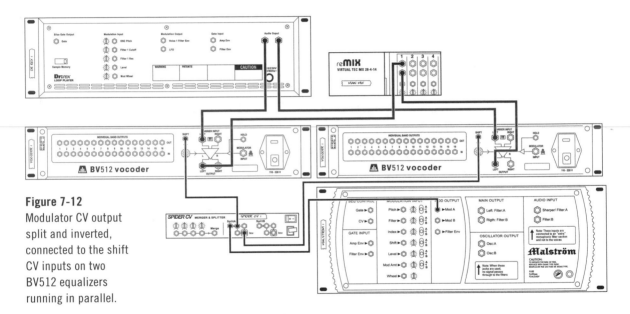

Figure 7-12
Modulator CV output split and inverted, connected to the shift CV inputs on two BV512 equalizers running in parallel.

1. In an empty rack, create a reMix mixer.
2. Bypass auto-routing and create two BV512 Vocoder modules.
3. Connect the Vocoder 1 left output to the mixer channel 1 left input.
4. Connect the Vocoder 2 left output to the mixer channel 1 right input.
5. Switch both vocoders to equalizer mode and set the band count to 32.
6. On Vocoder 1, set all of the even bands to $-\infty$ dB.
7. On Vocoder 2, set all of the odd bands to $-\infty$ dB.
8. Create a Spider CV Merger & Splitter.
9. Connect a Spider CV splitter A output to the Vocoder 1 shift CV input.
10. Connect the Spider CV splitter A inverted output to the Vocoder 2 shift CV input.
11. Bypass auto-routing and create a Malström Graintable Synthesizer.
12. Connect the Malström mod A output to the Spider CV splitter A input.
13. On the Malström, disable osc A, mod B, filter A, and filter B.

14. Set the Malström mod A rate to 24.
15. Bypass auto-routing and create a Dr.REX Loop Player.
16. Connect the Dr.REX left audio output to the Vocoder 1 left input and the Dr.REX right audio output to the Vocoder 2 left input.
17. Load the ReCycle loop "130_Clones_mLp_eLAB.rx2" from the Reason Factory Sound Bank\Music Loops\Variable Tempo (rex2)\Uptempo Loops directory.
18. Copy the REX slice data to the Dr.REX 1 sequencer track.
▶ Run the sequence.

Comb Filters

C omb filters impose attenuation of certain frequencies like normal filters, but they are actually a type of delay effect. A comb filter is a very short delay line with feedback. Because the delay time is short, certain frequencies within the delayed signal will be out of phase from the original signal. When the delayed signal is combined with the original signal, some frequencies are filtered due to phase cancellation.

DDL-1 Comb Filter

Using the DDL-1 Digital Delay Line, a basic comb filter effect can be created by setting the delay time to millisecond mode. This comb filter is limited, because feedback modulation is positive, and the delay times are set in one-millisecond intervals, but it demonstrates the properties of comb filters and the type of sounds they can produce. As the sequence plays, adjust the delay time to hear changes in the comb filter frequency. Because the delay time is fixed in millisecond increments, the actual frequencies are stepped, but some of the increments come close to chromatic notes. 3ms and 6ms settings are very close to the tuning in the key of E, and 1ms, 2ms, 4ms, and 8ms settings are close to tuning in the key of B.

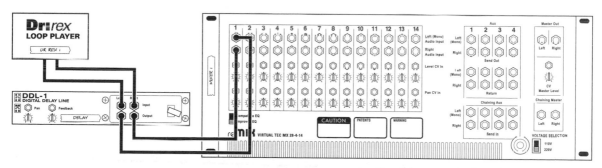

Figure 7-13

Using a delay line as a comb filter.

1. Start with an empty rack and create a reMix Mixer and a Dr.REX Loop Player.
2. Set the tempo to 135 BPM.
3. Load the ReCycle loop "Chm09_FatBoy_135_eLAB.rx2" from the Reason Factory Sound Bank\Dr Rex Drum Loops\Chemical Beats directory.
4. Copy the REX slice data to the Dr.REX 1 sequencer track.

5. Select the Dr.REX and insert a DDL-1 Digital Delay Line between it and the mixer.
6. Set the DDL-1 delay time to 4ms, feedback to 108, and dry/wet balance to 38.

▸ Run the sequence.

Malström Comb Filter

The Malström features comb filter algorithms, which provide finer control than the DDL-1. This configuration will demonstrate the differences between the two by using a Malström comb filter instead of the DDL-1. As the sequence plays, adjust the Malström filter A cutoff frequency knob to hear how much finer the resolution is with this comb filter effect.

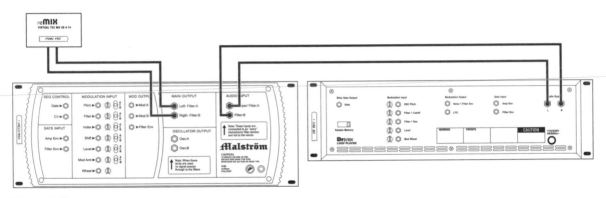

Figure 7-14
Dr.REX connected
into the Malström's
audio inputs.

1. Start with the song file you created in the previous example.
2. Delete the DDL-1.
3. Bypass auto-routing and create a Malström Graintable Synthesizer.
4. On the Malström, disable osc A, mod A, mod B, and filter B.
5. Set Malström filter A mode to comb+, filter frequency to 2, and resonance to 99.
6. Connect the Dr.REX left audio output left to the Malström shaper/filter A audio input.
7. Connect the Malström main output left to mixer channel 1 left input.

▸ Run the sequence.

Modulator-Controlled Comb Filter

A modulation source can be used to create a pattern-controlled effect synchronized to the tempo of the track.

1. Start with the Malström comb filter configuration described above.
2. Set the Malström filter A frequency to 64.
3. Enable mod B and turn on sync mode. Set the curve to 6, the rate to 1/8, and the mod B filter modulation amount to 51.

▸ Run the sequence.

Chapter 8
Vocoder Effects

A vocoder is special filter system known for creating synthetic vocal effects heard in science fiction films and countless songs in a variety of genres. It's a filter bank comprised of a number of bandpass filters set to different center frequencies along the audio spectrum. (The BV512 Crossover effect described in the previous chapter uses the BV512 Vocoder's bank of bandpass filters.) The vocoder requires two audio signals, a carrier and a modulator. Speech samples connect to the modulator input, and synthesizer sounds connect to the carrier input. The frequency characteristics of the modulator signal are analyzed and used to modulate the bandpass filters that process the carrier signal, thereby imparting the frequency spectrum of the modulator on the carrier.

There are two identical sets of bandpass filters in a vocoder. The modulator signal is processed through one set of filters, which separate the signal into frequency ranges. The output of each filter passes to an envelope follower, which generates a unipolar CV signal. The envelope follower CV signals modulate the output levels of the second set of filters, which process the carrier signal.

The BV512 has extensive CV modulation features and MIDI control, which provide other options for controlling the filters. The envelope follower CV signals are also routed to sockets on the rear of the BV512, and this opens up the possibility of utilizing frequency-dependent CV modulations elsewhere in Reason. Likewise, inputs for the bandpass filter levels can be connected to other CV sources for unique filter modulation effects.

Carrier Signal

The vocoder filters affect a broad range of frequencies, and for an effective vocoded sound, the carrier signal must be rich in harmonics with ample high-frequency information. If the carrier signal (synth) has few or no high harmonics, the information in the higher bands of the modulator (which would typically include the consonants in a vocal phrase) will be lost. The following examples illustrate a few methods of optimizing carrier signals for typical vocoding applications.

Classic Vocoder Effect

The typical vocoder sound uses a sawtooth wave from a synthesizer as a carrier signal. This example uses a Malström as the source, but a SubTractor sawtooth wave works as well. Sawtooth waves contain a fair amount of harmonics above the fundamental. The ReCycle loop is a sliced sample of spoken dialog, used as a modulator signal for this example.

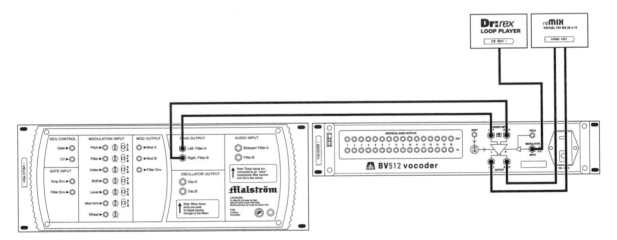

Figure 8-1
Malström connected to the BV512 carrier inputs, and Dr.REX (with a vocal ReCycle loop) connected to the BV512 modulator input.

1. In an empty rack, create a reMix Mixer.
2. Set the tempo to 136 BPM.
3. Create a Malström Graintable Synthesizer.
4. On the Malström, enable osc B. Set the Osc A graintable to Wave: Sawtooth*16 and the Osc B graintable to Wave: Sawtooth. Set the osc B octave setting to 5.
5. Insert a BV512 Digital Vocoder between the Malström audio outputs and the mixer inputs. The Malström is the carrier signal.
6. Set the Vocoder band count to 16.
7. Bypass auto-routing and create a Dr.REX Loop Player.

8. Load the ReCycle loop "Peff_VocoderText.rx2" from the *Power Tools for Reason* CD \ Dr.REX Loops directory.
9. Copy the REX slice data to the Dr.REX 1 sequencer track.
10. Patch the Dr.REX left audio output to the BV512 modulator input. This REX loop is the modulator signal.

▶ Enable MIDI through on the Malström 1 sequencer track, and run the sequence.

As the sequence plays the ReCycle loop slices, use a MIDI keyboard to play notes on the Malström to hear the classic vocoder sound of a sawtooth carrier wave. Try playing chords for more musical vocoding passages, and for robotic speech, play monophonic lines while working the pitchbend wheel or stick.

Bell Labs Style Vocoder

One of the earliest forms of a vocoder used a noise generator as carrier signal to accentuate sibilance. This example is inspired by a technique devised at Bell Labs, where the vocoder was in invented in the 1950s. Using the band level CV outputs, the modulation signal from one vocoder controls a second vocoder that processes a noise signal carrier input. The noise carrier signal is passed when frequencies in the higher ranges are sensed by the main vocoder, which emphasizes sibilance and hard consonant sounds.

Figure 8-2

Individual band levels from one vocoder modulating the filters on a second vocoder. A sawtooth carrier is processed by vocoder 1 and a noise carrier by vocoder 2.

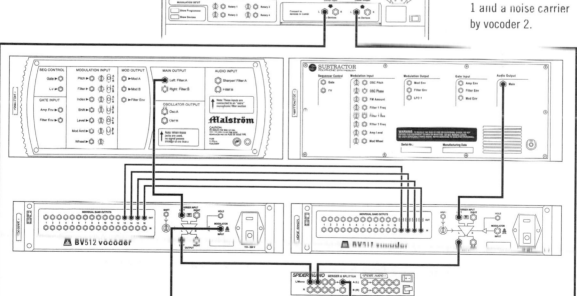

1. Start with an empty rack, create a reMix mixer, and set the tempo to 136 BPM.

Bell Labs Vocoder Combinator Patch

2. Create a Combinator. All of the devices listed in this section will be created in the Combinator sub-rack.
3. Create a Spider Audio Merger & Splitter.
4. Connect the merge output left to the Combinator From Devices input.
5. Bypass auto-routing and create two BV512 Digital Vocoders.
6. Connect the Vocoder left outputs to Spider merger left inputs. (This is a monophonic effect and only requires the left channel signals.)
7. Rename Vocoder 2 "Noise Bands."
8. Make sure the band count is set to 16 on both vocoders.
9. On Vocoder 1, set the frequency band levels 13, 14, 15, and 16 to $-\infty$ dB. Set decay to 6 (that is, the actual parameter value 6, not the "6" on the panel).
10. On Noise Bands, set the frequency band level adjustment 1 through 12 to $-\infty$ dB.
11. Connect the Vocoder 1 individual band level CV output 13 to the Noise Bands individual band level input 13. Repeat this for bands 14, 15, and 16.
12. Connect the Combinator To Devices left output to the Vocoder 1 modulator input.

Sawtooth & Noise Carrier Signals

13. Continuing within the Combinator sub-rack, bypass auto-routing and create a SubTractor Synthesizer.
14. Set the SubTractor polyphony to 1, enable the noise generator, set the noise color to 127, osc mix to 127, filter frequency 1 to 127, amp envelope sustain to 127, and master level to 72.
15. Connect the SubTractor audio output to the Noise Bands carrier left input.
16. Bypass auto-routing and create a Malström Graintable Synthesizer.
17. Set the Malström Osc A and Osc B graintables to Wave: Sawtooth, and set Osc B octave to 3.
18. Enable Osc B.
19. Disable Mod A, Mod B, Filter A, and Filter B.
20. Enable the routing of Osc A to the Shaper, Osc B to Filter B, and Filter B to Shaper.
21. Set Shaper mode to noise and Shaper amount to 127.
22. Connect the Malström left audio output to the Vocoder 1 carrier left input.
23. Open the Combinator Programmer and set the following modulation routings:

Device	Source	Target	Min	Max
Vocoder 1	Rotary 1	Decay	0	127
Vocoder 1	Rotary 2	Shift	−64	63
Vocoder 1	Button 1	Hold	0	1
Noise Bands	Rotary 2	Shift	−64	63

continued >

Device	Source	Target	Min	Max
SubTractor 1	Rotary 1	Amp Env Release	0	127
SubTractor 1	Rotary 3	Noise Level	0	127
SubTractor 1	Button 3	Noise Color	0	127
Malstrom 1	Rotary 1	Oscillator A Release	7	127
Malstrom 1	Rotary 4	Oscillator A Shift	−64	63
Malstrom 1	Button 2	Oscillator B On/Off	0	1
Malstrom 1	Button 4	Shaper On/Off	0	1
Malstrom 1	Rotary 1	Oscillator B Release	7	127
Malstrom 1	Rotary 4	Oscillator B Shift	−64	63

24. Rename the Combinator controls and set the parameters as follows:

Control	Name	Default Value
Rotary 1	Decay	9
Rotary 2	Shift	63
Rotary 3	Noise Level	127
Rotary 4	Carrier Shift	63
Button 1	Hold	Off
Button 2	OSC 2	Off
Button 3	Noise Color	Off
Button 4	Carrier Noise	Off

25. Save the patch as "Bell Labs-Style Vocoder.cmb."

Vocal Sample REX Loop Modulator

26. Bypass auto-routing and create, in the main rack, a Dr.REX Loop Player.
27. Connect the Dr.REX left output to the Combinator left input.
28. Load the ReCycle loop "Peff_VocoderText.rx2" from the *Power Tools for Reason* CD \ Dr.REX Loops directory.
29. Copy the REX slice data to the Dr.REX 1 sequencer track.
30. Route MIDI from a keyboard controller to the Combinator, and run the sequence.

Start playing single notes on the MIDI keyboard to hear the effect. Vocoder 1 filters 13 through 16 are disabled, but the CV signals generated by these bands are unaffected. These bands modulate the same filters on the second vocoder, which processes white noise generated by the SubTractor synthesizer. By patching one or two lower bands and adjusting the corresponding front panel band level adjust sliders in the same way, you can give the vocoded sound a breathy quality.

Vocoded Crowd Noise

Any sound can be used as a vocoder carrier signal. This effect demonstrates using a loop of a crowd cheering in a stadium as the carrier and a vocal sample as a modulator. The modulated cheering sample creates the effect of a large chanting crowd.

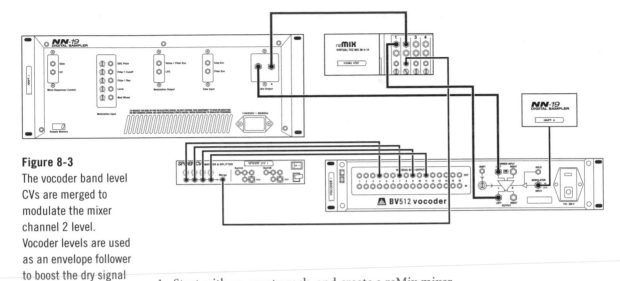

Figure 8-3
The vocoder band level CVs are merged to modulate the mixer channel 2 level. Vocoder levels are used as an envelope follower to boost the dry signal of the crowd noise.

1. Start with an empty rack, and create a reMix mixer.

Crowd Noise Carrier Signal

2. Bypass auto-routing and create an NN19 Digital Sampler.
3. Load the sample "Peff_Crowd.aif" from the *Power Tools for Reason* CD \ Audio Samples directory.
4. Connect the NN19 audio output right to the mixer channel 2 left input.
5. On the NN19 1 sequencer track, view the key lane and draw a note event on C3 from position 1.1.1 to position 9.1.1 (eight measures).

Vocoder Connections & Settings

6. Bypass auto-routing and create a BV512 Digital Vocoder.
7. Connect the NN19 audio output left to the BV512 carrier input left.
8. Connect the BV512 carrier output left to the mixer channel 1 left input.
9. Adjust the vocoder parameters as follows:

Crowd Noise BV512 Settings	
mode	vocoder
band count	32
hold	off
attack	0
decay	60
shift	6
HF emphasis	72
dry/wet	119

In a massive crowd, there's always background noise, and when the crowd chants, the levels sharply increase. To account for the dynamic changes, the vocoder acts as an envelope follower to modulate the level of the dry crowd signal. Several band level CV outputs are merged to create a modulator source for the dry signal mixer level control:

Envelope Follower for Dry Crowd Noise Level

10. Create a Spider CV Merger & Splitter.
11. Connect the BV512 individual band level outputs 4, 7, 9, and 11 to the Spider CV merger inputs.
12. Connect the Spider CV merge output to the mixer channel 2 level CV input.
13. Adjust the mixer channel 2 level CV trim to 56, and the fader level to 78.

Modulator Signal Source

14. Bypass auto-routing and create another NN19 Digital Sampler.
15. On NN19 2, load the sample "Peff_Vx_turnitup.aif" from the *Power Tools for Reason* CD \ Audio Samples directory.
16. Set the NN19 2 filter mode to HP 12 and the filter cutoff frequency to 44.
17. Connect the NN19 2 audio output left to the BV512 modulator input.
18. On the NN19 2 sequencer track, view the key lane and draw note events on C3 from measure 1 through measure 8. Each note should be one measure long. These events trigger the vocal sample to play every measure.
  ▸ Run the sequence.

This effect works best if the chant vocal also sounds like a large crowd. The vocal sample is a stereo mix of 24 different tracks of one person yelling the phrase with different gestures and at different pitches. This is easy to accomplish with any digital audio workstation or multitrack tape recorder. There are other ways to produce layered sound using Reason and several single samples.

Vocoder Freeze

This effect is a variation on one of the suggestions in the Reason Operation Manual. A noise source feeds into the vocoder carrier input, and a Matrix Pattern Sequencer triggers the hold feature of the BV512. Hold modulation freezes the modulation bands, filtering the noise generated from the SubTractor synthesizer and holding that curve until the gate event is released. This example also demonstrates using a drum loop as a modulation source. Drum loops vocoding a synthesizer carrier create interesting rhythmic textures.

1. In an empty rack, create a reMix mixer, and set the tempo to 150 BPM.
2. Bypass auto-routing and create a SubTractor Synthesizer.
3. Set the SubTractor polyphony to 1, enable the noise generator, and set the noise color to 85, osc mix to 127, filter 1 frequency to 127, amp envelope decay to 0, and amp envelope sustain to 82.
4. Create a Matrix Pattern Sequencer, and verify its connection to the SubTractor sequencer control inputs.
5. Set the Matrix pattern length to 1 step.

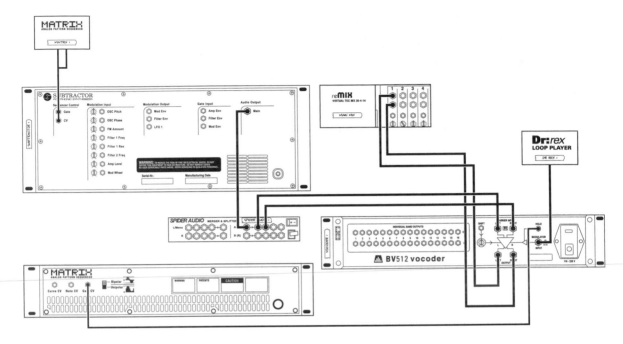

Figure 8-4
A Matrix gate CV triggering the vocoder's hold feature.

6. Program a tied note event on step 1 of the Matrix.

7. Create a Spider Audio Merger & Splitter.

8. Connect the SubTractor audio output to the Spider Audio splitter A input.

9. Bypass auto-routing and create a BV512 Digital Vocoder.

10. Connect the Spider Audio splitter A outputs 1 and 2 to the Vocoder carrier inputs.

11. Connect the Vocoder carrier outputs to the inputs on mixer channel 1.

12. Set the Vocoder's parameters as follows:

BV512 Vocoder Settings	
mode	vocoder
band count	32
hold	off
attack	0
decay	18
shift	−14
HF emphasis	48
dry/wet	127

13. Bypass auto-routing and create a Dr.REX Loop Player.

14. Connect the Dr.REX left output to the Vocoder 1 modulator input.

15. Load the ReCycle loop "Hco16_Piggy_150_eLAB.rx2" from the Reason Factory Sound Bank\Dr Rex Drum Loops\Hardcore directory.

16. Copy the REX slice data to the Dr.REX 1 sequencer track.

17. Bypass auto-routing and create a Matrix Pattern Sequencer.
18. Connect the Matrix gate CV output to the Vocoder hold input.
19. Program the following in Matrix pattern A1:

Matrix Pattern															
Step	1	2	3	4	5	6	7	8	9	10	11	12	13	14	15	16
Curve																
Note																
Gate		TH		TH		TH	TH	H		TH		TH	TH	TH	TH	TH

▸ Run the sequence.

While the sequence is playing, switch the Pattern on Matrix 2 to an empty pattern like A2 to hear the vocoding without the freeze effect.

Modulator Signals

Real-time vocoding is not possible in Reason because there is no audio input. Speech samples must be recorded using another application, then loaded into a Reason sampler. The sample can be sequenced to play back and used as the modulation signal for the vocoder. For musical applications, vocals should be synchronized with the tempo of the track. Ideally, a ReWire host application with recording features should be used. The song can be monitored while the vocal samples are recorded. Once recorded, the audio track can be edited and saved as one or more samples that can be loaded into an NN19 or NN-XT sampler.

Another useful technique is to process vocal samples with Propellerhead ReCycle and save them as REX files, then take the modulator signal from a Dr.REX. The timing of each word can be adjusted to fit with the rhythm of the track. Having the vocal phrase sliced into single-word segments adds flexibility if you want to remix the track or create stutter effects.

It's important to keep modulator vocal levels high. Low levels will still modulate the filters, but louder signals make the vocoding effect more discernable. If necessary, use an MClass Compressor to increase the loudness of modulator signal. This helps the subtle nuances of speech clearly translate in the vocoding process.

Although vocoders are intended for use with speech, other types of sounds can be used as modulator signals. Drum loops are fantastic because they contain energy in all parts of the frequency spectrum—kick drums in the bass and low midrange, snare drums and claps in the high midrange, and hi-hats and cymbals in the high frequency range. The following examples illustrate various synthesis techniques for modulating the vocoder bands for unique filtering effects.

Vocoder Band Sweep

A sine wave contains no harmonics other than the fundamental, and using a sine wave modulator signal provides a unique vocoder modulation. This example uses a sine wave from a SubTractor Synthesizer. The pitch is controlled by sequencer events and the portamento sweeps the pitch from a low C to a very high G. As the pitch changes, the different bands of the vocoder open.

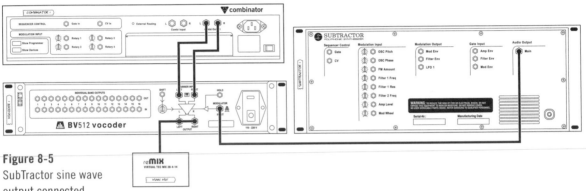

Figure 8-5

SubTractor sine wave output connected to the vocoder modulation input.

1. Start with an empty rack, and create a reMix mixer.
2. Create a Combinator.
3. Load the ReCycle loop "8 - FuzzyLogic mLp Source.cmb" from the *Power Tools for Reason* CD \ Combinator Patches directory.
4. Insert a BV512 Digital Vocoder between the Combinator and the mixer.
5. Adjust the BV512 parameters as follows:

BV512 Vocoder Settings	
mode	vocoder
band count	FFT
hold	off
attack	70
decay	74
shift	0
HF emphasis	60
dry/wet	127

Sine Wave Modulator

6. Bypass auto-routing and create a SubTractor Synthesizer.
7. Set the SubTractor mode to legato, portamento to 127, and polyphony to 1, and enable Low BW.
8. Set the SubTractor osc 1 waveform to a sine wave (wave 4).

9. Set the SubTractor filter 1 cutoff frequency to 127.

10. Set the SubTractor amp envelope A: 0, D: 0, S: 127, R: 34.

11. Set the SubTractor master level to 83.

12. Connect the SubTractor audio output to the BV512 modulator input.

Sequencer Control Track

13. On the SubTractor 1 sequencer track, enter edit mode to view the key lane.

14. Set the grid resolution to Bar.

15. Use the pencil tool and draw a sustained event on C1 for the duration of the transport loop.

16. Set the grid resolution to 1/4 and draw events of different durations on G8.

▶ Run the sequence.

The long portamento setting on the SubTractor slowly slides the pitch from C1 up toward G8. As the pitch rises, the modulator signal sweeps through the vocoder bands. Because the sine wave has no added harmonic content, the bandwidth is narrow. Experiment with other waveforms to create different sweeping effects, and try changing the decay parameter on the vocoder.

Formant-Controlled Vocoder

Vowel sounds created by the human voice are caused by frequency peaks called formants. Combinations of formants create distinct sounds like "ooh" or "aah." The Malström Throat graintable produces vowel formants, which can serve as a vocoder modulator source with voice-like filter characteristics.

Figure 8-6
Malström connected to BV512 modulator input. Matrix curve CV split to modulate the index and filter on the Malström.

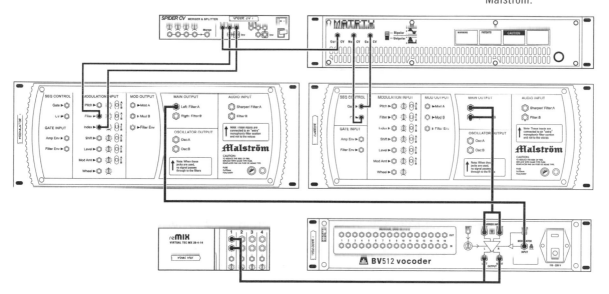

1. Start with an empty rack, and create a reMix mixer.
2. Bypass auto-routing and create a Malström Graintable Synthesizer. Rename the Malström "Modulator."
3. Set the Malström polyphony to 1 and the portamento to 67.
4. On Osc A, select the graintable Voice: Throat. Set motion to −64 and shift to 6, and enable routing into the shaper.
5. Set the filter A resonance to 36 and cutoff frequency to 82.
6. Set the filter envelope amount to 30.
7. Create a Matrix Pattern Sequencer.
8. Randomize pattern A1 by selecting Randomize Pattern from the Edit menu to randomize the curve CV settings.
9. Program the following on Matrix pattern A1:

Matrix Pattern															
Step	1	2	3	4	5	6	7	8	9	10	11	12	13	14	15	16
Curve																
Note	C3	C3	C3	C3	C3	C3	C3	C3	G3	G3	G3	G3	G3	G3	G3	G3
Gate	TH	TH	TH	TH	TH	TH	TH	H	TH	TH	TH	TH	TH	TH	TH

10. Bypass auto-routing and create a Spider CV Merger & Splitter.
11. Connect the Matrix curve CV output to the Spider CV splitter A input.
12. Connect the Spider CV splitter A out 1 to the Malström filter modulation input.
13. Connect the Spider CV splitter A out 2 to the Malström index modulation input, and set the index modulation trim to 127.
14. Create a second Malström and rename it "Carrier."
15. Enable osc B on the Carrier Malström, and Set the osc A and osc B graintables to Wave: Sawtooth*16.
16. Set osc A shift to −6 and cent tuning to 6.
17. Set osc B shift to 6 and cent tuning to −6.
18. Set the Carrier Malström spread to 83.
19. Create a BV512 Digital Vocoder as an insert between the Carrier Malström audio outputs and the mixer channel 1 inputs.
20. Connect the Modulator Malström's left main output to the Vocoder modulator input.
21. Set the BV512 band count to FFT and the shift to 12.
22. Set the MIDI enable on the Carrier Malström sequencer track, run the sequence, and play some chords from a MIDI controller.

Pattern-Controlled Vocoder Filtering

Pattern-controlled filtering is an exciting way to process signals, and using the vocoder for patterned-based filtering effects adds a dimension of multi-band filtering. Different bands of the frequency spectrum can be triggered by CV sources to create some bizarre filtering patterns.

Pattern-Controlled Vocoder

This effect could be created using a stack of Matrix Pattern Sequencers to trigger each of the individual band levels, but this would be tedious to edit. Instead, the individual channel gate CV outputs from a Redrum are connected to the BV512 band level inputs. This example only uses an 8-band vocoder to accommodate the limit of ten Redrum channels. Sixteen-band or 32-band mode could be used, but this would require more gate CV sources.

Figure 8-7
Combinator contains Redrum and BV512 connected as an effect device. Redrum gate CV outputs connect to the BV512 individual band level CV inputs.

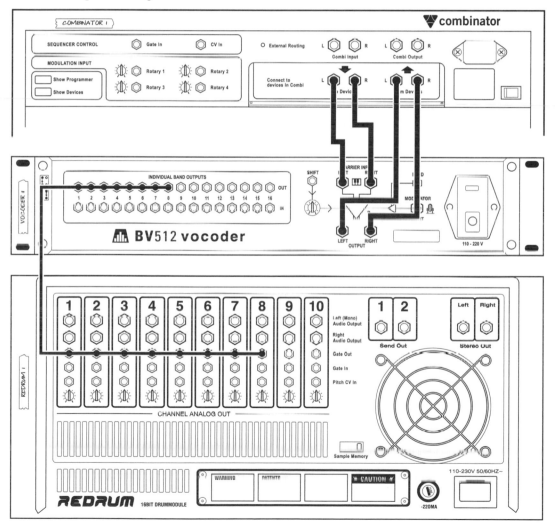

1. In an empty rack, create a reMix mixer.

Vocoder Section

2. Create a Combinator.
3. In the Combinator sub-rack, create a BV512 Digital Vocoder.
4. Adjust the BV512 parameters as follows:

BV512 Vocoder Settings

mode	vocoder
band count	8
hold	off
attack	0
decay	40
shift	0
HF emphasis	48
dry/wet	127

Redrum Gate CV Section

5. In the Combinator sub-rack, bypass auto-routing and create a Redrum Drum Computer.
6. Connect the Redrum channel 1 gate out socket to the Vocoder individual band level input 1. Repeat this for Redrum channels 2 through 8 and Vocoder bands 2 through 8.
7. Set Redrum channels 1 through 8 to decay/gate mode 1 (gate mode) and set the length to 50.
8. Program the following pattern into the Redrum pattern A1:

Redrum Pattern

	1	2	3	4	5	6	7	8	9	10	11	12	13	14	15	16
1	M				M				M				M			
2	M												M	M	M	
3	M								M							
4					M								M			
5					M								M			
6							M								M	
7			M	M							M		M			
8	S		M				M		S		M				M	
9																
10																

9. Save the Patch as "Pattern Controlled Vocoder.cmb."

Carrier Signal Source

10. In the Reason Rack, create a second Combinator.

11. ~~Create a second Combinator.~~

12. Load the patch "8 – REX Loop Source 1.cmb" from the *Power Tools for Reason* CD \ Combinator Patches directory.

▸ Run the sequence.

As the drum loop plays, the Redrum pattern triggers the individual filter bands on the BV512. When no events are triggered, the vocoder bands stay closed, completely silencing the loop signal from the Dr.REX. To make this pattern more colorful, you could create a SubTractor in the Combinator, set its LFO to a triangle wave, and use the LFO output to modulate the Shift parameter of the vocoder.

MIDI-Controlled Vocoder Filtering

The BV512 Vocoder responds to MIDI note events. To access these features, MIDI must be routed to the Vocoder from the Reason Hardware Interface or from a sequencer track. The individual band levels are velocity-sensitive, and this example demonstrates a method of created keyed filtering events that synchronize with a ReCycle groove.

Figure 8-8
MIDI note events starting at C1 control the Vocoder band levels.

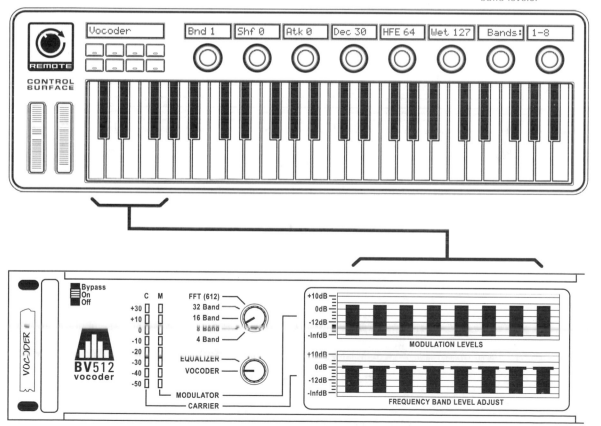

1. In an empty rack, create a reMix mixer.
2. Create a Dr.REX Loop Player.
3. Load the ReCycle file "125_StopStart_mLp_eLAB.rx2" from the Factory Sound Bank from the Music Loops\Variable Tempo (rex2)\Uptempo Loops directory.
4. Copy the REX slice data to the Dr.REX 1 sequencer track.
5. In the sequencer arrange window, select the grouped regions of the REX slice data, and then click on Get User Groove from the Edit menu.
6. Select the Dr.REX Loop Player and create a BV512 Vocoder.
7. Adjust the parameters on the BV512 as follows:

BV512 Vocoder Settings

mode	vocoder
band count	8
hold	off
attack	0
decay	0
shift	0
HF emphasis	0
dry/wet	127

8. Create a sequencer track and route the MIDI to Vocoder 1.
9. Enable MIDI input on the Vocoder sequencer track.
10. On the sequencer, enable Quantize Notes During Recording and set the quantize amount to User.
11. Enable the metronome and start recording notes to the vocoder sequencer track. The notes automatically quantize to the user groove, which has been set to match the REX note slices. In eight-band mode, playing notes between C1 and G1 triggers the vocoder bands. In 32-band mode, the range extends up to G3.

These events could be manually drawn in the sequencer, but recording them in real time has a natural feel. The automatic quantization synchronizes the events in time with the ReCycle slice data. When manually programming note events in the sequencer, you can re-quantize the events so the filter pattern matches the quantization of the REX slices.

Vocoder Band CV Modulation

The individual band level outputs of the Vocoder can be patched to different inputs so that filter bands are linked to each other. This is useful if you wish to group bands together or create random associations between bands. The Bell Labs style vocoder example earlier in this chapter demonstrated one use of routing band CV signals, and the following examples demonstrate a few other approaches.

Reverse Band Modulation

Using two BV512 Vocoders set to a band count of 16 or greater, a reverse band modulation can be configured by connecting the Band levels outputs in reverse order to a second BV512. The first vocoder analyzes the modulator audio and generates band level CV signals. The second vocoder filters are modulated by the incoming CV signals, and the carrier signal is processed in reverse.

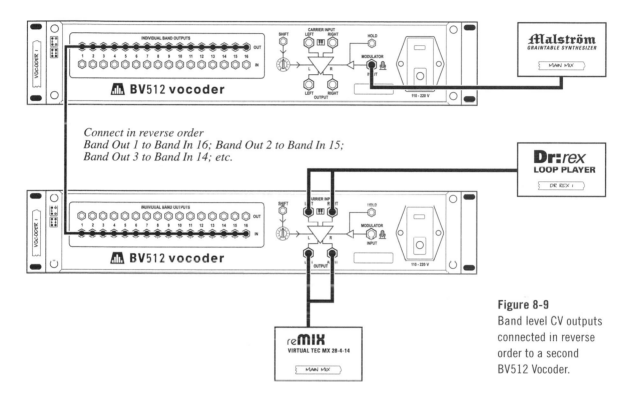

Figure 8-9
Band level CV outputs connected in reverse order to a second BV512 Vocoder.

1. In an empty rack, create a reMix mixer.
2. Bypass auto-routing and create a Malström Graintable Synthesizer.
3. Set the Malström osc A waveform to Sawtooth*16.

Vocoder & Reverse Vocoder Sections

4. Bypass auto-routing and create two BV512 Digital Vocoders. Rename them "Reverse" and "Main"
5. In reverse order, connect all 16 individual band level outputs from the Main BV512 to the individual band level inputs on the Reverse BV512. In other words, connect band out 1 to band in 16, band out 2 to band in 15, band out 3 to band in 14, etc.

6. Adjust the Reverse BV512 as follows:

Reverse BV512 Vocoder Settings

mode	vocoder
band count	32
hold	off
attack	0
decay	30
shift	10
HF emphasis	32
dry/wet	127

7. Adjust the Main BV512 as follows:

Main BV512 Vocoder Settings

mode	vocoder
band count	16
hold	off
attack	0
decay	40
shift	0
HF emphasis	64
dry/wet	127

8. Connect the Malström audio outputs to the Reverse BV512 carrier inputs.
9. Connect the Reverse BV512 carrier outputs to the mixer channel 1 inputs.

Modulator Signal Source

10. Bypass auto-routing and create a Dr.REX Loop Player.
11. Load the ReCycle loop "Rnb29_Sweet_080_eLAB.rx2" from the Reason Factory Sound Bank\Dr Rex Drum Loops\RnB HipHop directory.
12. Copy the REX slice data to the Dr.REX 1 sequencer track.
13. Set the Dr.REX master level to 127.
14. Connect the Dr.REX left audio output to the Main BV512 modulator input.
▸ Run the sequence.

The Malström is used as a carrier source that is processed by this configuration. In order to hear the reverse band modulation, route MIDI to the Malström and play some chords on a MIDI controller as the sequence plays. This configuration can also be used to create a highpass filter effect in which a SubTractor used as a noise generator is assigned to the Main Vocoder modulator. Sweeping the lowpass cutoff frequency of the SubTractor contours the frequency response, which is inverted by the Reverse BV512. The carrier signal is then processed as if it were passing through a highpass filter.

DOWNLOAD.

For more details on this effect, consult the Propellerhead Software Discovering Reason article "Filer Up" at www.propellerhead.se.

Chapter 9
Delay Effects

Mother Nature is the likely inspiration for delay effects. People are always fascinated by echoes one hears when yelling into a deep canyon or in a large hall. A natural echo occurs when sound waves travel a certain distance over a period of time, reflect against a surface, then travel back until, a few moments later, they are heard at the source.

Technology introduced new forms of echo machines like the early tape delay systems. A tape delay is a recording device with a ribbon of tape spliced end-to-end to form a loop. The machine records incoming audio signals to the tape loop, and the tape loop cycles from the record head to the playback head, where the signal is played back a moment later. Increasing or decreasing the tape speed changes the timing of the echoes. Most contemporary delay systems are now digital: The signals are sampled and stored in a memory buffer and retriggered at specific intervals. But the concept is basically the same: A delay line is simply a device that accepts a signal at the input and waits for a specified period of time before sending the signal on to the output.

The delay line is the fundamental unit for a very large number of effects, ranging from simple echoing to flanging and complex reverberation effects. The DDL-1 Digital Delay Line, the CF-101 Chorus/Flanger, and the RV-7 and RV7000 reverbs are all time-based effects processors that use delay in some form. When using any time-based effect, keep in mind that the effect usually doubles whatever signal is already introduced into the mix. Delay effects can add density to a sparsely orchestrated track, but can overwhelm a mix that is already rich with sounds.

The DDL-1 Digital Delay Line is Reason's all-purpose digital delay. It's ideal for basic delay effects as well as tempo synchronous effects. The RV7000 Advanced Reverb also has delay algorithms, which include features for making interesting stereophonic delay effects. This chapter will focus on some general applications of the delays.

The CF-101 Chorus/Flanger unit uses very short delays to create lush stereo effects. The principles behind short delays will be discussed below; the chorusing and flanging applications of the CF-101 will be described in a later chapter.

Phase Shifting

When signals are delayed by very short intervals—no greater than 1ms—and the non-delayed signal is then mixed with the delayed signal, a phenomenon called phase shifting occurs. Certain overtones in the time-shifted signal will be out of phase with respect to the same overtones in the non-delayed signal, which will result in phase cancellation. Comb filters rely on this type of phase cancellation.

The concept of wave phase comes from trigonometry. It refers to the momentary position of a wave in relation to its total cycle (wavelength). Phase is measured in terms of angles (radians) of a circle, or in degrees of arc. A complete cycle around the circle represents a full cycle of the wave. A single cycle of a 250Hz sine wave is four milliseconds long. At 0ms, the wave starts at 0 radians. At 1ms from the start of the wave, the cycle peaks at $\pi/2$ radians (90 degrees). At 2ms, half the cycle has passed, and the phase is π radians (180 degrees). After 3ms, the sine wave reaches the trough at $3\pi/2$ radians (270 degrees), and the wave cycle completes at 2π radians after 4ms. Note that 2π radians is the same as 0 radians.

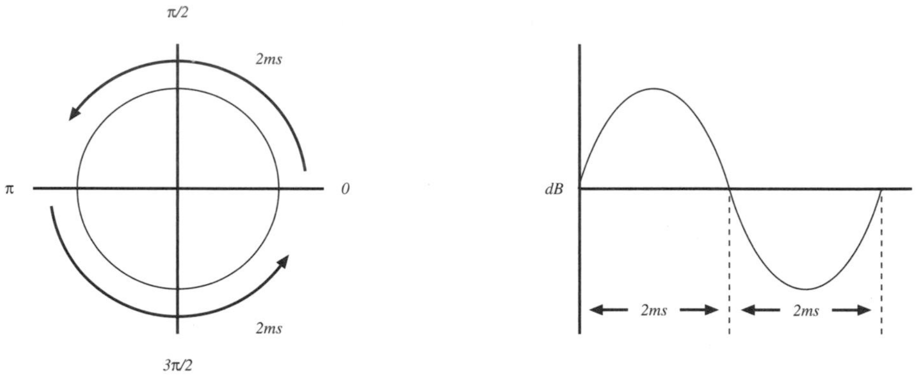

Figure 9-1

The phase of a sine or cosine wave is measured in terms of the angle of arc within a circle.

Normally, a sine wave will start at the beginning of the cycle at 0 (2π) radians, however a delay can offset the start time so that the phase is shifted relative to the original signal. Delaying the 250Hz sine wave by 2ms will offset the phase by π radians relative to the original, at which point the delayed signal will be out of phase. When the delayed signal is combined with the original, the two will cancel each other out, resulting in silence (see Figure 9-2). Since most sounds consist of a number of partials (sine waves at various frequencies), after any given delay time some of the partials are likely to be out of phase while others are in phase.

Very Short Delay

The heart of the CF-101 is a digital delay. Chorusing and flanging effects are based on very short delay times, ranging from 1ms to 20ms. When the modulation and feedback parameters are disabled, the CF-101 becomes a digital delay. In the example below, a Dr.REX loop provides the audio, which demonstrates this effect. Panning the input channels to the far stereo extremes demonstrates how the very short delay creates a subtle stereo widening effect.

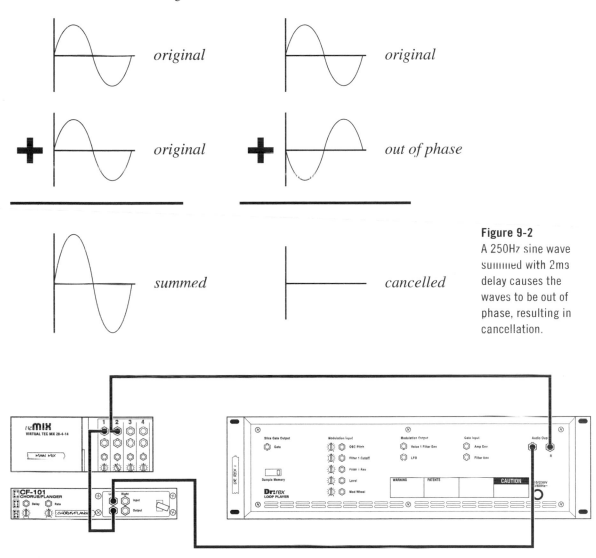

Figure 9-2
A 250Hz sine wave summed with 2ms delay causes the waves to be out of phase, resulting in cancellation.

Figure 9-3
Dr.REX right output connected directly to the mixer. The left output is delayed through the CF-101.

1. In an empty rack, create a reMix mixer.
2. Bypass auto-routing and create a Dr.REX Loop Player.
3. Load the ReCycle loop "Trh22_Pharzyde_110_eLAB.rx2" from the Reason Factory Sound Bank\Dr Rex Drum Loops\Abstract HipHop directory.
4. Copy the REX slice data to the Dr.REX 1 sequencer track.

5. Connect the Dr.REX right audio output to the mixer channel 2 left input.
6. Bypass auto-routing and create a CF-101 Chorus/Flanger.
7. Connect the Dr.REX left audio output to the CF-101 left input.
8. Connect the CF-101 left output to the mixer channel 1 left input.
9. Set the CF-101 delay to 36 and LFO mod amount to 0, and enable send mode.

▸ Run the sequence.

Setting the delay time between 1 and 6 will create a comb filter effect, which is a normal phenomenon with short delays. With a delay time of 0 the output signal actually decreases, which indicates that phase cancellation is occurring. To hear more extreme comb filtering, mute mixer channel 2 and pan mixer channel 1 to 0. Adjust the feedback to below –60 or above 55.

Fattening

Delay times in the range between 1ms and 30ms can be useful to fatten up a sound. A dry signal and a delayed signal are usually panned hard left and right for really wide stereo placement, but these signals can be panned anywhere in between to control the width. Feedback should be set at zero when using the DDL-1 for fattening signals, as otherwise comb filtering will occur. The next few examples demonstrate how to use the DDL-1 to create the fattening effect.

Figure 9-4

Using a DDL-1 as an insert effect, the right audio output from a Dr.REX Loop Player is delayed by 12ms. The left output from the Dr.REX is connected directly to a mixer.

Basic Fattening

This technique is useful for moving signals away from the center of a mix, and while it's most effective with high frequencies, it can thicken bass well. As the sequence plays, switch the DDL-1 into bypass mode to hear the loop without the fattening. It's obvious that the original signal is monophonic, as the loop plays from dead center in the stereo field. Try panning the input signals to different positions, and keep the settings balanced—for instance, channel 1 pan to –33 and channel 2 pan to 32.

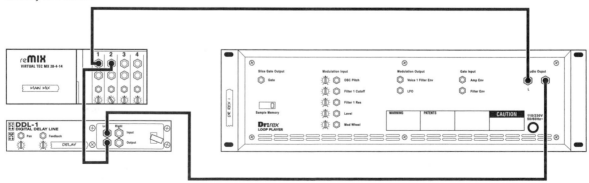

1. Start with an empty rack, and create a reMix mixer.
2. Bypass auto-routing and create a Dr.REX Loop Player.
3. Load the ReCycle file "130_Cycle_mLp_eLAB.rx2" from the Factory Sound Bank from the Music Loops\Variable Tempo (rex2)\Uptempo Loops directory.
4. Copy the REX data to the Dr.REX 1 sequencer track.
5. Bypass auto-routing and connect the Dr.REX left output to the mixer channel 1 left input.
6. Bypass auto-routing and create a DDL-1 Digital Delay Line.
7. Set the DDL delay time to 12ms and set feedback to 0.
8. Connect the Dr.REX right output to the DDL-1 left input.
9. Bypass auto-routing and connect the DDL-1 left output to the mixer channel 2 left input.
10. Pan mixer channel 1 to –64 and mixer channel 2 to 63.
   ▶ Run the sequence.

Stereo Fattening Send Effect

This example is a basic delay-based fattening technique implemented as a send effect. A mono send signal is split and directed to two DDL-1 delays with different time settings. This configuration is not as colored as a chorus, yet the delayed signal creates a dense stereophonic effect. The signal is tripled by the use of two delays mixed with the source signal.

Figure 9-5

An aux send from the mixer is sent to this Combinator and split to two DDL-1 delays. The Combinator output is connected to the mixer's aux return inputs.

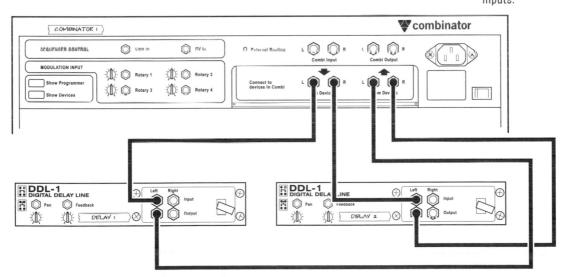

1. Start with an empty rack, and create a reMix mixer.
2. Create a Dr.REX Loop Player.

3. Load the ReCycle file "Hhp_Keybed_092_Chronic.rx2" from the Factory Sound Bank from the Dr Rex Instrument Loops\Various Hip Hop Loops directory.
4. Copy the REX data to the Dr.REX 1 sequencer track.

Stereo Fattening Combinator Patch

5. Bypass auto-routing and create a Combinator.
6. Connect the mixer aux 1 send outputs to the Combinator inputs.
7. Connect the mixer aux 1 return inputs to the Combinator outputs.
8. In the Combinator sub-rack, bypass auto-routing and create two DDL-1 Digital Delay Lines.
9. Bypass auto-routing and connect the Combinator's To Devices left output to the Delay 1 left input.
10. Bypass auto-routing and connect the Delay left output to the Combinator's From Devices left input.
11. Connect the Combinator's To Devices right output to the Delay 2 left input.
12. Connect the Delay 2 left output to the Combinator's From Devices right input.
13. On Delay 1, set delay time to 11ms and feedback to 0.
14. On Delay 2, set delay time to 7 ms and feedback to 0.
15. Save the Combinator Patch as "Stereo Fattener.cmb."
  ▸ Run the sequence.

As the sequence plays, raise the mixer channel 1 aux 1 send to hear the loop processed with the fattening send effect. To complete the Combinator effect, route a rotary control to the Delay Time (ms) parameter on both delays. Keep the 4ms offset when assigning modulation routing: The Min/Max range for Delay 1 can be 11 through 31, the range for Delay 2 can be 7 through 27. You can take this configuration even further by routing a rotary control to the feedback parameters, as well as the Dry/Wet parameters on both delay units, to create an interesting comb filter effect.

Doubling & Slapback

Short delay intervals become perceptible to the human ear as separate events at about 20ms. At about 100ms they start sounding like distinct echoes. Doubling and slapback are useful delay effects that can be created with delay times that fall into this 20–100ms range. Doubling is more commonly created by recording two different performances of the same part, but a delay with a setting in the range of 20–50ms can be used to create the "doubled" track. Slapback is a common effect applied to vocal tracks, where the signal is processed through a delay with a setting of 60–100ms. Slapback delay times are usually tweaked so they fit with the groove of a track and occur close to a 32nd-note offset.

The DDL-1 can be used to calculate delay times in milliseconds based on the tempo of the track. First set the DDL-1 delay time to 1 step, then switch the units to ms. The number that appears on the time display is the duration of a sixteenth-note in milliseconds. Useful slapback settings are usually half this amount.

The dry/wet balance is important when using slapback. The effect should be very subtle, so the delay sounds like a ghost note. Try experimenting with shifting the delay time up or down to change the feel of the groove.

Doubled Guitar

This example uses a multi-sampled guitar to demonstrate doubling. Doubling and slapback are most effective with acoustic sounds because they create a synthetic or *processed* (effected with digital signal processing) feel to an audio signal. Using these effects on synthesized sounds can easily muck things up, unless the synth envelopes have fast decay times and low sustain levels. Loud sustained synth sounds don't really benefit from doubling.

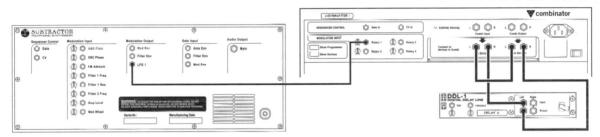

Figure 9-8

A Combinator being used as a stereo doubler insert effect. The left input is connected directly to the output, while the right input passes through a DDL-1 delay. The SubTractor LFO modulates delay time.

1. Start with an empty rack, and create a reMix mixer.
2. Set the reMix channel 1 pan to –38, the channel 2 pan to 37.

Doubler Combinator Patch

3. Bypass auto-routing and create a Combinator.
4. Connect the Combi left output to the reMix channel 1 left input, and the Combi right output to the reMix channel 2 left input. This is a stereo insert effect and requires both inputs. The left channel passes through unchanged.
5. In the Combinator sub-rack, bypass auto-routing and connect the To Devices left output to the From Devices left input.
6. Bypass auto-routing and create a DDL-1 Delay.
7. Connect the Combinator To Devices right output to the DDL-1 left input.
8. Connect the DDL-1 left output to the Combinator From Devices right input.
9. Set the delay feedback to 0 and units to ms.
10. Open the Combinator programmer, and assign rotary 1 to Delay 1: Delay-Time(ms). Min: 37. Max: 39. Then Adjust rotary 1 to 87.

11. In the Combinator sub-rack, create a SubTractor Synthesizer. The LFO will be used to modulate the delay time.
12. Connect the SubTractor LFO 1 modulation output to the Combinator rotary 1 CV input.
13. Set the SubTractor LFO 1 rate to 32.
14. Save the patch as "Doubler.cmb."

Sound Source

15. In the Reason rack, create a second Combinator. Verify that it's connected to the "Doubler" Combi inputs.
16. Load the patch "9 - Clean Guitar Loop Source.cmb" from the *Power Tools for Reason* CD \ Combinator Patches directory.

▸ Run the sequence.

The guitar doubling effect is similar to fattening (described earlier), but the longer delay gives the impression of two different string plucks. The shorter delays for fattening still sound like a single pluck. The LFO modulation of the delay time adds a slight hesitation and rush to the doubled track for a slight variation in the doubling.

Echoes

Delay times longer than 100 milliseconds with a moderate amount of feedback can be used to create spatial effects and rhythmic delay effects. The delay algorithms in the RV7000 Reverb and DDL-1 Digital Delay Line both have synchronization settings so that delay time can be set in relation to the song tempo. Usually tempo-synchronized delays are placed fairly high in the mix so that they are perceived as separate events. A single delay can be used with the dry signal panned to one channel and the delay panned to the other, but multi-tap and ping-pong delays can be created for more complex delay effects.

Multi-Tap Delay

A multi-tap delay is usually several delays in series. The connection between each delay is tapped and routed to a mixer input channel. This example uses six DDL-1 delay lines connected in series. Each of the tapped delay signals can be attenuated and panned to create a cascading delay effect. The send effect is routed through the same mixer as the combined delay tap signals on the aux 4 bus. The aux 4 send bus will provide feedback control from any of the incoming tap signals.

1. In an empty rack, create a reMix mixer.
2. Set the mixer channel 1 aux send 1 amount to 68.
3. Create a Redrum Drum Computer.
4. On Redrum channel 1, load the sample "Studio54_eLAB.aif" from the Reason Factory Soundbank\Other Samples\Chords-Phrases-Pads-Stabs directory.

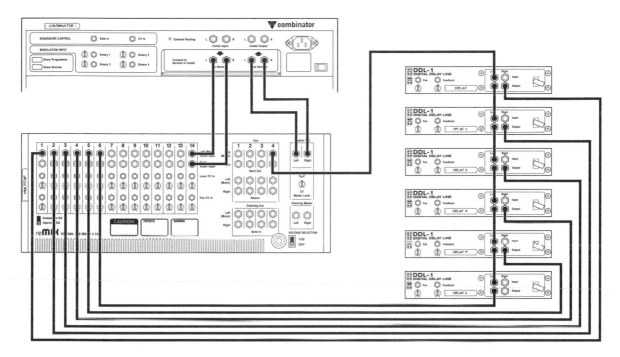

Figure 9-7
Six DDL-1 delays
connected in a series.
The right outputs are
used as taps and
combined in a mixer.

5. Select Redrum channel 1 and program a medium hit on step 1.

6. Bypass auto-routing, and create a Combinator.

7. Connect the Mixer aux 1 send outputs to the Combi inputs, and the Combi outputs to the aux 1 return inputs.

Multi-Tap Delay Combinator

8. In the Combinator sub-rack, create another reMix mixer.

9. Rename Mixer 2 "Multitap."

10. Set the Multitap mixer channel 14 fader level to 0, aux 4 send to 100, and enable pre-fade for the aux send.

11. Connect the Combinator To Devices outputs to the Multitap mixer channel 14 inputs.

12. Still in the sub-rack, bypass auto-routing and create a DDL-1.

13. Set the delay time to 1 step and feedback to 0.

14. Duplicate the DDL-1 five times. Rename the duplicates "Delay 2," "Delay 3," etc.

15. Connect the Multitap mixer aux 4 send left to the Delay 1 DDL-1 left input.

16. Bypass auto-routing, and connect the Delay 1 left output to the Delay 2 left input. Continue this procedure for each delay up to Delay 6.

17. Connect the Delay 1 right output to the Multitap mixer channel 1 left input. Connect the Delay 2 right output to the Multitap channel 2 left input, and repeat through Delay 5. On the last delay, Delay 6, connect the left output to the Multitap mixer channel 6 left input.

18. Set the pan on the Multitap mixer as follows: channel 1: –64; channel 2: –29; channel 3: –12; channel 4: 11; channel 5: 28; channel 6: 63.
19. Assign rotary 1 to the DelayTime (steps) target on all six delay units.
20. Rename rotary 1 "Delay Steps" and adjust rotary 1 to 0.
21. Assign rotary 2 to the Multitap mixer channel 4 aux 4 send, Min 0, Max 75.
22. Rename rotary 2 "Delay Input" and adjust rotary 2 to 90.
23. Save the patch as "Multi-Tap Delay.cmb."

▸ Run the sequence.

As the sequence triggers the sample, observe the Multitap Mixer VU meters as each delay tap feeds into the input channels. The Aux send 4 bus carries the send signal and channel 4 is "tapped" to send feedback through the bank of delay units. The Combinator feedback control is limited to prevent an overload, but be cautious with high input signals. Try experimenting with different fader levels on each of the taps to create effects of decaying or increasing loudness, or change the panning to random positions in the stereo field.

Cross-Feedback Delays

The next effect configuration is also known as a "ping-pong" delay because the delay signals move across the stereo field like a ping-pong ball skipping back and forth across a table. This effect uses the DDL-1 step delay mode to create a rhythmic ping-pong delay effect. Cabled feedback is attenuated and routed between two delay devices. The feedback signal from one delay drives the second delay, and the output from the second delay feeds back to the first delay.

Figure 9-8
Feedback cabled between the two DDL-1 Delay Lines.

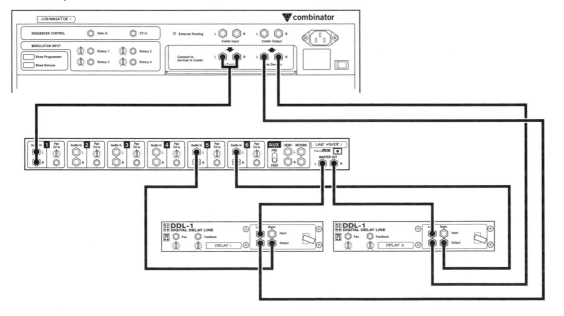

1. Start with an empty rack, create a reMix mixer.
2. Set the mixer channel 1 aux send 1 to 81.
3. Create a Redrum Drum Computer.
4. On Redrum channel 1, load the sample "Clp_Beltram.wav" from the Reason Factory Soundbank\Redrum Drum Kits\xclusive drums-sorted\04_Claps directory.
5. Select Redrum channel 1 and program a medium hit on step 1.

Cross-Feedback Delay Combinator Patch

6. Bypass auto-routing and create a Combinator.
7. Connect the Mixer aux 1 send outputs to the Combi inputs, and the Combi outputs to the aux 1 return inputs.
8. In the Combinator sub-rack, bypass auto-routing and create a microMix mixer.
9. Rename Line Mixer 1 "Cross FB."
10. Pan the Cross FB mixer channel 1 to –64, channel 5 to 63, and channel 6 to –64.
11. Set the Cross FB mixer channel 5 and channel 6 levels to 63.
12. Still in the sub-rack, bypass auto-routing and create two DDL-1 delays.
13. Rename the DDL-1 delays "Left" and "Right."
14. Set the feedback to 0 on both the Left DDL-1 and Right DDL-1.
15. Connect the Combinator To Devices output to the Cross FB mixer channel 1 inputs.
16. Connect the Cross FB mixer master out left to the Left DDL-1 left input.
17. Connect the Cross FB mixer master out right to the Right DDL-1 left input.
18. Connect the Left DDL-1 left output to the Combinator From Devices left input.
19. Connect the Left DDL-1 right output to the Cross FB mixer channel 5 left input.
20. Connect the Right DDL-1 left output to the Combinator From Devices right input.
21. Connect the Right DDL-1 right output to the Cross FB mixer channel 6 left input.
22. Open the Combinator programmer and set the following modulation routings:

Device	Source	Target	Min	Max
Cross FB	Rotary 2	Channel 5 Level	0	75
Cross FB	Rotary 2	Channel 6 Level	0	75
Left	Rotary 1	DelayTime (steps)	1	16
Left	Rotary 1	DelayTime (ms)	1	2000
Left	Button 1	Unit	0	1
Right	Rotary 1	DelayTime (steps)	1	16
Right	Rotary 1	DelayTime (ms)	1	2000
Right	Button 1	Unit	0	1

23. Rename the Combinator controls and set the parameters as follows:

Control	Name	Default Value
Rotary 1	Delay Time	20
Rotary 2	Feedback	66
Button 1	MS – Steps	On

24. Save the patch as "Cross Feedback Delay.cmb."

▸ Run the Redrum pattern.

Ping-Pong Delay

The RV7000 Advanced Reverb has a multi-tap delay algorithm that is different from using a series of DDL-1 delay modules. The multi-tap algorithm has damping and diffusion features that make the echoes decay naturally. Unlike the DDL-1, the RV7000 is a stereo effects processor, unless a monophonic signal is connected to the input. For this example, the ping-pong delay is more effective when the RV7000 is connected in mono.

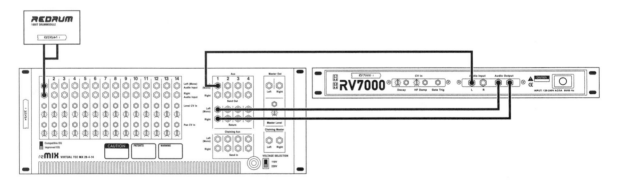

Figure 9-9

RV7000 connected in mono from the mixer.

1. Start with an empty rack, and create a reMix mixer.
2. Set the mixer channel 1 aux send to 81, and pan to –64.
3. Create an RV7000 Advanced Reverb.
4. Disconnect the cable from the RV7000 right input.
5. Open the RV7000 Remote Programmer.
6. Set the RV7000 algorithm to multi-tap, turn tempo sync on, and set the diffusion to 0, LF damp to 1,000Hz, tap 1 delay time to 6/16, tap 2 delay time to 3/16, and repeat tap repeat time to 6/16.
7. Create a Redrum Drum Computer.
8. On Redrum channel 1, load the sample "Clp_Photek.wav" from the Reason Factory Soundbank\Redrum Drum Kits\xclusive drums-sorted\04_Claps directory.
9. Select Redrum channel 1 and program a medium hit on step 1.

▸ Run the sequence.

Long Feedback Effects

With repeating echoes, the output levels increase as the feedback is combined with the input signal. The RV7000 decay parameter controls the feedback amount for the delay algorithms. A decay setting of 0 means no feedback, while a setting of 127 is 100% feedback. The next few examples use delays with high feedback settings. Delay parameters can easily be automated using sequencer tracks, but these examples use Matrix pattern sequencers to create rhythmic patterns of feedback control.

Gated Echoes

This effect uses a Matrix-controlled mixer channel to gate the effect send to an RV7000 echo delay. The echo delay effect has a long decay setting, and short keyed gate events will send bursts of signal to the RV7000. The master output from the "Send Gate" mixer is the source for the RV7000 echo. The effect send is going to be monophonic, so only use the master output left. The ReCycle drum loop provides the audio signal source for this example. The send signal on the aux send 1 bus will be connected to the Matrix-controlled gate.

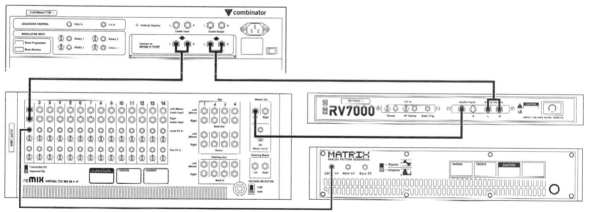

Figure 9-10

A Matrix gate controlling the RV7000 input signal.

1. Start with an empty rack, and set the tempo to 92 BPM.
2. Create a reMix mixer, and adjust the channel 1's aux send 1 to 70.
3. Create a Dr.REX Loop Player.
4. Load the ReCycle loop "Rnb14_Original_100_eLAB.rx2" from the Reason Factory Sound Bank\Dr Rex Drum Loops\RnB HipHop directory.
5. Copy the REX slice data to the Dr.REX 1 sequencer track.
6. Bypass auto-routing, and create a Combinator.
7. Connect the mixer aux 1 send outputs to the Combi inputs, and the Combi outputs to the aux 1 return inputs.

Gated Echo Combinator Patch

8. In the Combinator sub-rack, bypass auto-routing and create a second reMix mixer.
9. Rename Mixer 2 "Send Gate."
10. Set Send Gate mixer channel 1 fader level to 0.
11. Still in the sub-rack, create a Matrix Pattern Sequencer.
12. Connect the Matrix curve CV output to the Send Gate mixer channel 1 level CV input.
13. Program a curve CV event on step 13 with a value of about 65%.
14. Still in the sub-rack, bypass auto-routing and create an RV7000 Advanced Reverb.
15. Connect the Combinator To Devices outputs to the Send Gate mixer channel 1 inputs.
16. Bypass auto-routing and connect the Send Gate mixer master output left to the RV7000 left audio inputs.
17. Connect the RV7000 audio outputs to the Combinator From Devices inputs.
18. Open the RV7000 Remote Programmer and set the parameters according to the following chart:

RV7000 Parameters	
EQ	Off
Gate	Off
Decay	123
HF Damp	40
Hi EQ	0
Dry/Wet	127
Algorithm	Echo
Tempo Sync	On
Echo Time	1/16
Diffusion	58
LF Damp	242
Spread	127
Predelay	0

19. Save the patch as "Gated Echo.cmb."
   ▸ Run the sequence.

The Matrix gates the aux send signal, allowing only the snare on beat 4 to echo. The Combinator patch can be modified with rotary control over the Echo Time (steps) parameter and Decay parameters for a little more flexibility. Different gate patterns can be programmed into the matrix and also saved with the patch.

Feedback Hold Effect

The feedback parameter of a DDL-1 can be automated by a CV input. When the CV setting is 0 there is no feedback, and when the CV signal is 127, feedback is 100%. Full feedback can be used to create a repeating hold effect in which a sample is looped. Using a gate CV signal from a Matrix, a feedback hold pattern initiates stuttering sample textures.

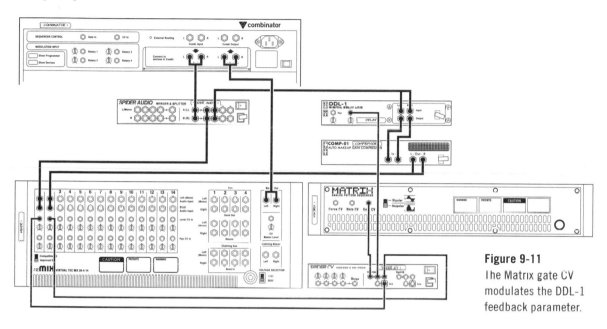

Figure 9-11
The Matrix gate CV modulates the DDL-1 feedback parameter.

1. Begin with an empty rack, and set the tempo to 90 BPM.

Feedback Hold Combinator Patch

2. Create a Combinator.
3. In the Combinator sub-rack, create a Spider Audio Merger & Splitter.
4. Connect the Combinator To Devices outputs to the Spider splitter inputs.
5. Still in the sub-rack, create a reMix mixer and set the channel 2 fader level to 0.
6. Connect the Spider splitter output 1 to the mixer channel 1 inputs.
7. Bypass auto-routing and create a DDL-1 Digital Delay Line in the sub-rack.
8. Connect the Spider Audio splitter output 2 to the DDL-1 inputs.
9. Connect the DDL-1 output to the mixer channel 2 inputs.
10. Set the DDL-1 delay time to 62ms, and feedback to 0.
11. Insert a Comp-01 Compressor/Limiter between the DDL-1 and mixer channel 2.
12. Set the Comp-01 ratio to 106, threshold to 70, attack to 0, and release to 86.
13. Create a Matrix Pattern Sequencer in the sub-rack.
14. Bypass auto-routing and create a Spider CV Merger & Splitter.

15. Connect the Matrix gate CV output to the Spider CV split A input.
16. Connect Spider CV split A output 1 to the DDL-1 feedback CV input.
17. Set the DDL-1 feedback CV trim to 127.
18. Connect Spider CV split A output 2 to the mixer channel 2 level CV input.
19. Set the mixer channel 2 level CV trim to 30.
20. Connect Spider CV split A output 4/inv to the mixer channel 1 level CV input.
21. Set the mixer channel 1 level CV trim to 127.
22. Program the following on Matrix pattern A1:

Matrix Pattern																
Step	1	2	3	4	5	6	7	8	9	10	11	12	13	14	15	16
Curve																
Note																
Gate			TH	TH			TH	TH	TH	TH				TH	TH	H

23. Open the Combinator Programmer and set the following modulation routings:

Device	Source	Target	Min	Max
Mixer 1	Rotary 4	Master Level	0	127
Delay 1	Rotary 1	DelayTime (ms)	1	2000
Delay 1	Button 1	Unit	1	0
Delay 1	Button 2	Step Length	0	1
Delay 1	Rotary 1	DelayTime (steps)	1	16
Matrix 1	Button 4	Pattern Enable	1	0

24. Rename the Combinator controls and set the parameters as follows:

Control	Name	Default Value
Rotary 1	Delay Time	24
Rotary 4	Level	96
Button 1	Unit	Off
Button 2	Step Length	Off
Button 4	Bypass	Off

25. Save the patch as "Feedback Hold.cmb."

Sound Source

26. In the main rack, Create a Dr.REX Loop Player.
27. Load the ReCycle loop "Gt_Wah_A7_07_085.rx2" from the Reason Factory Sound Bank\Dr Rex Instrument Loops\Guitar Loops\WahWah 085 bpm directory.
28. Copy the REX slice data to the Dr.REX 1 sequencer track.
29. Set the Dr.REX master level to 128.
   ▸ Run the sequence.

Delay Time Modulation

The Reason 3.x audio engine has undergone changes that directly improve the sound quality of digital delay effects. Delay time modulation has always been a feature available in Reason, but before version 3.0, changing the delay time would introduce artifacts. Used in conjunction with the modulation routing features of the Combinator, digital delay time modulation can yield very interesting pitch-shifting effects that in years past were only featured on very expensive digital signal processors. The following example is an LFO-driven pitch modulation effect.

1. Start with an empty rack, and create a reMix mixer.

Delay Time Modulator Combinator Patch

2. Create a Combinator.
3. In the Combinator, bypass auto-routing and create two DDL-1 Digital Delay Lines.
4. Set the units of both DDL-1s to ms and the delay time to 62ms.
5. Connect the Combinator To Devices left output to the Delay 1 left input.
6. Connect the Combinator To Devices right output to the Delay 2 left input.
7. Connect the Delay 1 left output to the Combinator From Devices left input.
8. Connect the Delay 2 left output to the Combinator From Devices right input.
9. Create an NN-19 Digital Sampler in the sub-rack.
10. Connect the NN-19 LFO CV output to the Combinator rotary 1 CV input.
11. Set the rotary 1 input trim to a value between 4 and 10.
12. Open the Combinator Programmer and set the following modulation routings:

Device	Source	Target	Min	Max
Delay 1	Rotary 1	DelayTime (ms)	1	330
Delay 1	Rotary 2	Feedback	0	127
Delay 2	Rotary 1	DelayTime (ms)	30	356
Delay 2	Rotary 2	Feedback	0	127
NN19 1	Rotary 3	LFO Rate	0	50
NN19 1	Rotary 4	LFO Wave	0	5
NN19 1	Button 3	LFO Sync Enable	0	1

13. Rename the Combinator controls and set the parameters as follows:

Control	Name	Default Value
Rotary 1	Delay Time Mod	15
Rotary 2	Feedback	44
Rotary 3	LFO Rate	0
Rotary 4	LFO Wave	0
Button 3	Sync	On

14. Save the patch as "Delay Time Modulator.cmb."

Sound Source Section

15. In the main Reason rack, create a Dr.REX Loop Player.
16. Load the ReCycle loop "100_PhaseRhodes_mLp_eLAB.rx2" from the Reason Factory Sound Bank\Music Loops\Variable Tempo (rex2)\Downtempo Loops directory.
17. Copy the REX slice data to the Dr.REX 1 sequencer track.

▸ Run the sequence.

The time modulation is slightly different for the two delays, which provides the stereo thickening effect, and as the delay time changes, it creates a subtle pitch shift. Moving the Delay Time Mod rotary control manually will create pitch-shift effects. Adding more feedback, increasing the delay time, and pushing up the rear-panel input CV trim for rotary 1 will create a pitch-shifting cascade effect. The rotary 1 CV can be driven by other modulation sources like a matrix pattern or envelopes as the basis of unique pitch modulation effects.

Chapter 10
Reverb

Digital reverbs simulate room acoustics and add the sense of ambience to instruments in a mix. The reverb effect fills silent gaps between notes with an ambient wash, giving recorded music a more natural feel. The effect should be subtle and just loud enough to smooth out the gaps. Reverbs are also used as an element of sound design, to give a special character to single sounds within a mix. Using reverberation to enhance a mixdown or add a spatial element to a sound is ultimately a matter of taste.

There are some general rules when applying reverb, but breaking these rules can be interesting. It depends on the style of the music being created. If reverb is applied to vocal samples, string sections, or acoustic drums, then using the traditional techniques for realistic ambience may be a good idea. To create the impression that the listener is floating in space, then atypical reverberation techniques would be more useful. An example of unconventional reverb came about in dub and reggae music, where the sound of spring reverb is part of the genre.

Reason has two reverb devices, the RV-7 Digital Reverb and the RV7000 Advanced Reverb. The RV7000 is a far superior device to the RV-7, and given the choice between the two, most people will use the RV7000. On occasion, subtle reverberation is required, in which case the RV-7 is suitable. The RV7000 is more complicated to program, having parameters for several aspects of reverberation.

The main parameter for both the RV-7 and RV7000 is the *algorithm* setting. The algorithm is the set of mathematical operations that control what happens to the signal. User inputs to the algorithm include such parameters as decay time, reflection diffusion, and so on, which create the reverberation effect. When approaching the mixdown of a track, decide on the type of acoustics that work with the track. Algorithms are typically named after the space being simulated, and having a mental picture of the acoustic space will make algorithm choice simple.

Acoustic Space Simulation

The RV7000 has several algorithms that are used primarily for simulating the acoustics of various structures. The arena algorithm creates the ambience of an enormous empty building with many reflective surfaces. The other extreme is the small space algorithm, which simulates the sound of a closet or even a metal box. The hall algorithm emulates the characteristics of concert halls and other long spaces with high ceilings. The room algorithm simulates the characteristics of rooms with lower ceilings and less volume than a hall. Hall and room reverbs are the most common choices for acoustic space simulation, while arena and small space reverbs are more suited for creating special ambient effects.

Reverberation effects can incorporate dozens or even hundreds of delays to emulate the reflection of sounds of an acoustic space. Two types of echoes are created by the hall and room algorithms—*early reflections* and *reverberation*. Early reflections are short digital delays panned around the stereo field to simulate the echoes heard directly from surfaces in the room. Reverberation is the sound of echoes that bounce off surfaces many times before returning to the listener. The delay and pan patterns of early reflection and reverberation are controlled by the *room shape* parameter. When you set the size to the maximum setting, the early reflection time and amplitude levels can be seen on the graphic time line representation on the RV7000 Remote Programmer.

Size & Decay

The size and decay parameters are analogous to the delay time and feedback parameters of the DDL-1 Digital Delay. The room size parameter determines the delay time of early reflections and the length of the reverberation. Higher size settings will have slightly longer delay times, and the time between early reflection echoes becomes a bit more distinct. The decay parameter controls feedback of the delays in the reverb algorithm to control the duration of the reverb tail. Just as with the DDL-1 feedback control, longer decay settings will increase the duration of the decay.

As a general rule for reverb applied to drum sounds, the size and decay parameters are adjusted so that the reverb tail from a snare hit does not overlap and obscure the attack of the next kick drum. This concept can be applied to vocals and solo instruments as well, so the reverb tail masks out silence between words and syllables or notes without intruding on the next word or note. This means the tempo of the track will affect the size and decay time of the reverberation.

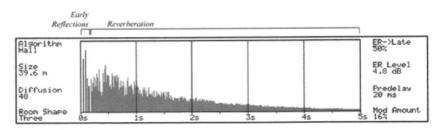

Figure 10-1
The early reflections and reverberation parts of the hall algorithm.

Damping

The materials used in building construction have a tendency to filter high frequencies when sound is reflected. A harder wall surface will reflect more highs, while a softer surface will absorb more highs. The damping parameter causes the algorithm to filter frequencies from the reflections. The HF Damp knob controls the rate at which high frequencies decay, which simulates the nature of reflections in acoustic spaces. If no high-frequency damping is applied, the reflections and reverb will sound more metallic and have a brighter sound. Some of the algorithms have low-frequency damping parameters, which cause low frequencies to decay faster than the high frequencies.

Predelay & ER->Late

Human perception defines space in terms of the delay time and attenuation—long delays should sound softer than short delays. The shorter and louder the delay, the smaller the acoustic space feels. Under normal atmospheric conditions at sea level, sound travels at 342 meters per second. This is the fundamental constant for calculating the initial reflection time of a reverb algorithm. The length of an echo from a wall 34 meters away is about 200 milliseconds—100ms for the sound to travel to the wall, and another 100ms for the echo to return.

For natural-sounding reverberation, a slight delay occurs before the reverberation. The predelay setting controls this time offset. The predelay influences how far away a sound seems to be in a room. If the sound is distant from the listener, it occurs only a few milliseconds ahead of the reverb, but if the sound is close, there's a gap (the predelay) between the original sound and the reverberant echoes.

The ER->Late parameter offsets the time between early reflections and the reverb. This controls the sensation of the proximity to the walls of a room. Sounds that are distant from the listener's perspective arrive about the same time as the early reflections, and the offset should be set to 0%. Sounds close to the listener's position will have a slight delay between the early reflections and the reverberation, so the ER->Late parameter should be set higher.

Diffusion

The density of the reverb reflections is controlled by the diffusion parameter. Lower diffusion settings will make the reflections sound more distinct, while a higher diffusion setting will make the individual reflections less discernible. In most cases, high levels of diffusion are appropriate since the reflections are smoothed.

Setting the diffusion to zero will help you understand the different room shapes and the reflections in the algorithms. Set the decay to zero, HF Damp to zero, and size to maximum. Route a sparse and slow drum loop through the reverb and start modifying the room shape parameter. With no diffusion applied to the reverb, the distinct echo characteristics of each room shape become apparent. This is a good way to determine which room shape is appropriate for a track. Once the shape has been selected, the diffusion setting can be adjusted back up.

Modulation

The Mod Amount parameter controls a modulation feature that adds a chorusing character to the reverberation. Modulation seems to affect the reverb tail more than the initial delays of the algorithm and adds a variation that gives the reverb tail a smoother, more natural decay sound. With long sustained notes, the modulation can be heard, as if a subtle chorus effect has been inserted in front of the RV7000. Keep the mod setting low to minimize this effect. The effect is barely noticeable with drums and percussion.

Plate & Spring Reverbs

The plate and spring algorithms simulate electro-mechanical devices that themselves were used to simulate room reverberation. A plate reverb is large sheet of metal suspended in an isolated room or box. Amplified signals are connected to a driver coil attached to the metal sheet, causing it to vibrate. A microphone or pickup captures the sound of the vibration. The plate reverb is the descendent of the spring reverb, which works on a similar principle using one or more metallic springs. Audio signals would induce vibrations in the springs, and the vibrations were captured by a pickup.

These types of reverb were used so often in the history of recorded music that their sound is often desired for productions. Plate reverb is often added to vocal tracks because it does not have the hard reflective characteristics induced by room and hall algorithms. The echoing effect of discrete reflections can add a type of chorusing that will distract the listener from an outstanding vocal performance. Because plate reverbs do not have early reflection characteristics, the effect is smooth and ideal for long spatial effects as well.

Infinite Reverb

Using electronic reverberation, one can create acoustic environments not found in the real world. One example of this is the "infinite" reverb, which is a reverb with an infinite decay time. Any of the reverberation algorithms can be used for this effect, but this example uses the plate reverb because it has a parameter to control low-frequency damping. Instead of using the decay, the high-frequency and low-frequency damping features will be used to attenuate the reverb tail.

1. Start with an empty rack, and create a reMix mixer.
2. Create an NN-XT Advanced Sampler.
3. Load the NN-XT patch "InfiniteHit.sxt" from the *Power Tools for Reason* CD \ NN-XT Patches directory.
4. Switch the sequencer to edit mode and view the NN-XT 1 track key lanes.
5. Pencil in a C3 note event with a one-measure duration on measure 1, and do the same on measure 5.

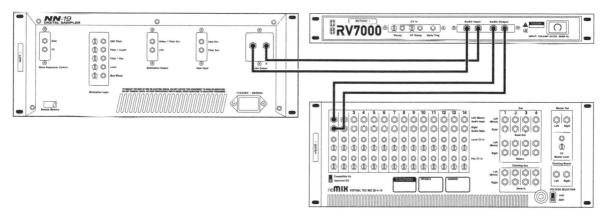

Figure 10-2
In this patch, the
plate reverb decay is
set to 127.

6. Insert an RV7000 Advanced Reverb between the NN-XT audio outputs and the mixer channel 1 inputs.

7. Open the RV7000 Remote Programmer and set the parameters according to the following chart:

RV7000 "Infinite Reverb" Parameters	
EQ	Off
Gate	Off
Decay	127
HF Damp	0
Hi EQ	0
Dry/Wet	81
Algorithm	Plate
LF Damp	20Hz
Predelay	75ms

▸ Run the sequence.

As the sequence plays, you'll hear a dense lingering reverb tail from the initial sample hit. While the sequence plays, adjust the HF Damp parameter up to 127 and listen as high frequencies decay while the low frequencies continue to trail. This creates a dark and cavernous-sounding ambient space. HF Damp is similar to an equalizer or lowpass filter in that it cuts the high frequencies of the reflections in the reverb algorithm.

The LF Damp parameter of the plate algorithm is similar to HF Damp in that it filters low frequencies from the reverb tail. Set the HF Damp back to 0 and increase the LF Damp parameter to 93Hz. The density is gone, which gives the reverb an airy quality, as if it's ascending.

Dub-Style Spring Reverb

This effect uses a DDL-1 in combination with the RV7000 spring reverb algorithm to create a rhythmic echo and spring reverb effect. The eighth-note triplet delay time adds the syncopated rhythmic element found in dub and reggae music. One modification that can be made to this configuration is to connect the DDL-1 right output to the mixer aux return 2 input. Use the aux return knob to mix the level of the delayed signal.

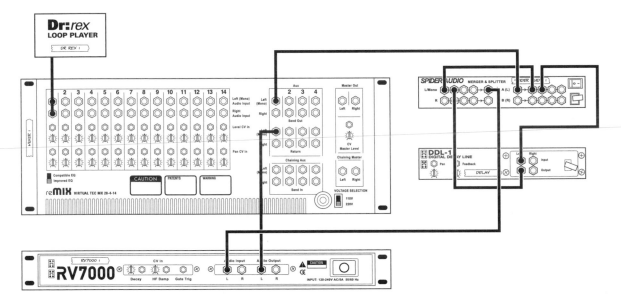

Figure 10-3
Delay inserted before the RV7000.

1. Start with an empty rack, and set the tempo to 72 BPM.
2. Create a reMix mixer.
3. Set the mixer channel 1 aux send 1 amount to 59.
4. Create a Dr.REX Loop Player.
5. Load the ReCycle loop "Dub04_Scientist_070_eLab.rx2" from the Reason Factory Sound Bank\Dr Rex Drum Loops\Dub directory.
6. Copy the REX slice data to the Dr.REX 1 sequencer track.
7. Create a Spider Audio Merger & Splitter.
8. Bypass auto-routing and connect the mixer aux send 1 left output to the Spider Audio split A input.
9. Connect the Spider Audio split A out 1 to the Spider Audio L/mono merge input 1.
10. Bypass auto-routing and create a DDL-1 Digital Delay Line.
11. Connect the Spider Audio split A out 2 to the DDL-1 left input.
12. Connect the DDL-1 left output to the Spider Audio merge L/mono input 2.

13. Set the DDL-1 delay time to 1 step, step length to 1/8T, feedback to 84, and dry/wet balance to 87.
14. Bypass auto-routing and create an RV7000 Advanced Reverb.
15. Connect the Spider Audio merge L/mono output to the RV7000 left input.
16. Bypass auto-routing and connect the RV7000 left output to the mixer aux return 1 left input.
17. Enable EQ on the RV7000 and set the decay to 82 and HF Damp to 18.
18. Open the RV7000 Remote Programmer panel and program the following:

RV7000 Spring Reverb Parameters	
EQ	On
Gate	Off
Decay	82
HF Damp	18
Hi EQ	0
Dry/wet	127
Algorithm	Spring
Length	.37m
Diffusion	127
Disp Freq	873Hz
LF Damp	373Hz
Stereo	Off
Predelay	24ms
Disp Amt.	100%

19. Switch the RV7000 Remote Programmer to EQ edit mode.
20. Set the EQ parametric gain (not the low gain) to 8.9dB, parametric frequency to 1104Hz, and Q to 0.5.
   ▸ Run the sequence.

Gated Reverb

Reverb can add a lot of density to the sound of drums. The right setting yields massive-sounding drums. One problem with this is that the drums will overpower everything else, and the reverb tail will obscure the attack of the next drum hit. A method made popular with recordings in the '80s is to apply a noise gate after the reverb output. The noise gate threshold settings are set at a high enough level to cut off the tail of the reverb, while the dense reverberation in the early part of the decay is retained, giving a huge sound.

Typically, gated reverb should not be applied as a send effect for all devices. If certain sounds require gated reverb, a second reverb device should be added on a different aux effect bus on the mixer. The gate can be triggered in the conventional manner by carefully setting the threshold and envelope settings, or it can be triggered using gate CV signals from another device. This can be especially useful to create the gated drum sound for Redrum patterns—the gate trigger CV output from a snare sample can be connected to the RV7000 gate trigger input. The reverb gate will open only when a snare drum hit occurs.

Gated Drums

This example demonstrates using the RV7000 as an insert device to create the gated drum sound effect. Using the RV7000 as a mono insert effect allows the effect to be panned in a specific position in the mix, and the sounds processed through the gated reverb will sound like they are down a hallway or a tube.

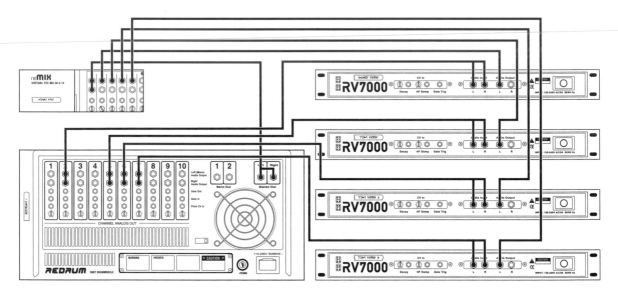

Figure 10-4
RV7000 reverbs inserted between Redrum channels and mixer inputs.

1. Start with an empty rack. Set the tempo to 105 BPM and pattern shuffle to 10.
2. Create a reMix mixer.
3. Create a Redrum Drum Computer and load the patch "Groovemasters Rock Kit 3.drp" from the Reason Factory Sound Bank\Redrum Drum Kits\Rock Kits directory.
4. Set the pan to 0 on Redrum channels 5, 6, and 7.
5. Enable shuffle and set the Redrum flam amount to 108.

6. Program the following on Redrum pattern A1:

Redrum Pattern

	1	2	3	4	5	6	7	8	9	10	11	12	13	14	15	16
1	M							M			S				S	
2				M									M			
3																
4																
5	M			M												
6							M			M						
7												S			M	
8	M		M	S	M	S	Sf		M		M	S	M	Sf	M	
9		S						S		S					S	
10																

7. Bypass auto-routing and create a RV7000 Advanced Reverb. Rename it "Snare Verb."
8. Load the patch "ALL 1st Hall" from the Reason Factory Sound Bank\RV7000 Patches directory.
9. Connect the Redrum channel 2 outputs to the RV7000 inputs.
10. Connect the RV7000 outputs to the mixer channel 2 inputs.
11. Set the RV7000 dry/wet mix to 54, and enable the gate.
12. Open the RV7000 Remote Programmer and switch to gate edit mode.
13. Adjust the gate threshold to -10.5dB and the gate release time to 100ms.
14. Bypass auto-routing, create an RV7000 Advanced Reverb, and rename it "Tom Verb 1."
15. Load the patch "ALL Small Room" from the Reason Factory Sound Bank\ RV7000 Patches directory.
16. Connect the Redrum channel 5 outputs to the Tom Verb 1 inputs.
17. Connect the Tom Verb 1 left output to mixer channel 3 left input.
18. Set the Tom Verb 1 dry/wet mix to 86, and enable the gate.
19. Open the Tom Verb 1 Remote Programmer and switch to gate edit mode.
20. Adjust the gate threshold to -12.6dB and the gate release time to 100ms.
21. Make two duplicates of the Tom Verb 1 RV7000, and rename them "Tom Verb 2" and "Tom Verb 3."
22. Connect the Redrum channel 6 outputs to the Tom Verb 2 inputs and the Redrum channel 7 outputs to the Tom Verb 3 inputs.
23. Connect the Tom Verb 2 left output to mixer channel 4 left input and the Tom Verb 3 left output to mixer channel 5 left input.

24. Set the mixer channel 3 pan to −56, channel 4 pan to −17, and channel 5 pan to 59.

▸ Run the Redrum pattern.

This patch can be edited in various ways. Try soloing each of the tom channels in the mixer and playing with the reverb settings for it. Switch the toms to gate mode 1 and shorten their length, so that the dry tom sound will also be gated.

Modulated RV7000 Gate & Decay

This example of a gated reverb uses a Matrix Pattern Sequencer to trigger the RV7000 gate. The gate threshold settings are disabled when the trigger source is switched to the MIDI/CV setting.

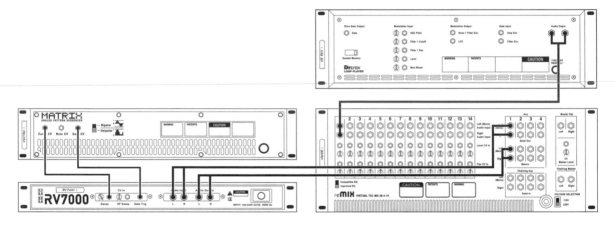

Figure 10-5
Matrix gate CV connected to the RV7000 gate trig CV input.

1. Start with an empty rack, and create a reMix mixer.
2. Create an RV7000 Advanced Reverb and load the patch "DRM AMS PrcPlate.rv7" from the Reason Factory Sound Bank\RV7000 Patches directory.
3. Set the RV7000 decay to 0, enable the gate, open the Remote Programmer, and set the gate trig source to MIDI/CV.
4. Create a Matrix Pattern Sequencer.
5. Verify that the Matrix curve CV is automatically cabled to the RV7000 decay input and that the Matrix gate CV output is connected to the RV7000 gate trig input.
6. Set the RV7000 decay CV trim to 127.
7. Program the following on Matrix pattern A1:

Matrix Pattern

Step	1	2	3	4	5	6	7	8	9	10	11	12	13	14	15	16
Curve					128	72	48	0					64	48	32	0
Note																
Gate	TH	TH	TH		TH	TH	TH	TH				TH	TH	TH	TH	TH

8. Create a Dr.REX Loop Player.

9. Load the ReCycle loop "Chm07_Skint_130_eLAB.rx2" from the Reason Factory Sound Bank\Dr Rex Drum Loops\Chemical Beats directory.
10. Copy the REX slice data to the Dr.REX 1 sequencer track.
11. Set the mixer channel 1 aux send 1 to 100.
  ▸ Run the sequence.

Reverse Reverb

Reverse reverb is an effect that originated in the '60s. It was originally produced by reversing the playback direction of a tape, sending the tape output (a guitar solo, for instance) into a reverb, and recording the reverb to a new track. Then the tape would be flipped over and played in its normal direction again, causing the reverb tail to appear before each note, growing from silence to a high level.

This effect can't be simulated perfectly in a digital reverb's reverse algorithm, but it can be approximated. In a reverse algorithm, the reverb tail gets louder rather than softer.

Reverse Drums

Using the reverse reverb as a send effect, the events from a ReCycle loop are ghosted and delayed to create an overlapping echo and reverse reverb pattern. As the pattern plays, adjust the RV7000 length parameter to hear the interesting rhythmic variations with the reverse algorithm. Also, try setting the RV7000 decay to 127 to hear the full reverse hit rather than the crescendo. This works best with shorter lengths up to three sixteenth-note steps.

1. Start with an empty rack, and create a reMix mixer.
2. Set the mixer channel 1 aux send 1 amount to 91.
3. Create an RV7000 Advanced Reverb.
4. Open the RV7000 Remote Programmer and set the parameters according to the following chart:

RV7000 Parameters	
EQ	Off
Gate	Off
Decay	97
HF Damp	20
Hi EQ	44
Dry/Wet	127
Algorithm	Reverse
Length	5/16
Density	127
Tempo Sync	On
Rev Dry/Wet	64

5. Create a Dr.REX Loop Player.
6. Load the ReCycle loop "Trh06_RZA_100_eLAB.rx2" from Reason Factory Sound Bank\Dr Rex Drum Loops\Abstract HipHop directory.
7. Copy the REX slice data to the Dr.REX 1 sequencer track.
▸ Run the sequence.

Pre-Verb

The dry/wet parameter controls the level between the reversed reverb and delayed signal. The default setting of 64 mixes equal levels of the reverse and delayed signal, while a setting of 127 will only pass the reverse reverb signal. This example uses two identical samples. One sample, processed with a reverse reverb insert, is triggered four steps ahead of the second. The reverse reverb creates a build-up leading to the second sample.

Figure 10-6

Reverse reverb inserted on Redrum channel 2.

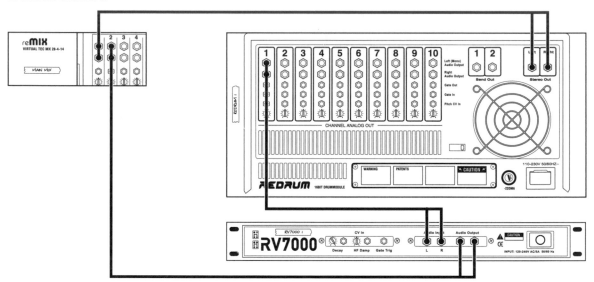

1. In an empty rack, create a reMix mixer.
2. Create a Redrum Drum Computer.
3. On Redrum channels 1 and 2, load the sample "PianoStab2_eLAB.aif" from the Reason Factory Sound Bank\Other Samples\Chords-Phrases-Pads-Stabs directory.

4. Program the following on Redrum pattern A1:

Redrum Pattern

	1	2	3	4	5	6	7	8	9	10	11	12	13	14	15	16
1	M															
2					M											
3																
4																
5																
6																
7																
8																
9																
10																

5. Bypass auto-routing and create an RV7000 Advanced Reverb.
6. Connect the Redrum channel 1 outputs to the RV7000 audio inputs.
7. Connect the RV7000 audio outputs to the mixer channel 2 input.
8. Open the RV7000 Remote Programmer and set the parameters according to the following chart:

RV7000 Pre-Verb Parameters

EQ	Off
Gate	Off
Decay	76
HF Damp	0
Hi EQ	0
Dry/Wet	127
Algorithm	Reverse
Length	4/16
Density	127
Tempo Sync	On
Rev Dry/Wet	127

▸ Run the Redrum pattern.

Equalization

B ecause many delays are summed in the process of creating a reverb effect, certain frequency ranges will be boosted. To balance the effect with the rest of the mix, it is often necessary to equalize the signal. For instance, string arrangements with cello parts that fall into the low midrange will cause a bellowing sound from the reverb. When combined with the rest of the mix, this creates muddiness. Using the RV7000's built-in EQ to roll off the bass and low mids will allow the reverb to sit above the string arrangement without overloading the mix.

The RV7000 has a shelving EQ control on the main panel. This is simply a treble control similar to the reMix's treble EQ. There is also a dedicated EQ section, which has a low shelving equalizer and a single-band parametric EQ. Instead of using the RV7000 EQ, a PEQ-2 Parametric Equalizer can be inserted between the mixer aux send and the RV7000 inputs. Troublesome frequencies like the low midrange can be attenuated before processing. To pad down the low mids, set the PEQ-2 center frequency in the range between 22 and 50, Q set to 0, and a gain amount of between –10 and –22.

Feedback

Using reverb devices wired into feedback loops can simulate the harmonic howling of a guitar pickup feeding back through an amplifier. A similar phenomenon occurs with a spring reverb pickup when the sound coming from an amplifier causes the spring to oscillate. The following examples demonstrate how to recreate these techniques using cabled feedback loops with reverbs.

RV-7 Feedback Resonance

In the world of hardware, it's common to find bits and pieces of odd gear sitting in the rack next to high-performance devices. One might wonder why a producer would choose to use an inexpensive reverb when a high-end reverb is available. Signal processing devices have their own characteristic nuances, which may be exactly what the mix calls for. Like using a spring reverb algorithm instead of a hall algorithm, choosing the RV-7 can be useful to create a certain sound. This example shows how the RV-7 can be used to create a nice feedback effect. The feedback loop will be used as a send effect. The feedback resonance from the RV-7 algorithms sounds a lot like old science fiction film sound effects.

1. Start with an empty rack, and create a reMix mixer.
2. Set the mixer channel 1 aux send 1 amount to 99.

RV-7 Feedback Combinator Patch

3. Bypass auto-routing and create a Combinator.
4. Connect the mixer's aux 1 sends to the Combi inputs.
5. Connect the Combi outputs to the mixer's aux 1 return inputs.
6. In the Combinator sub-rack, create a reMix mixer.
7. Set this mixer's channel 14 aux 4 send amount to 115, and switch on the EQ for channel 14.
8. Connect the Combinator To Devices outputs to the Mixer 1 channel 1 inputs.
9. Still in the sub-rack, bypass auto-routing and create an MClass Compressor.
10. Connect the Mixer 1 aux 4 sends to the Compressor audio inputs.

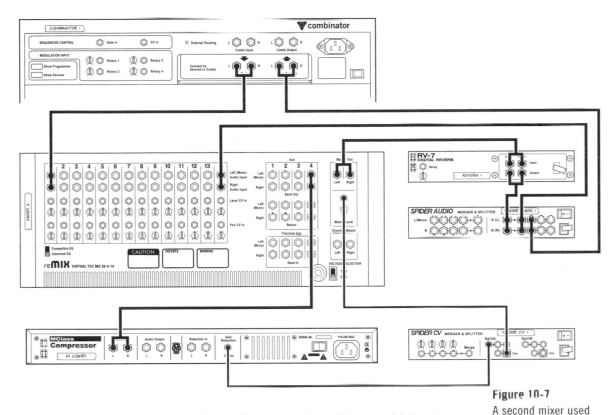

Figure 10-7

A second mixer used to create a feedback loop with an aux send.

11. Set the MClass Compressor threshold to –28.1 dB, soft knee enabled, ratio ∞:1, attack 100ms, release 236ms, adapt release enabled.

12. Bypass auto-routing and create a Spider CV Merger & Splitter.

13. Connect the compressor's gain reduction CV out to the Spider split A input.

14. Connect the Spider split 4 (inv) output to the Mixer 1 master level CV input.

15. Set the Mixer 1 master level CV trim to 127. This CV section is a protection circuit that should prevents overloading feedback loops.

16. Bypass auto-routing and create an RV-7 Digital Reverb.

17. Connect the Mixer 1 master outputs to the RV-7 inputs.

18. Create a Spider Audio Merger & Splitter.

19. Connect the RV-7 outputs to the Spider Audio splitter inputs.

20. Connect the Spider split 1 outputs to the Mixer 1 channel 14 inputs.

21. Connect the Spider Split 2 outputs to the Combinator's From Devices inputs.

22. Open the Combinator Programmer and set the following modulation routings:

Device	Source	Target	Min	Max
Mixer 1	Rotary 1	Channel 14 Level	21	75
Mixer 1	Rotary 4	Channel 14 Bass Amt.	–22	–64
Mixer 1	Button 1	Master Level	100	0

continued >

Device	Source	Target	Min	Max
Mixer 1	Button 2	Channel 14 Mute	0	1
Reverb 1	Rotary 2	Size	−25	39
Reverb 1	Rotary 3	Decay	−64	−12
Reverb 1	Rotary 4	Damping	0	49

23. Rename the Combinator controls and set the parameters as follows:

Control	Name	Default Value
Rotary 1	Feedback	104
Rotary 2	Size	17
Rotary 3	Decay	76
Rotary 4	Damping	86
Button 1	EMERGENCY!	Off
Button 2	Mute Feedback	Off

24. Save the patch as "RV7 Feedback.cmb."

Sound Source

25. In the Reason song rack, create a second Combinator.
26. Load the patch "10 – Harmonic Sound Source" from the *Power Tools for Reason* CD \ Combinator Patches directory.
   ▸ Run the sequence.

The slight sound of metallic ringing is the circuit resonating through the feedback loop. To increase the ringing, turn up the feedback and decay knobs in the Combinator and turn down the damping. Turning the size knob will change the color of the feedback. As the pattern plays, enable the Mute Feedback button to hear the straight reverb effect. The limited parameter range and level CV modulation are designed to prevent overloading feedback loops. In the event of an overload, the Combinator emergency button will disable the feedback loop, as will the Mute Feedback button. Different algorithms will create interesting effects, especially the low density and the pan room algorithms.

Chapter 11
Chorusing Effects

Chorusing effects thicken and add stereo width to sounds. Even a simple monophonic sound can be transformed into a lush stereo texture by chorusing. Stereo chorusing is based on the principles of comb filtering and fattening using delay modules. The main difference is that the delay time changes under the control of a modulation signal like a triangle wave LFO.

Reason has three devices for creating stereo effects based on the principles of short delay times. The CF-101 Chorus/Flanger and PH-90 Phaser use the principles of comb filtering, but the delay time is modulated with an LFO to produce variations. The UN-16 Unison module is another device used for creating stereo chorusing effects. While it's not designed as a stereo chorusing device, the MClass Stereo Imager can enhance or spatialize signals for stereophonic effects.

Chorusing

A chorus effect typically has a delay time between 15ms and 30ms, and it's very similar to using delays for doubling. The LFO modulation should be subtle, with a moderate amount of feedback to add density to the signal.

The CF-101 Chorus/Flanger can be used as either a send or an insert effect. The "send mode" button is like a dry/wet balance switch. When send mode is enabled, only the processed signal is output. When send mode is disabled, the dry signal and processed signal are mixed together. There is no dry/wet balance control, thus it's better to use it as send effect. Adjust the wetness using the effect send and return knobs.

The CF-101 processes both monophonic and stereophonic signals. Unlike the DDL-1 Delay and RV-7 Reverb, the CF-101 processes stereo signals discretely. The stereo image that comes in remains unchanged at the output, and the CF-101 acts like two independent monophonic chorusing devices. This changes when only one input signal cables to the left audio input: The CF-101 will take a monophonic input and create a pseudo stereo effect.

Simple Stereo Chorus

Stereo chorusing is enabled when the CF-101 receives a mono input signal and the modulation amount is set greater than zero. There are really no set rules for creating a chorus effect, but this example gives the basic settings for an all-purpose stereo chorusing effect using the CF-101.

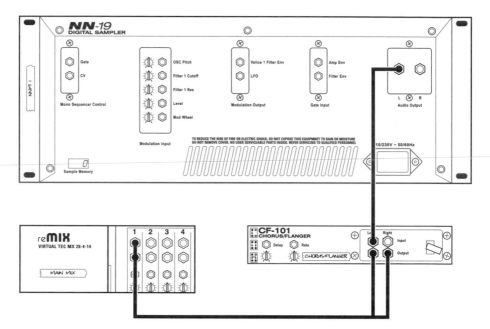

Figure 11-1

The CF-101 produces stereo modulation when it receives only a mono input signal.

1. Start with an empty rack, and set the tempo to 85 BPM.
2. Create a reMix mixer.
3. Bypass auto-routing and create an NN19 Digital Sampler.
4. Load the sample "170_Gated_mLp_eLab.aif" from the Reason Factory Sound Bank\Music Loops\Fixed Tempo (wave, aiff) directory.
5. Bypass auto-routing, and create a CF-101 Chorus/Flanger.
6. Set the CF-101 delay to 64, feedback to 10, LFO rate to 0, and LFO mod amount to 38.
7. Connect the NN19 left audio output (mono) to the CF-101 left input.
8. Connect the CF-101 left and right outputs to the mixer channel 1 inputs.
9. View the key lane on the NN19 sequencer track.
10. Use the pencil tool and draw two-measure note events on C3.
    ▶ Run the sequence.

Experiment with various settings of the CF-101's delay, feedback, rate, and mod amount knobs to get a feel for the sound of basic chorusing.

Flanging

O riginally, flanging was created by running two synchronized tape machines that were playing the same audio signal. While the machines played the identical tracks, an engineer would press down on the flange of the tape reel on one machine, which would induce a slight pitch shift and delay. When the two signals were mixed, a comb filtering effect would be heard as the signals from the two machines fell slightly out of sync.

Signal processors like the CF-101 create a different type of flanging than the original tape technique. DSP flanging sounds more like a Doppler shift—a bit like the sound of a jet engine passing by the listener. A subtle phase shift created by delays with durations less than 10ms causes comb filtering. The LFO modulation sweeps the delay time, creating the Doppler shift sound. Unlike tape flanging, DSP flanging uses feedback to enhance the comb filtering to get a deeper resonating effect.

Stereo Flanger

This example demonstrates using the CF-101 stereo mode to create a lush stereo flanging effect. To hear the difference between the stereo flanging effect and the CF-101 used with stereo input signals, connect the right channel from the NN19 into the CF-101. This configuration is an insert device, so send mode is disabled.

1. Start with the patch created in the chorusing example, above.
2. Set the tempo to 130 BPM.
3. Load the sample "130_PlanetE_mLp_eLab.aif" from the Reason Factory Sound Bank\Music Loops\Fixed Tempo (wave, aiff) directory.
4. Set the CF-101 delay to 4, feedback to –42, LFO rate to 48, and LFO mod amount to 8.
5. Select the NN19 sequencer track and enter edit mode to view the key lane.
6. Set the sequencer resolution to Bar.
7. Use the pencil tool and draw several four-measure events on C3.
  ▶ Run the sequence.

Malström Stereo Flanger

Digital Flangers work on the principles of modulating a comb filter, and a stereo flanger can be created using the comb filter mode in Malström's filter section. This effect uses two Malström filters with the same mode settings, and a Combinator modulation routing changes the frequency controls in opposite directions.

1. Start with an empty rack and set the tempo to 135 BPM.
2. Create a reMix mixer.
3. Bypass auto-routing and create a Dr.REX Loop Player.
4. Load the ReCycle loop "Tec12_Cologne_135_eLAB.rx2" from the Reason Factory Sound Bank\Dr Rex Drum Loops\Techno directory.
5. Copy the REX slice data to the Dr.REX 1 sequencer track.

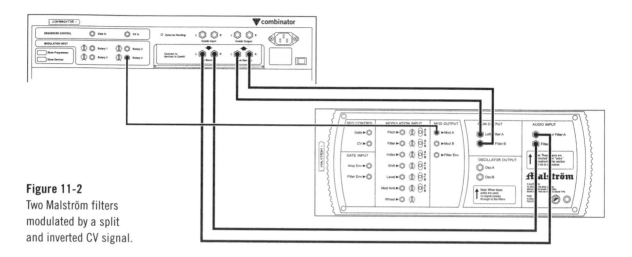

Figure 11-2
Two Malström filters
modulated by a split
and inverted CV signal.

Malström Stereo Flanger Combinator Patch

6. Insert a Combinator between the Dr.REX and the reMix inputs.
7. In the Combinator sub-rack, create a Malström Graintable Synthesizer.
8. Connect the Combinator 'To Devices' outputs to the Malström Audio inputs.
9. On Malström 1, disable all sections except Mod A, Filter A, and Filter B.
10. Set Filter A and Filter B modes to comb+, and set Spread to 128.
11. Connect the Malström Mod A CV output to the Combinator Rotary 4 input.
12. Open the Combinator Programmer and set the following modulation routings:

Device	Source	Target	Min	Max
Malstrom 1	Rotary 1	Modulator A Curve	0	30
Malstrom 1	Rotary 2	Modulator A Rate	0	127
Malstrom 1	Rotary 3	Filter B Resonance	0	127
Malstrom 1	Rotary 4	Filter B Freq	63	127
Malstrom 1	Button 1	Modulator A Sync	0	1
Malstrom 1	Rotary 3	Filter A Resonance	0	127
Malstrom 1	Rotary 4	Filter A Freq	127	63

13. Rename the Combinator controls and set the parameters as follows:

Control	Name	Default Value
Rotary 1	Curve	8
Rotary 2	Rate	45
Rotary 3	Resonance	47
Rotary 4	Freq MOD	63
Button 1	Sync	On

14. Save the patch as "Malstrom Flanger.cmb."
▸ Run the sequence.

The stereo sweeping caused by the inverted modulation sounds a lot like a phase-shifting effect, discussed later in this chapter. For a more subtle effect, change the Malström filter modes to comb– and reduce the Combinator resonance setting. This configuration is also the basis for a large number of other stereo processing effects. Try changing the filter modes to lowpass and bandpass, and try adjusting the Combinator Curve and Rate controls.

Phaser

The basic principle behind a phaser effect is the principle of phase shifting described in Chapter 8. Phasers behave like notch filters, but they filter specific frequencies using phase cancellation. Phasers, such as hardware devices and the Reason PH-90, have stages that apply different amounts of phase shift to the signal to cancel several different frequencies. This is different from using a delay to create a phase-shift, because the delay has only has one stage.

The PH-90 is a four-stage phaser, and in essence it behaves like a four-band notch filter. The frequency knob controls the base cutoff frequency of the first notch filter. The split parameter determines the spacing between the center frequencies of the other three notch filters. The width parameter controls the bandwidth: Higher width settings increase the bandwidth filtered by the notch filters—similar to the PEQ-2 Q parameter. The feedback parameter attenuates the feedback level of the filtered signal. Higher feedback settings will cause the phaser to resonate and increase the depth of the filters.

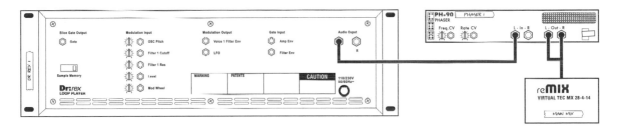

Figure 11-3
"Fake stereo" created by connecting a mono input to the PH-90 left input socket.

Classic Stereo Phaser

The PH-90 Phaser behaves differently depending on how it is cabled. Only connecting a signal to the left audio input will enable a special pseudo-stereo mode that creates the classic stereo phaser sound found on contemporary and vintage phaser devices. In order to enable the stereo effect, the PH-90 a mono signal connects to the left audio input. The PH-90 modulates the right channel with an inverse phase to create the stereo effect. When connected in stereo, both channels are modulated in the same manner.

1. Start with an empty rack, and create a reMix mixer.
2. Create a Dr.REX Loop Player.
3. On the Dr.REX, load the Recycle file "135_TechChords_mLp_eLAB.rx2" from the Factory Sound Bank from the Music Loops\Variable Tempo (rex2)\ Uptempo Loops directory.
4. Copy the REX data to the Dr.REX sequencer track.
5. Insert a PH-90 Phaser between the Dr.REX and the mixer channel 1 input.
6. Disconnect the Dr.REX right output from the PH-90 right input.
▶ Run the sequence.

This configuration can be changed back to the standard phaser effect by reconnecting the Dr.REX Audio Output Right to the PH-90 right input. The audible difference between the modes is that the pseudo stereo phaser provides a swirling panning feeling caused by the inverted modulation. The standard mode will sound centered and monophonic with subtle sweeps that move from the center phantom image outward towards the stereo monitors.

Pattern-Controlled Phaser

The PH-90 can be used as a pattern-controlled device like the ECF-42 Envelope Controlled Filter to create interesting pattern-based notch filtering. The pattern in this example sustains a fixed level for several steps. Phasers are commonly used as a filter device in the dub music, and this example uses a DDL-1 inserted before the phaser to recreate the rhythmic syncopation induced by a 1/8T delay.

Figure 11-4

The Matrix curve CV is cabled to the PH-90 frequency CV input. A DDL-1 is inserted before the phaser to create a dub-style echo.

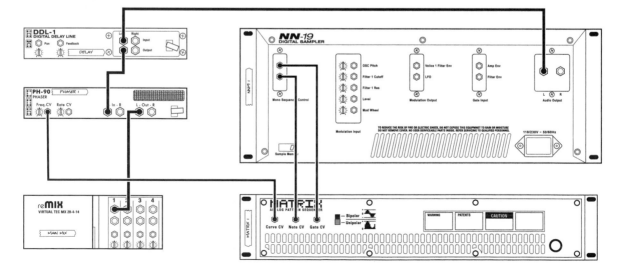

1. Start with an empty rack, and set the song tempo to 70 BPM.
2. Create a reMix mixer.
3. Bypass auto-routing and create an NN19 Digital Sampler.
4. Open the NN19 Patch Browser, and open the ReCycle loop "090_DubStrat_ mLp_eLab.rx2" from the Reason Factory Sound Bank\Music Loops\Variable Tempo (rex2)\Downtempo Loops directory.
5. Set the NN19 oscillator octave transpose to 3 and semitone to 10.
6. Create a Matrix Pattern Sequencer.
7. Program the gate and note events as follows:

Matrix Pattern

Step	1	2	3	4	5	6	7	8	9	10	11	12	13	14	15	16
Curve	50%	50%	50%	75%	75%	75%	40%	40%	40%	40%	20%	20%	20%	20%	80%	80%
Note	C3	C3	G2	C3	C3	C3	E2	C3	C3	C3	B2	C3	C3	C3	A2	C3
Gate			TH				TH				TH				TH	

8. Switch to curve edit mode.
9. Use the line tool (hold down the Shift key) and draw a flat line at 50% from step 1 through step 16.
10. From step 3 to step 6, draw a line at 75%.
11. From step 7 to step 10, draw a line at 40%.
12. From step 11 to step 14, draw a line at 20%.
13. From step 15 to step 16, draw a line at 80%.
14. Bypass auto-routing and create a DDL-1 Digital Delay Line.
15. Bypass auto-routing and connect the NN19 left output to the DDL-1 left input.
16. Set the DDL-1 delay time to 1 step, step length to 1/8T, feedback to 88, dry/wet balance to 32.
17. Bypass auto-routing and create a PH-90 Phaser.
18. Bypass auto-routing and connect the DDL-1 left output to the PH-90 left input.
19. Bypass auto-routing and connect the PH-90 left output to the mixer channel 1 left input.
20. Connect the Matrix curve CV output to the PH-90 frequency CV input.
21. Set the PH-90 frequency to 54, LFO F.Mod to 0, and feedback to 82.
▶ Run the Matrix pattern.

Unison

The UN-16 Unison module can be considered the ultimate chorus effect. While based on principles of pitch shifting and delay doubling, the UN-16 Unison module operates differently than a CF-101. The UN-16 splits the incoming signal from four to 16 times depending on the voice count parameter. Each of the duplicate signals is processed in parallel through delays and pitch shifters. Unlike the CF-101, which uses a triangle wave to modulate the delay time, the UN-16 uses random noise to modulate the pitch shifting amount. The detune parameter scales the depth of the pitch modulation.

Like the CF-101 and PH-90, the UN-16 runs in mono, stereo, or fake stereo mode depending on the input and output cabling. The UN-16 can be used to thicken up any input signal, but it really shines as a stereo chorusing device. Either cabled as an insert effect or a send effect, a mono input signal on the UN-16 left input and stereo outputs will create a massive chorus sound.

Unison SubTractor

This example describes a basic method of using the UN-16 as an insert device. Adjusting the Dry/Wet mix allows for some of the original mono signal to pass through, but for the widest possible stereo separation, set the Dry/Wet Mix to 127 (default). The UN-16 Detune setting seems to work best at 40 (the default), but this should be adjusted for taste.

1. Start with an empty rack, and create a reMix mixer.
2. Create a Combinator.
3. In the Combinator sub-rack, create a SubTractor synthesizer.
4. Load the patch "In To My Head.zyp" from the Reason Factory Sound Bank\ SubTractor Patches\PolySynths directory.
5. Select the SubTractor, and insert a UN-16 Unison module between the SubTractor and the Combinator 'From Devices' inputs.
6. Save the Combinator patch as "Unison Subtractor.cmb."
  ‣ Play notes on a MIDI controller.

Big Brass Section

The UN-16 Unison module has a dry/wet balance control, which makes it very suitable as an insert effect. Signals processed through the UN-16 are dramatically different from the original, and getting the most out of the effect often requires careful balancing between processed and dry signals. This example demonstrates how subtle use of the UN-16 enhances a trumpet section multisample.

1. Start with an empty rack, and create a reMix mixer.
2. Create a NN-XT Advanced Sampler.
3. Load the patch "TRPS SfzC.sxt" from the Orkester Sound Bank\Brass\Trumpet Section (TRPS) directory.
4. Insert a UN-16 Unison module between the NN-XT and the mixer.
5. Set the UN-16 detune to 22, and the dry/wet mix to 89.
6. Insert an RV7000 Advanced Reverb between the UN-16 and the mixer.
7. Set the RV7000 decay to 30 and the dry/wet mix to 44.
8. Open the RV7000 Remote Programmer.

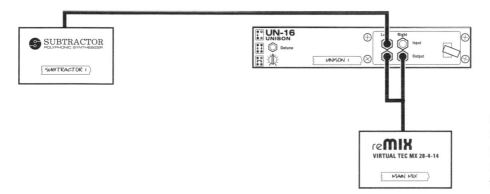

Figure 11-5
UN-16 in fake stereo mode with a mono input signal connected to the left input socket.

9. Set the RV7000 algorithm to hall, size to 26.5m, diffusion to 127, room shape to three, early reflection delay to 69%, early reflection level to 0.0dB, predelay to 30ms, and modulation amount to 42%.
▸ Play some notes on a MIDI controller keyboard.

Stereo Drum Processing

Most of the drum samples included in Reason Factory Sound Bank are monophonic, and the drum patterns usually end up as monophonic sources panned center in the mix. These sounds can be enhanced with a subtle bit of stereo processing through a UN-16 to spread the drum sounds across the stereo field.

1. Start with an empty rack, and create a reMix mixer.
2. Create a Redrum Drum Computer.
3. Connect the Redrum channel 1 outputs to the mixer channel 2 inputs.
4. Load the Redrum patch "Electronic Kit 3.drp" from the Reason Factory Sound Bank\Redrum Drum Kits\Electronic Kits directory.
5. Program the following on Redrum pattern A1:

Redrum Pattern

	1	2	3	4	5	6	7	8	9	10	11	12	13	14	15	16
1	M										M					
2							M									
3													M			
4			M									S				
5					M			S		S			M			S
6																
7																
8	M	S	S	S	M	S	S	S	M	S	S	S	M	S	S	S
9	M								M							
10														M		

6. Insert a UN-16 Unison module between the Redrum stereo outs and the mixer channel 1 inputs.

7. Set the UN-16 voice count to 8, detune to 18, and dry/wet mix to 90.

▸ Run the Redrum pattern.

The bass drum sample, which bypasses the UN-16, remains a mono sound in the mix, but the other samples processed through the UN-16 sound spread out between the left and right channels of the mix.

MClass Stereo Imager

The MClass Stereo Imager device is a spatialization effect used primarily for mastering to enhance stereo separation. An incoming signal is split by a crossover into two frequency ranges determined by the X-over parameter. The lower range of frequencies is directed to the Lo Band processor, and the higher range is processed through the Hi Band section.

While set to the center *Original* position, the signals pass through unaffected by the processors. When adjusted counterclockwise, the processor merges the stereo signals into a mono signal. When adjusted clockwise toward the Wide setting, the processors induce phase shifting between the stereo channels to create the impression of greater stereo separation. The amount of shift is determined by the difference between the incoming stereo channels, so the imaging process only works with stereo signals.

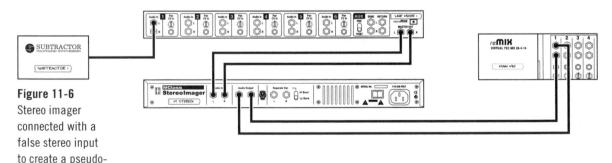

Figure 11-6
Stereo imager connected with a false stereo input to create a pseudo-stereo effect.

Pseudo-Stereo Imaging

This example should also illustrate how the stereo imager can dramatically change the stereo spread. It takes a mono signal on the right channel and converts it to a full stereo signal in both channels. This is useful as a chorusing effect; however, it should not be used with maximum settings when mastering a song.

1. In an empty rack, create a reMix Mixer.
2. Bypass auto-routing and create a SubTractor synth.
3. Bypass auto-routing and create a MicroMix Line mixer.

4. Connect the SubTractor Audio output to the MicroMix Channel 1 Input.
5. Bypass auto-routing and create a MClass Stereo Imager.
6. Connect the MicroMix Master outputs to the Stereo Imager inputs.
7. Connect the Stereo Imager outputs to the reMix Channel 1 inputs.
8. Play and hold a note or chord, and observe that the stereo imager meters do not change.
9. While holding the notes, adjust the MicroMix Channel 1 Pan from hard left to hard right. Observe the Stereo Image meters increase as you pan the signal further from center.
10. Pan the MicroMix Channel 1 hard right.
11. Adjust the Stereo Imager Lo Band Width: 63, and Hi Band Width: 63.

▸ Play some notes and hear the pseudo-stereo effect generated with the stereo imager. While listening, adjust the width of the Hi Band to full mono (–64) and sweep the crossover frequency back and forth to hear an interesting filter sweep effect.

In order for the stereo imaging process to work, both inputs must be connected to incoming signals. Using the Micromix, the incoming signals are offset with the pan control to trick the processor into thinking that there is a separation in signals.

Chapter 12
Distortion Effects

Since the invention of electrified music instruments, the sound created by over-driven amplifiers has defined the music known as rock and roll. Electronic music has drawn upon the technical innovations created for rock, and distortion is commonly used to process synthesizers, drum loops, and even vocals. In analog electronics, distortion is easy to achieve simply by overloading a circuit. In digital audio, overloading a circuit results in clipping, which sounds nothing like analog distortion and is generally very undesirable. In digital effects, distortion must be simulated using software algorithms that emulate analog circuits.

Reason has three distortion effects. The Scream 4 and D-11 are dedicated devices for distortion, and signals can be routed through the Malström Shaper section to distort them. The Scream 4 is the best distortion effect in the traditional sense, but the results differ on each device. In some cases the D-11 or Malström Shaper is more suitable. The Scream 4 parameters can be saved as patches, and there are number of presets available in the Reason Factory Sound Bank.

Distortion works best when used as an insert rather than as an aux send effect, and the examples provided below do not really explore special routing techniques like feedback. Some of the examples use distortion effects in parallel or several distortion units in series, but nothing more exotic. Distortion is normally a dramatic effect, but very subtle use of distortion can add slight harmonic changes that excite an ordinary tone.

Instrument Distortion

Distortion is a dynamics-dependent effect, which means it's sensitive to signal level. The louder the incoming signal, the more the signal distorts. The Scream 4 has two controls for adjusting levels—the damage control knob and the master output knob. Damage control is used to boost or cut the gain of the signal at the input of the effect.

Adjusting this parameter to a high level is like overloading the input of an analog device to increase the distortion. Using a low damage control setting is useful to add subtle coloring to a signal. The master output control is an attenuator like a fader: Unity gain is 100, and settings above 100 add gain.

When turning up the damage control, it's often useful to turn down the master output so that the distorted signal doesn't overpower the mix. By switching the Scream in and out of bypass mode, you can match the perceived levels of the undistorted and distorted tones if you need to.

The Scream 4 has several algorithms that simulate classic analog effects. The overdrive, distortion, and fuzz algorithms are the most suitable for simulating transistor-based distortion circuits. The tube algorithm does not have a strong distortion character, but the bias control is a useful feature to add harmonics to a signal.

Preamp & Distortion

Electric guitar rigs usually have several devices that can create distortion. The combination of pedals, amplifiers, and cabinets creates a unique distortion tone. This chain of devices inspired the following example, which uses two Scream 4 units connected in series to create a fuller distortion tone. The first unit uses the tube algorithm to add density to the raw tone. The bias setting controls DC offset, a setting of 63 being zero offset. A slight upward offset shifts the waveform, adding harmonic content to the tone. The second unit distorts the signal with the distortion algorithm. The Combinator modulation routings govern several parameters simultaneously to simplify dialing up a tone. Having several Scream 4 units wired in series makes it possible to create unique-sounding distortion modules within the Combinator.

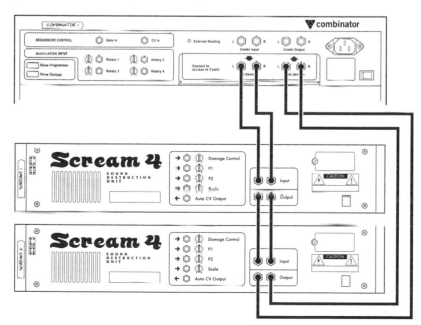

Figure 12-1
Two Scream 4 units connected in series.

1. In an empty rack, create a reMix mixer.
2. Create a Dr.REX Loop Player.
3. Load the ReCycle loop "Jh_DI_Guitar_heavyriff.rx2" from the *Power Tools for Reason* CD \ Dr.REX Loops directory.
4. Copy the REX slice data to the Dr.REX 1 sequencer track.
5. Insert two Scream 4 units in series between the Dr.REX and the mixer.
6. Rename the first Scream 4 (connected right after the Dr.REX) "Preamp" and the second Scream 4 "Distortion."

Preamp & Distortion Combinator Patch

7. Select the two Scream 4 units and click on Combine in the Edit menu.
8. On the Preamp Scream 4, set the Algorithm to Tube.
9. Open the Combinator Programmer and set the following modulation routings:

Device	Source	Target	Min	Max
Preamp	Rotary 1	Damage Control	0	63
Preamp	Rotary 2	Parameter 1	32	127
Preamp	Rotary 1	Master Level	43	94
Preamp	Rotary 1	Parameter 2	52	97
Distortion	Rotary 1	Damage Control	70	41
Distortion	Rotary 2	Parameter 1	0	127
Distortion	Rotary 3	Parameter 2	0	127
Distortion	Rotary 4	Damage Type	0	2
Distortion	Rotary 1	Master Level	127	85

10. Rename the Combinator controls and set the parameters as follows:

Control	Name	Default Value
Rotary 1	Drive	71
Rotary 2	Tone	103
Rotary 3	Presence	124
Rotary 4	Type	99

11. Save the patch as "Preamp & Distortion.cmb."

▸ Run the sequence.

The Tube algorithm gives the signal a lot of body, and the combination of algorithms is useful for all types of input signal including synthesizers and drum loops. Try different algorithms on the Distortion Scream 4.

Acid MonoSynth

Distortion has become as common with synthesizer as it is with electric guitar. The most common use of distortion with synthesizers is perhaps with bubbly acid-style monophonic synthesizer patterns. The Scream 4 can take a seemingly harmless monophonic synth line and turn it into an aggressive and ripping lead.

1. In an empty rack, create a reMix mixer.
2. Create a Combinator.
3. Load the ReCycle loop "12 – 303 Loop Source.cmb" from the *Power Tools for Reason* CD \ Combinator Patches directory.
4. Insert a Scream 4 Distortion module between the Combinator and the mixer.
5. Load the Scream 4 patch "Hollow303.scr" from the Reason Factory Sound Bank\Scream 4 Patches\Instrument Tweaks directory.

▸ Run the sequence.

Resonant filters make the distortion effect interesting. The resonant filter peak around the cutoff frequency is most distorted, and sweeping the cutoff frequency creates a very dynamic distortion effect. Set the Dr.REX filter resonance to 80, then start sweeping the cutoff frequency as the loop plays.

Foldback Distortion

The D-11 Foldback Distortion unit creates a digital type of distortion based on clipping. When the foldback setting is 63, the output clipping is flat. Settings above 63 engage the foldback process, in which the signal levels over the clipping threshold are subtracted from the threshold level. The result looks as if the peaks are folded back down. While the effect does cause distortion, it does not have the character of analog distortion. One useful application of the D-11 is with monophonic synthetic sounds, such as sine waves, which have little or no harmonic content. The clipping transforms the signal into a square wave.

A 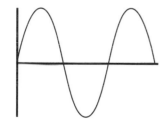   *B*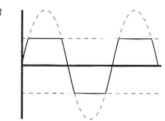

C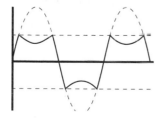

Figure 12-2
Sine wave (A) clipping
(B) and foldback (C).

1. In an empty rack, create a reMix mixer.
2. Create a Malström Graintable Synthesizer.
3. Set the polyphony to 1, Mod A rate to 46, OSC A release to 90, and master level (volume) to 118.
4. Insert a D-11 Foldback Distortion module.
5. Set the D-11 amount to 42, and Foldback to 63.
6. Select the Malström and D-11 and click on Combine in the Edit menu.
7. Assign rotary 1 to Dist 1 Foldback: Min 63, Max 127.
8. Connect the Malström Mod A CV output to the Combinator rotary 1 CV input.

Play a note on a MIDI keyboard, and listen to the foldback affect on the harmonic content of the sine wave. As noted before, this works best with simple waveforms because the effect changes the harmonic content very drastically. Complex waveforms and polyphonic signals can create harsh gritty noises through the D-11. The Malström Shaper Saturation and Clipping algorithms simulate the clipping effect, but they do not fold back the peaks. Saturation induces a DC offset like the Scream 4 tube algorithm, which sounds slightly warmer.

Speaker Cabinet Emulation

The Scream 4 Body section is designed to simulate the filter characteristics of a speaker cabinet. Body is a specialized resonant filter algorithm, and the parameters are similar to filter controls, but the results are different than with a typical lowpass filter.

The Type switch selects among five different types of simulated cabinets. Types A, B, and C are smaller cabinets, and are ideal for simulating guitar amplifiers. Types D and E simulate large housings, like a bass cabinet. The Scale control determines the size of the cabinet, much like a room size parameter on a reverb, but the behavior is more like the cutoff frequency of a filter. As in a filter, higher resonance settings make the cutoff frequency more noticeable. The Auto parameter is the scale modulation control from the envelope follower in the Scream 4.

Full Stack

This example uses two Scream 4 Distortion units running in parallel. The distortion algorithm and parameter settings are the same for both units, but different EQ and body parameters are used to simulate having two different speaker sources.

1. In an empty rack, create a reMix mixer, and set the tempo to 86 BPM.

Full Stack Combinator Patch

2. Create a Combinator.
3. In the Combinator sub-rack, create a microMix Line Mixer.
4. Set the microMix channel 1 level to 82, and channel 2 level to 74.
5. Insert an MClass Compressor between the microMix Master outputs and the Combinator From Devices inputs.

6. Set the Compressor threshold to −14.7dB, soft knee enabled, attack 83ms, release 158ms, adapt release on, output gain 4.9dB.
7. Still in the sub-rack, create a Spider Audio Merger & Splitter.
8. Connect the Combinator To Devices outputs to the Spider splitter inputs.
9. Bypass auto-routing and create a Scream 4 distortion unit.
10. Connect the Spider Audio split 1 outs to the Scream 4 inputs.
11. Connect the Scream 4 outputs to the microMix channel 1 inputs.
12. Program the following settings on Scream 1:

Scream 1 Settings

Damage: *on*	Damage Control	72
	Algorithm	Distortion
	P1	75
	P2	99
Cut: *on*	Lo	17
	Mid	20
	Hi	13
Body: *on*	Reso	75
	Scale	81
	Auto	0
	Type	E
	Master	85

13. Bypass auto-routing and create a DDL-1 Digital Delay Line.
14. Set the DDL-1 delay time to 15ms and feedback to 0.
15. Connect the Spider Audio split 2 outputs to the DDL-1 inputs.
16. Bypass auto-routing and create a second Scream distortion unit.
17. Connect the DDL-1 outputs to the Scream 2 inputs.
18. Connect the Scream 2 outputs to the microMix channel 2 inputs.
19. Program the following settings on Scream 2:

Scream 2 Settings

Damage: *on*	Damage Control	92
	Algorithm	Distortion
	P1	20
	P2	97
Cut: *on*	Lo	11
	Mid	24
	Hi	4
Body: *on*	Reso	78
	Scale	34
	Auto	8
	Type	C
	Master	85

20. Open the Combinator Programmer and set the following modulation routings:

Device	Source	Target	Min	Max
Line Mixer 1	Rotary 1	Master Level	90	85
Line Mixer 1	Rotary 4	Channel 1 Pan	−3	−14
Line Mixer 1	Rotary 4	Channel 2 Pan	7	14
M Comp 1	Button 4	Enabled	2	1
Scream 1	Rotary 1	Damage Control	74	127
Scream 1	Rotary 2	Parameter 2	0	127
Scream 1	Rotary 3	Body Scale	82	127
Scream 1	Button 1	Cut On/Off	0	1
Scream 1	Button 2	Body On/Off	0	1
Scream 1	Button 3	Body Auto	0	4
Delay 1	Rotary 4	DelayTime (ms)	15	30
Scream 2	Rotary 1	Damage Control	92	127
Scream 2	Rotary 2	Parameter 2	0	127
Scream 2	Rotary 3	Body Scale	34	79
Scream 2	Button 1	Cut On/Off	0	1
Scream 2	Button 2	Body On/Off	0	1
Scream 2	Button 3	Body Auto	0	4

21. Rename the Combinator controls and set the parameters as follows:

Control	Name	Default Value
Rotary 1	Drive	85
Rotary 2	Presence	93
Rotary 3	Scale	85
Rotary 4	Separation	41
Button 1	EQ	On
Button 2	Body	On
Button 3	Body Auto	On
Button 4	Compressor	On

22. Save the patch as "Full Stack.cmb."

D.I. Guitar Signal Source

23. Create a second Combinator and verify the connection into Combinator 1.
24. Load the patch "12 – Jh Finger Lick Source.cmb" from the *Power Tools for Reason* CD \ Combinator Patches directory.

▸ Run the sequence.

As the sequence runs, switch both Scream 4 devices into bypass mode to hear the raw signal. The difference is stunning. This full stack configuration makes use of the Body (speaker simulator) feature of the Scream 4 by creating two distinct cabinet sizes and placing them slightly off center in the stereo field. Try switching to different algorithms, making sure that both Scream 4 devices are using the same algorithm.

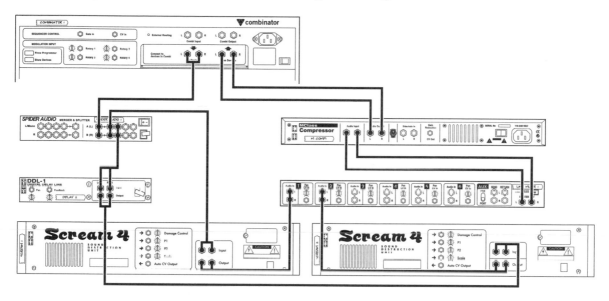

Figure 12-3
Two Scream 4 units
running in parallel.

Tone Enhancer

This example demonstrates using only the body function of the Scream 4. The specialized filter can be used in a subtle manner to add presence to a signal. Body algorithms D and E affect the bass and low-mid frequency ranges. Resonant settings using these body types adds fullness to the sound.

1. In an empty rack, create a reMix mixer.
2. Create a Dr.REX Loop Player.
3. Load the ReCycle loop "Rnb20_Vibey_090_eLAB.rx2" from the Reason Factory Sound Bank\Dr Rex Drum Loops\RnB HipHop directory.
4. Copy the REX slice data to the Dr.REX 1 sequencer track.
5. Create a Scream 4 Sound Destruction Unit as an insert device between the Dr.REX and the mixer.
6. Program the following settings on the Scream 4:

Scream 4 Tone Enhancer Settings

Damage: *off*	Damage control	–
	Algorithm	–
	P1	–
	P2	–
Cut: *off*	Lo	–

continued >

Scream 4 Tone Enhancer Settings		
	Mid	–
	Hi	–
Body: *on*	Reso	81
	Scale	85
	Auto	0
	Type	E
	Master	85

▸ Run the sequence.

As the drum loop cycles, toggle the Scream 4 in and out of bypass mode to hear the difference between the original and processed signals. The subtle resonance from the body section adds fullness and color to the tone without drastically boosting the bass frequency range.

Low-Fidelity Effects

The Scream 4 "digital" algorithm simulates the sound of downsampling and bit depth reduction of digital audio. Downsampling occurs when the sampling rate of a digital audio signal is decreased. The rate parameter controls the sample rate, and a maximum setting is full sample rate. As the sample rate drops, digital artifacts occur. Bit reduction is the process of decreasing the size of the audio data word. The resolution parameter decreases the word length from 16 bits down to 1 bit, with a resolution setting of 127 being the full bit depth.

8-Bit Audio

This example uses the Scream 4 digital algorithm to change a ReCycle loop into a drum loop that sounds generated from an old console video game or computer.

1. In an empty rack, create a reMix mixer.
2. Create a Dr.REX Loop Player.
3. Load the ReCycle loop "Trh19_KingBeat_125_eLAB.rx2" from the Reason Factory Sound Bank\Dr Rex Drum Loops\Abstract HipHop directory.
4. Copy the REX slice data to the Dr.REX 1 sequencer track.
5. Insert a Scream 4 Distortion unit between the Dr.REX audio outputs and the mixer channel 1 inputs.
6. Program the following settings on the Scream 4:

8-Bit Audio Settings		
Damage: *on*	Damage Control	70
	Algorithm	Digital

continued >

8-Bit Audio Settings		
	P1	31
	P2	76
Cut: *off*	Lo	–
	Mid	–
	Hi	–
Body: *off*	Reso	–
	Scale	–
	Auto	–
	Type	–
	Master	85

▶ Run the sequence.

The parameter controls (P1 & P2) on the Scream 4 control the bit depth and sample rate. Lowering the bit depth and sample rate creates quantization noise, useful in simulating video game noises from old hand-held game devices. To add a little more character to this downsampling effect, insert a Malström between the Scream 4 and the mixer input channel, and use the Shaper set to Quant. The Quant (quantize) algorithm also truncates a signal for creating low-fidelity digital effects.

Scream Auto CV Modulation

The Scream 4 envelope follower was described in detail in Chapter 3. The next examples further demonstrate uses of the auto CV modulation feature on the Scream 4.

Auto-Wah

The Body section of the Scream 4 is a resonant filter, and can create filter effects such as wah-wah. This example uses envelope follower modulation to control the scale parameter, which causes the body section to filter automatically.

1. In an empty rack, create a reMix mixer, and set the tempo to 86 BPM.
2. Create a Dr.REX Loop Player.
3. Load the ReCycle loop "Jh_D1_Guitar_finger lick.rx2" from the *Power Tools for Reason* CD \ Dr.REX Loops directory.
4. Set the Dr.REX master level to 127.
5. Copy the REX slice data to the Dr.REX 1 sequencer track.
6. Create a Scream 4 Sound Destruction Unit as an insert device between the Dr.REX and the mixer.

7. Program the following settings on the Scream 4:

Scream 4 Auto-Wah Settings

Damage: *on*	Damage control	40
	Algorithm	Fuzz
	P1	70
	P2	50
Cut: *off*	Lo	–
	Mid	–
	Hi	–
Body: *on*	Reso	111
	Scale	12
	Auto	111
	Type	B or C
	Master	85

▸ Run the sequence to hear the guitar riff distorted and processed with the auto-wah.

Auto CV Parameter Modulation

Using the auto CV output from the envelope follower on the Scream 4 is a way to add dynamic parameter changes to the effect. The envelope follower CV signal can be routed other CV destinations to add modulations determined by audio signals.

1. Start with an empty rack, and create a reMix mixer.
2. Create a Dr.REX Loop Player.
3. Load the ReCycle loop "Chm28_TwoFour_125_eLAB.rx2" from the Reason Factory Sound Bank\Dr Rex Drum Loops\Chemical Beats directory.
4. Copy the REX slice data to the Dr.REX sequencer track.
5. Insert a Scream 4 Distortion unit between the Dr.REX audio outputs and the mixer channel 1 inputs.
6. Program the following settings on the Scream 4:

Scream 4 Auto CV Modulate Settings

Damage: *on*	Damage Control	62
	Algorithm	Modulate
	P1	50
	P2	91
Cut: *off*	Lo	–
	Mid	–
	Hi	–
Body: *off*	Reso	–
	Scale	–
	Auto	–
	Type	–
	Master	85

7. Create a Spider CV Merger & Splitter.
8. Connect the Scream 4 auto CV output to the Spider CV split A input.
9. Connect the Spider CV split A out 1 to the Scream 4 P1 CV input.
10. Connect the Spider CV split A out 4/inv to the Scream 4 P2 CV input.
 ▸ Run the sequence.

Waveshape Distortion

The Malström Shaper is a distortion effect based on waveshaping synthesis where amplitude is shaped based on a shape function. The function converts a signal amplitude to a different amplitude value. Each shaper modes is a different function, and the *amount* control governs the intensity of shape modulation.

Figure 12-4 depicts a type of quantization shape function where the smooth sine wave curve transforms into a jagged waveform. The clip mode has a function that functions like the D-11 Distortion unit where the peaks are clipped off (see Figure 12-2B).

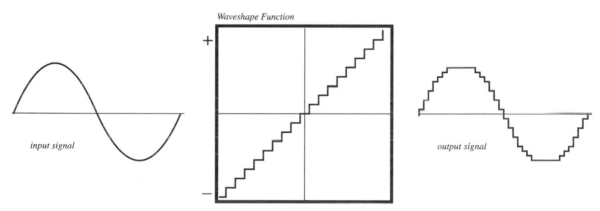

1. Start with an empty rack, and create a reMix mixer.

Stereo Waveshaper Combinator Patch

2. Create a Combinator.
3. In the Combinator sub-rack, bypass auto-routing and create a microMix Line Mixer.
4. Connect the To Devices Combi outputs to the microMix channel 1 inputs.
5. Set the microMix channel 1 aux send to 100. The mixer is used to add gain to the incoming signals.
6. Bypass auto-routing and create two Malström synths.
7. Disable all oscillators, filters, and modulators and enable the shaper on both Malströms.

Figure 12-4
Waveshape distortion imposes an amplitude change based on the shaping function. This illustration depicts a type of staircase shape function. The sine wave is converted into a quantized wave.

8. Connect the microMix left output to Malström 1 Shaper/Filter: A input.
9. Connect the microMix right output to Malström 2 Shaper/Filter: A input.
10. Connect the Malström 1 Left: Filter: A output to the Combinator From Devices left input.
11. Connect the Malström 2 Left: Filter: A output to the Combinator From Devices right input.
12. Bypass auto-routing and create an MClass Compressor.
13. Connect the microMix aux sends to the Compressor audio inputs.
14. Connect the Compressor gain reduction CV output to the Combinator rotary 2 CV input. The compressor acts as an envelope follower to apply modulation to the shapers.
15. Open the Combinator Programmer and set the following modulation routings:

Device	Source	Target	Min	Max
Line Mixer 1	Rotary 1	Master Level	100	127
Line Mixer 1	Rotary 1	Channel 1 Level	35	127
Malstrom 1	Rotary 2	Shaper Amount	0	127
Malstrom 1	Rotary 3	Shaper Mode	0	4
Malstrom 1	Rotary 4	Master Level	0	127
Malstrom 1	Button 1	Shaper On/Off	1	0
Malstrom 1 – Receive Notes Disabled				
Malstrom 2	Rotary 2	Shaper Amount	0	127
Malstrom 2	Rotary 3	Shaper Mode	0	4
Malstrom 2	Rotary 4	Master Level	0	127
Malstrom 2	Button 1	Shaper On/Off	1	0
Malstrom 2 – Receive Notes Disabled				
MComp 1	Button 2	Enabled	0	1

16. Rename the Combinator controls and set the parameters as follows:

Control	Name	Default Value
Rotary 1	Drive	70
Rotary 2	Shaper Amount	46
Rotary 3	Shaper Mode	45
Rotary 4	Level	87
Button 1	Bypass	Off
Button 2	Follower	Off

17. Save the patch as "Stereo Waveshaper.cmb."

Sound Source

18. Create a second Combinator and verify that it's automatically connected to the Stereo Waveshaper inputs.

19. Load the patch "12 – Ahp13 Live Loop Source.cmb" from the *Power Tools for Reason* CD \ Combinator Patches directory.

▸ Run the sequence to test the waveshape distortion patch. As the loop plays, try the different shape functions and the envelope follower feature.

Chapter 13
Mastering

Mastering is the process that makes a track as presentable as possible to listeners, so that (we all hope) they'll enjoy the song. Traditionally, mastering is the first stage of the duplication process, in which a master tape, CD, or lacquer is prepared for pressing. The first stage involves balancing levels and equalization, features incorporated into Reason as the MClass devices and MClass Mastering Suite. In earlier chapters you've seen the MClass Compressor, Equalizer, Maximizer, and Stereo Imager at work, but using them together as mastering tools is a different process.

Certain audio principles may help clarify what mastering does for music, but in reality, the task is ultimately a matter of taste. The topic is subjective and difficult to describe, especially in words. Mastering a Reason song will accomplish several things: balance the frequency response so playback is more consistent on different systems; smooth out dynamic fluctuations to increase playback fidelity; increase the overall loudness to maximize headroom; and prevent clipping to avoid digital distortion.

Mastering is a subtle process, and the parameter settings you choose should gently enhance and accentuate an already good mix. A track can sound dramatically different once mastered, and problems may become more apparent. Contrary to some myths, mastering does not improve a mediocre mix. If problems become apparent, go back into the song and adjust mixer levels or apply equalization to individual sound modules.

Monitoring for Mastering

The listening environment is crucial for proper mastering, and a pair of quality nearfield monitors is a minimum requirement. One stage of mastering is balancing the frequency response so mixes will sound good through any playback medium. If the listening environment does not accurately reproduce sounds, then mastering can be ineffective. Using headphones to master (or to mix, for that matter) is not recommended.

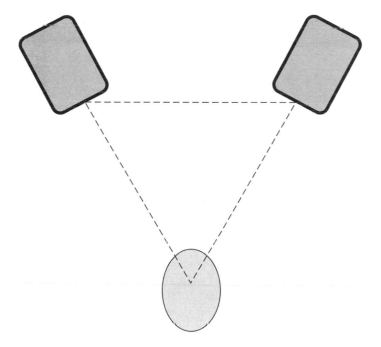

Figure 13-1
Position monitors along the points of an equilateral triangle, equidistant between each other and the listening position.

Arrange the monitors at the points of an equilateral triangle with your listening position being the third corner. If the monitors are spaced four feet apart, the sweet spot is the point four feet away from each monitor. The optimal height is ear level. If possible, position monitors away from walls with enough space to walk behind them.

Listen to some compact discs through your nearfield monitoring system. Become familiar with songs similar to the style of the work you're producing. Carefully study how these tracks sound in order to mentally compare the sound with your Reason tracks. Listen for tonal characteristics like bass, low-mids, high-mids, and highs, as well as loudness levels.

Mastering Suite Combinator

In a Reason song file, mastering effects are inserted in series between the main mixer and the Reason Hardware Interface, and auto cable routing recognizes the insertion of mastering effects at this point. In a Reason song that you have previously created, select the Reason Hardware Interface. On the Create menu, click on MClass Mastering Suite Combi. The MClass mastering suite inserts automatically below the Interface.

The MClass mastering suite has several preset configurations, which can help you quickly find settings that suit your track. Use the patch scroll buttons or the contextual menu to audition the patches with your song. While auditioning each MClass Suite configuration, try adjusting a few parameters to become familiar with the features.

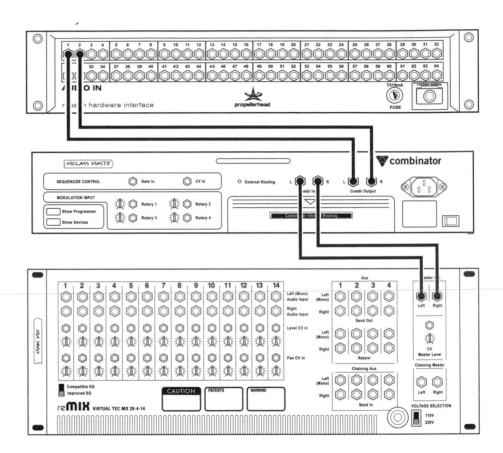

Figure 13-2
Mastering effects connected in series between the reMix outputs and the Reason Hardware Interface inputs.

Inspection of the MClass Default Mastering Combinator rack reveals the typical order of mastering effects. This is a series connection starting with the Equalizer, the Stereo Imager, the Compressor, and lastly, the Maximizer.

Mastering an Audio file
You may find yourself in a situation where your computer has insufficient resources to add a set of mastering tools to the Reason song rack. If so, render the song to a 24-bit, 48kHz audio file and load it back into the sampler, and then process the audio from the sampler through the mastering effects.

1. Start with an empty rack.
2. Set the tempo to 122 BPM and the right loop locator to 40.1.1.
3. Create an MClass Mastering Suite Combi.
4. Create an NN-XT Advanced Sampler.
5. Load the sample "Peff_SKR_122bpm.aif" from the *Power Tools for Reason* CD \ Audio Samples Directory.

6. Enable high quality interpolation and disable the filter.
7. Set polyphony to 1 and amp envelope gain (level) to 8.0dB.
8. Enter the key lane on the NN–XT 1 sequencer track and pencil in a 40-measure note event on C3 starting at position 1.1.1.

▸ Run the sequence.

The audio file was previous produced within Reason at 122 BPM for 40 measures, and setting the tempo and loop position helps when monitoring the track. Provided your system requirements can accommodate many large samples, you could set up an entire set of songs for playback and mastering. The one disadvantage of this technique is that playback can't be started in the middle of the song.

Equalization

Equalization in the mastering process balances the tonal qualities between each track on an album, and it can correct troubling signals in individual tracks. Equalization changes the loudness of the signal, so the frequency contouring normally occurs before dynamics processing. The MClass Equalizer features several stages for applying both types of changes to the frequency response of a track. Equalizing a mix is not an exact science, and frequency settings vary according to each song. It's easier to balance the frequency response between album tracks because each song provides a reference for the next track.

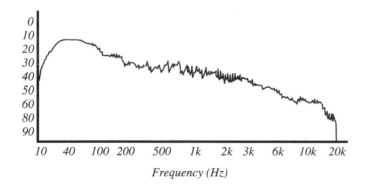

Figure 13-3
Typical distribution of frequencies of a mastered song.

The typical frequency response of a pop or electronic song carries most of the energy in the bass and low midrange region, while high frequency information is significantly less intense. The mixdown should achieve this type of response as closely as possible. Bear in mind that every track is different, and equalization is subjective, but you have to consider other systems that will play your music. Use this as a guideline, and then make subtle adjustments that work with the track and appeal to your tastes.

Bass Rolloff

The first stage of the MClass Equalizer is the Lo Cut filter. This highpass filter cuts out low-frequency rumble that might be lingering below the audible range. There might be an occasional sample with ambient noise or a resonant filter oscillating in a range below 30Hz, neither of which benefit the mix, and the Lo Cut stage filters these frequencies out. It's common practice to always have this filter enabled.

Contouring Frequency Response

When using the MClass Equalizer to contour the frequency response, limit the gain settings to +/– 5dB with no more than 6dB of variation between one peak and another. The Hi and Lo Shelf bandwidth settings should usually be quite broad; for general contouring, settings between .50 Q and 1.0 Q are a good starting point. The parametric stages should have a 1.0 Q to 3.0 Q. Even though the MClass Equalizer can impose drastic changes on the frequency response, when used for mastering, the slight settings are still quite effective.

1. Start with an empty rack, and create a reMix mixer.
2. Create a Combinator.
3. Load the patch "13 – TransP Source.cmb" from the *Power Tools for Reason* CD \ Combinator Patches directory.
4. Insert an MClass Equalizer between the reMix mixer and the Reason Hardware Interface.
5. On the MClass EQ, enable Lo Cut, Lo Shelf, and Hi Shelf.
6. Set the Lo Shelf frequency to 326.6 Hz, gain to 1.7dB, and Q to 0.83.
7. Set the Hi Shelf frequency to 4.0Khz, gain to –1.7dB, and Q to 0.79.

Run the Combinator patch, and as the Combinator loop plays, bypass the EQ to compare the difference. There is a subtle boost to the bass, and the kick drum is slightly more pronounced. By raising the low shelf by 1.7dB and lowering the high shelf by 1.7dB, the equalizer applies almost 3.5 dB of difference between the bass and treble ranges.

8. Continue from the previous example.
9. Set the Lo Shelf Gain: –1.7dB.
10. Set the Hi Shelf Gain: 1.4dB.

Run the Combinator Patch, and continue to compare the sound with the EQ in bypass mode. The frequency response with this equalization tilts the output with 3dB greater response in the treble range. The high end sounds more open above the bass, and the cymbals sizzle a bit more.

Midrange Contouring

Approach equalization in terms of what can be boosted and what can be cut simultaneously. A similar approach can be applied to midrange frequencies by either cutting or boosting both the bass and treble ranges. With midrange contouring, follow the general rule of gentle cut and boost gain settings. More than 6dB will often be excessive. After finding the right frequency, Q, and gain settings, try decreasing the gain setting by 20% and carefully listen.

1. Start with an empty rack, and create a reMix mixer.
2. Create a Combinator.
3. Load the patch "13 – Peff_FP Source.cmb" from the *Power Tools for Reason CD \ Combinator Patches* directory.
4. Insert a Default MClass Mastering Suite Combinator between the reMix Mixer and the Reason Hardware Interface.
5. Click on the Show Devices button of the MClass Mastering Suite and observe the Equalizer display.
6. Set the MClass Mastering Suite Loudness Curve to 14.
▸ Run the sequence.

As the sequence plays, adjust the Loudness Curve parameter and listen as the gain changes on the Lo Shelf and Parametric 2 equalizer parameters.

Surgical Equalization

The equalizer can also be used to notch out a problem frequency in the mix. You might encounter a spot where overlapping sounds generate odd overtones that sound strange in the mix. Using a narrow parametric curve, you can cut out the problem frequency range.

7. Continue from the previous example.
8. Enable the Equalizer's Param 1 stage.
9. Set the Param 1 gain to 18dB, and Q to 32.0.
10. While running the sequence, slowly sweep the frequency parameter of the Param 1 stage. Every so often, a dramatic spike in loudness occurs when the EQ boosts a range of frequencies where there is a lot of activity in the audio signal. When you find one of these spikes, stop adjusting the frequency. If you can't seem to find a specific frequency, try 494.8, 2.198 kHz, or 3.805 kHz.
11. Change the Param 1 gain to 0dB and listen. Next, change the gain to –8dB, and listen to how the sharp EQ notches out the sliver of the frequency spectrum.

Notching out problem frequencies is a common practice, but it's better to go into the Reason song, isolate the source of the problem, and change the mix. Adjust the problem signal within the mixdown, rather than making dramatic cuts with the equalizer.

Stereo Imaging

The Stereo Imager adds separation and depth between frequency ranges, which sometimes helps a complicated mix. Moderate processing of the Lo Band and Hi Band narrows the separation of bass frequencies towards the center and spreads the high frequencies between the stereo channels. Some engineers don't like these spatialization effects because they induce phase shifting that dramatically alters the original, but usually a touch improves the sound.

Centering Bass

The power that drives the volume of a track is principally in the bass region of the frequency range. Keeping the bass and kick drums centered in a mix helps deliver power equally to speakers and opens up the stereo field for other instrumentation. One function of the MClass Stereo Imager is to tighten up the low-frequency content and center it in the stereo field.

1. Start with an empty rack, and create a reMix mixer.
2. Create a Combinator.
3. Load the patch "13 – SKR Source.cmb" from the *Power Tools for Reason* CD \ Combinator Patches Directory.
4. Insert an MClass Stereo Imager between the Reason Hardware Interface and the mixer.
5. Run the Combinator to hear the sound source before processing.
6. On the Stereo Imager, click on Solo Lo Band.
7. Adjust the X-Over Frequency to 210 Hz.
8. Adjust the Low Band Width to –38.
9. Click on Solo Normal to hear the mono processing of the low-frequency info with the unprocessed high band.

As the song loops, switch the Stereo Imager into bypass mode and compare the unprocessed signal. The bass and kick sound slightly more defined through the stereo imager.

Imaging Lo & Hi Bands

Using a combination of Lo and Hi Band imaging can help give a mix a polished sound. Use the Lo Band to center the bass and the Hi Band to add a subtle stereo spread to the high-frequency range.

10. Continue from the previous example.
11. On the Stereo Imager, click on Solo Hi Band.
12. Adjust the X-Over Frequency to 470 Hz.
13. Adjust the Low Band to –20.
14. Adjust the Hi Band to 14.

15. Click on Solo Normal to hear the subtle mono processing and slight stereo width through the high band.

This is a typical setting for the Stereo Imager. A subtle amount of bass definition and stereo width adds a bit of clarity to the mix. This is especially noticeable with the cymbals and hi-hats.

High-Frequency Enhancement

16. Continue from the previous example.
17. On the Stereo Imager, click on Solo Hi Band.
18. Adjust the X-Over Frequency to 6.0 kHz.
19. Adjust the Lo Band to 0.
20. Adjust the Hi Band to 37.
21. Click on Solo Normal to hear the extreme width on the high band.

In this example, most of the mix occupies the region below the 6kHz crossover threshold, so only the very high frequency range is processed through the Hi Band imager. Notice how the cymbals seem to spread throughout the stereo field and sound slightly more excited. The hi-hats and tambourine are more lively as well.

Mastering Dynamics

Mastering dynamics is essentially the process of managing headroom and loudness. A number of processes can be applied when mastering a track, but this is where mastering becomes convoluted. Ideally, the perfect mix should not require compression. This perfect mix should only require level adjustment to take advantage of available headroom.

Normalizing a signal is a basic dynamics process that adjusts the peak levels to near 0dBFS—the relative dynamic range is unchanged. Hard compression and peak limiting that squeezes the audio in a 2dB range is probably the most extreme. Mastering is as subjective as music creation, and the type of dynamics should reflect the style of music and its intended audience.

Normalizing

Normalizing the audio is a process of minimizing headroom by increasing the loudness of the audio signal up to 0dBFS. The loudest peak of the track is at or near 0dB without exceeding the threshold. This is merely a gain adjustment; no dynamics processing is involved.

1. In an empty rack, create a reMix mixer.
2. Create a Combinator.
3. Load the patch "13 – R2B Source.cmb" from the *Power Tools for Reason* CD \ Combinator Patches Directory.

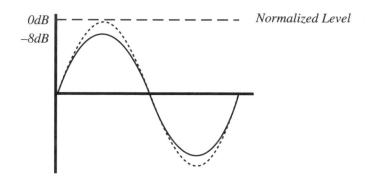

Figure 13-4
Original signal peak maximum of –8dB. Increasing the gain by 8dB normalizes the signal and fills the small gap of headroom.

4. Insert an MClass Default Mastering Suite between the Reason Hardware Interface and the Mixer.
5. On the MClass Mastering Suite, click on the Show Devices button.
6. On the MClass Maximizer, set limiter off and soft clip off.
7. Run the R2B Source Combinator, and monitor the Maximizer peak meter.
8. Let the song loop through and take a mental note of the peak meter ballistics. You should notice that the peaks reach –2dB.
9. On the MClass Maximizer, adjust the gain to 5.1dB. This is just over 2dB greater than the previous setting.
10. Continue observing the meter and keep an eye on the Audio Out clipping indicator to see if the signal peaks above 0dBFS.

Compression

The general idea of using a compressor for mastering is to tighten up the dynamic range of the final mix. Compression alters the overall loudness of the mix by reducing the difference between the loud and soft peaks of the track. Make-up gain compensates for the reduced levels, and when adjusted, the lower dynamics are louder while the louder peaks are about the same as the original level. The difference between loud to soft peaks, or dynamic range, is decreased.

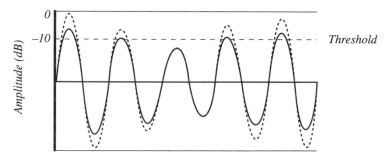

Figure 13-5
Compressed peaks are closer to the uncompressed peaks—a decrease in dynamic range.

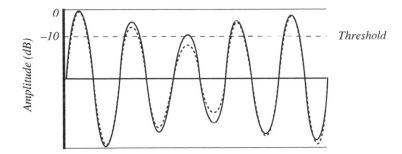

Figure 13-6
After makeup gain
is applied, the
uncompressed peaks
are louder while the
compressed peaks are
about the same level
as before.

Typical compression settings for mastering should be restricted to very subtle settings. The trick is to apply gain reduction without noticeable effects. Start with low ratio settings around 1.7:1 to 3.0:1, and high threshold settings around −12dB to −10dB. Once these parameters are set, adjust the input gain, attack, and release parameters to maintain consistent reduction that ranges from 2dB to no more than 6dB of gain reduction. These gentle settings achieve the desired *transparent* compression.

1. In an empty rack, create a reMix mixer.
2. Create a Combinator.
3. Load the patch "13 – Noesis Source.cmb" from the *Power Tools for Reason* CD \ Combinator Patches Directory.
4. Insert an MClass Default Mastering Suite between the Reason Hardware Interface and the Mixer.
5. On the MClass Mastering Suite, click on the Show Devices button.
6. Set the Maximizer input gain to 0dB, limiter off, and soft clip off. Put the meter in VU mode. The Maximizer Peak/VU meter will monitor levels.
7. Run the Noesis Source Combinator to monitor the audio signal processed through the Mastering Suite.
8. Enable the MClass Compressor, set the ratio to 1:1, attack to 1ms, and release to 474ms.
9. On the MClass Compressor, increase the input gain until the VU meter ballistics reach −5dB. The setting should be around 4.0 dB.
10. Switch the Maximizer meter to peak mode. Occasional peaks should clip above 0dBFS.
11. On the Compressor, slowly increase the ratio setting and watch as the peak levels decrease. Stop when the peaks settle around 0dB. The ratio setting should be about 2.08:1.
12. Adjust the compressor output gain slowly upward until peaks start going into the red OVER range. Then adjust the gain back until the peaks fall around 0dB. The output gain setting should be about 1.5dB.

As the song loops, compare the uncompressed signal with the compressed signal to hear the difference in overall loudness. The gain reduction meter shows that compression is safely in the 6dB range. The VU meter indicates the increase in loudness. Before compression, the signal averages around −12dB, and with the increased gain and compression, the loudness averages around −8dB. An average level anywhere between −15dB and −5dB is desired.

Limiting

Peak limiting is usually inserted last in the mastering signal chain. The Maximizer primarily serves to prevent unwanted digital distortion, and even if peaks are below the 0dB limit, it's a good idea to have brick wall settings enabled. This provides peace of mind: You can rest assured that the occasional imperceptible transient does not clip.

Overs Protection

A basic form of peak limiting protects from digital distortion and clipping caused by signals that exceed the 0dBFS limit. To prevent overs always apply a form of brickwall peak limiting using either the Soft Clip or the 4ms Look Ahead features.

13. Continue from the previous example.
14. On the Maximizer, enable the Limiter, switch 4ms Look Ahead on, attack fast, release fast.

Run the Combinator and observe the peak meter ballistics. In the previous example, an occasional transient would clip, but with the Limiter in Look Ahead mode, these occasional spikes are restrained.

Maximizing

The brickwall limiter settings allow you to compact the dynamic range in the small window below the 0dB threshold, so it's possible to squeeze out a little more loudness. This step is ultimately a matter of taste. When you push the Maximizer input gain, you destroy the dynamics of the song, but this doesn't stop people from excessive compression because the result is a louder track that overshadows the competition.

15. Continue from the previous example.
16. On the Maximizer, disable the limiter and switch the meter into VU mode.
17. Run the Noesis Source Combinator and observe the VU meter. It should normally peak around −4dB, and average below this point.
18. Increase the Maximizer unput gain until the VU meter peaks −1dB to −2dB. The gain setting should be around 3dB.
19. Enable the limiter, and observe the gain reduction ballistics. Make sure they stay in the range of −4dB to −6dB.

As the audio signal loops, compare the original signal with the processed signal by switching the MClass Mastering Suite in and out of bypass mode. The signal is much louder due to the dynamics processing. The signal is 11dB louder at the expense of lost dynamic range. Dynamics processing balances loudness, and the song will translate when played through systems outside the studio.

Punch

The settings described previously are tight and clamp down on transient spikes quickly. Slower attack times and faster release times allow you to contour the behavior of transients to add more punch to the master.

1. In an empty rack, create a reMix mixer and a Combinator.
2. Load the patch "13 – SKR Source.cmb" from the *Power Tools for Reason* CD \ Combinator Patches Directory.
3. Insert an MClass Default Mastering Suite between the Reason Hardware Interface and the Mixer, and click on Show Devices.
4. Set the Compressor input gain to 9.6dB, threshold to –14.7dB, ratio to 2.40:1, attack to 45ms, release to 201ms, and adapt release enabled. The longer attack allows for a gentle compression that allows the transients to pass to add punch to the mix.
5. Take the Compressor out of bypass mode.
6. Set the Maximizer input gain to 0.9dB, limiter on, 4ms Look Ahead off, attack slow, release auto, soft clip on, amount 42.

Run the SKR Source Combinator and listen to the song loop with the dynamics processing. Besides the increased loudness, you should hear the bass, snare, and kick drum slightly more pronounced than the original track. This is the result of the slow attack settings on the Compressor and Maximizer. The peaks pass through the chain until the Maximizer Soft Clip suppresses them.

Rendering the Mastered Audio

Once you've tweaked the mastering effects to perfection, the Reason song is ready for output. The process of exporting a Reason song to an audio file is also called *rendering*. There are two Export to Audio File items in the Reason file menu. Export Loop creates an audio file of the material between the left and right locators, and is suited for rendering loops or sections, while Export Song is suited for a mastered track.

Before rendering the audio file, insert a leader of silence at the beginning of the song. This space should only be one or two bars in duration. Use the sequencer edit item to insert bars between locators after setting the loop locators. The end of the song should have a trailer of silence as well. Make certain that the song end marker is positioned ten bars past the last sequencer event. If a long reverb tail extends past the last sequencer event, it can be cut short when the song is exported.

When you select Export Song to Audio File and choose a location to which to save the file, a prompt window asks for the word length (bit depth) and sample rate. Files destined for CD or MP3 should be rendered at 16-bit and a 44.1kHz sample rate with Dither switched on. If you're planning to further edit the audio files in other software, you should use 24-bit resolution and a 48kHz or 96kHz sample rate.

Dither is a low-level noise field spread through the audio signal. While too quiet to be audible, the noise is especially useful when rendering to 16-bit audio because it helps shape very quiet digital audio signals and reduce harmonic distortion, especially in reverb tails. Dither should only be applied to a given audio file once, so it's usually reserved for the very last possible stage. It's common for software to apply dither after reducing the word length from 24-bit to 16-bit.

Professional Mastering

Obtaining the services of an experienced engineer working in a mastering room is the best way to master a CD. Besides their talent and experience, mastering engineers provide you with an objective set of ears and can execute changes accurately in the critical listening environment of a mastering studio. While some of the configurations described above are useful for preparing individual tracks for distribution, it's better to master an album with editing software or in a mastering studio. Once all of the songs are finished, the rendered tracks should be prepared for mastering.

Unless various tracks fade at different rates, fade-out and fade-in automation should be disabled at the beginning and end of the song. Not only is a mastering console or software more suited to create fades, track spacing is more flexible when fades are added during the mastering process. If the songs are rendered with the fades, then the timing between tracks will be forced to fit the fade. It's better to set the fade-out in context between two tracks. Duplicate the fade-out measures a few extra times just in case you want to extend the fade a little longer.

If you're going to use a professional mastering house, render your final tracks at a 24-bit word length. The sample rate should be at least 44.1kHz, but 96kHz files have the greatest frequency range, and the difference is noticeable. Most mastering software and studios can accommodate 96kHz files, and it's best to use the highest resolution possible.

Try mastering your album project at home before taking it to a mastering studio. In the context of an album, the individual songs often sound different. Make a preview CD to hear how the song ordering works. This kind of decision should not be made at the very last moment, especially when you're paying an engineer to wait for your decision. Listening through the preview CD will also give you a better idea of how the levels and EQ should change for each track.

Chapter 14
Redrum Methods

When the first rhythm machines appeared, they were limited in both sounds and patterns. Early devices had simple percussion sounds, which played fixed rhythms named after various styles of music: Machines with buttons labeled "Waltz," "Bossa Nova," and "Cha-Cha" were common. As technology progressed, rhythm machines became more flexible, allowing users to create their own patterns on a step sequencer interface. The Redrum Drum Computer is the descendant of these early programmable drum machines, and features an interface with which you can create your own patterns using buttons.

Redrum is a sample playback device, and audio files are loaded directly into each Redrum channel using the sample browser. Alternatively, complete sample sets can be loaded from patch files. Patches contain file location information that tells Redrum where to find samples for each channel. Patches also contain parameter information such as pitch, panning, and envelope settings. Whether you choose to load individual samples or a patch that configures the entire device, no sound emits from Redrum until one or more samples are loaded.

Hardware drum machines feature a pattern mode and a song mode. Once programmed into the drum machine, patterns are placed in the necessary order using the song mode editor. In Reason, the song mode is programmed by entering pattern changes in the Redrum sequencer track.

Pattern Programming

Most Reason users are familiar with programming Redrum patterns using the 16-step pattern interface. This section illustrates some unorthodox methods for programming Redrum to achieve exotic syncopated rhythms using a variety of methods, including gate CV triggering from other devices.

Vintage Drum Machine Swing

Older programmable drum machines didn't have a *shuffle* feature to add a swing to the beat. However, some of them allowed for programming triplets, which allowed the user to create patterns with a lively swing. Even though Reason has shuffle, the sound of a 16-step pattern with shuffle on does not quite capture the same feel as using sixteenth-note triplet steps.

1. Start with an empty rack and set the tempo to 126 BPM.
2. Create a mixer and a Redrum Drum Computer.
3. Load the patch "House Kit 04" from the Reason Factory Sound Bank\Redrum Drum Kits\House Kits directory.
4. Set the Redrum pattern length to 24 steps and the resolution to 1/16T.
5. Set the Redrum edit steps to 1–16 and program the following pattern:

Redrum Pattern Steps 1–16

	1	2	3	4	5	6	7	8	9	10	11	12	13	14	15	16
1	M						S						S			
2							M									
3							M									
4																
5																
6																
7																
8			S			M						S			M	
9				M						M						M
10			S				M									

6. Set the Redrum edit steps to 17–32 and program the following pattern:

Redrum Pattern Steps 17–24

	17	18	19	20	21	22	23	24
1			S					S
2			M					
3			M					S
4								
5								
6								
7								
8		M			M			
9						M		
10						M		

This technique is widely used in producing house music tracks and is useful for other music styles that require a strong shuffle. The closed hi-hats and snare fills groove nicely when programmed in this manner. Try programming a snare roll from step 19 through step 24.

Grooved Redrum Patterns

ReCycle drum loops are rarely sliced to perfect sixteenth notes, and it's not always possible to synchronize Redrum patterns with ReCycle loops. A solution for this is to convert Redrum patterns to sequenced note events. Once the notes are converted, quantize them using a user groove established from the slice data sequence of a REX loop.

1. Start with an empty rack, and set the tempo to 97 BPM.
2. Create a reMix mixer.
3. Create a Dr.REX Loop Player.
4. Load the ReCycle loop "Rnb08_Seductive_090_eLAB.rx2" from the Reason Factory Sound Bank\Dr Rex Drum Loops\RnB HipHop directory.
5. Copy the REX slice data to the Dr.REX 1 sequencer track.
6. Select a group in the Dr.REX sequencer track and click on Get User Groove in the Edit menu.
7. Create a Redrum Drum Computer.
8. Load the patch "Chemical Kit 03.drp" from the Reason Factory Soundbank\Redrum Drum Kits\Chemical Kits directory.
9. Program the following on Redrum pattern A1:

Redrum Pattern

	1	2	3	4	5	6	7	8	9	10	11	12	13	14	15	16
1	M							M						M		
2																
3					M							M		M		
4																
5																
6																
7																
8	H	S	M	S	H	S	M	M	H	M	M	S	H	S	M	S
9			M													
10																

10. Select Copy Pattern to Track from the Edit menu. The Redrum pattern converts to MIDI note events.
11. On the Redrum, switch off pattern playback by clicking on the Enable Pattern Selection lamp.
12. Select all drum lane events, and then quantize them by clicking on the Quantize button. The quantization resolution should already be set to User.
▸ Run the sequence.

Matrix Multi-Quantization Patterns

Drum pattern programming is normally limited to the resolution and number of steps of the Redrum pattern. Using the Redrum gate inputs, however, a Matrix can trigger a drum channel. The Matrix pattern can have alternative length and resolution settings in which variations with syncopated timing are programmed using gate CV events.

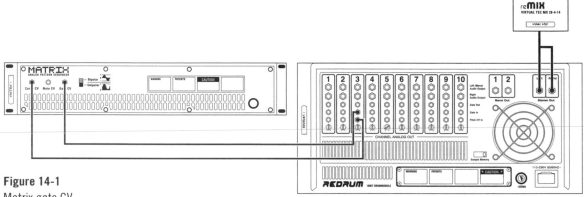

Figure 14-1

Matrix gate CV connected to the Redrum channel 3 gate CV input. The curve CV is controlling drum pitch.

1. Start with an empty rack, and set the tempo to 160 BPM.
2. Create a reMix mixer and a Redrum Drum Computer.
3. Load the patch "DrumNbass Kit 04" from the Reason Factory Sound bank.
4. Adjust the Redrum channel 3 level-to-velocity setting to 63.
5. Program the following Redrum pattern in pattern A1:

Redrum Pattern

	1	2	3	4	5	6	7	8	9	10	11	12	13	14	15	16
1	S						S						S			
2					S								S			
3																
4																
5					S								S			
6	S										S					
7																
8	M		S		M		S		M		S		M		S	
9																
10																

6. Bypass auto-routing and create a Matrix Pattern Sequencer.
7. Switch the Matrix into bipolar mode.

8. Connect the Matrix gate CV socket to the Redrum channel 3 gate in socket.

9. Connect the Matrix curve CV output to the Redrum channel 3 pitch CV input.

10. Set the Redrum channel 3 pitch CV trim to 8.

11. Set the Matrix pattern length to 24 steps, and the resolution to 1/16T.

12. On the Matrix, program gate events at steps 7, 13, 22, and 23. The gate event at step 7 should be the loudest, while the others should be less than 50%.

13. Program curve events above and below the zero crossing on steps 7, 13, 22, and 23. The settings are arbitrary as long as they are different.

▸ Run the sequence.

While the Redrum pattern is based on 16 steps, the Matrix is playing a pattern through the Redrum based on 24 steps divided into sixteenth-note triplets. It's not practical to use a Matrix for every Redrum channel, but this is useful for snare samples where you want to create some intricate syncopation or flams. This technique is also useful for a flam that decreases in loudness.

For drum 'n' bass patterns with a tempo around 160 BPM, try a 32-step pattern with 32nd-note resolution and enable shuffle. Set the master shuffle amount to 118. The shifted notes seem to syncopate nicely for ghosted snare hits.

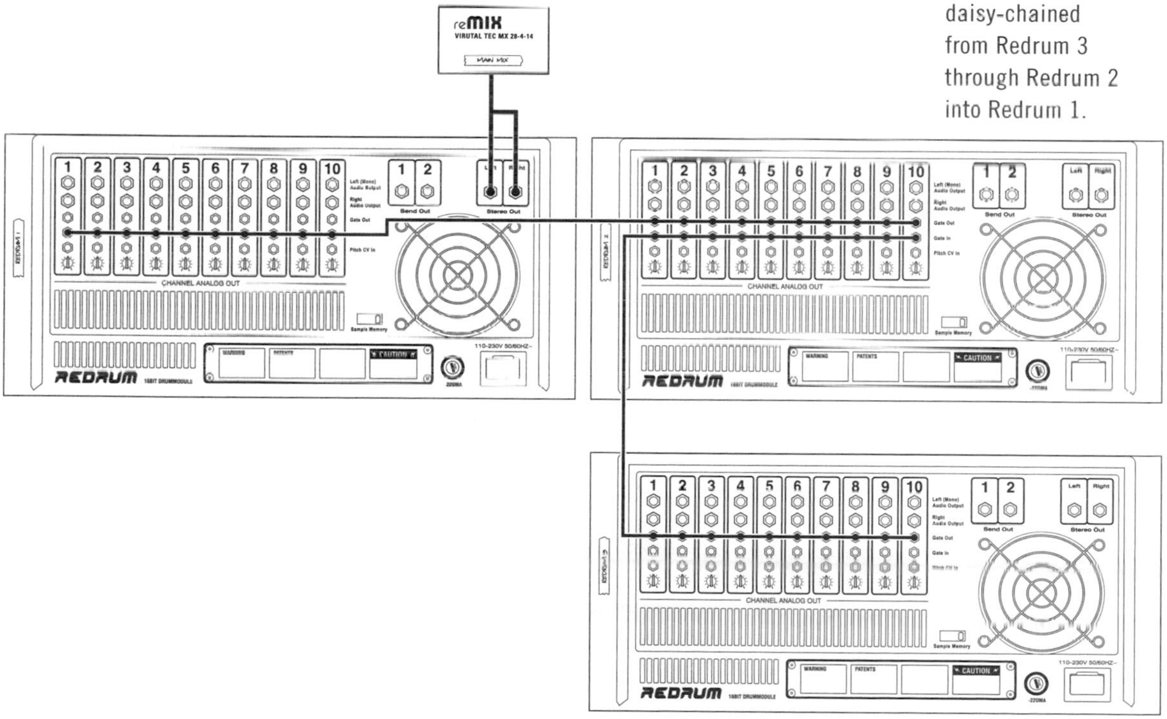

Figure 14-2
Gate CV signals daisy-chained from Redrum 3 through Redrum 2 into Redrum 1.

Layered Redrum Patterns

The Redrum can be used as a pattern-based gate CV source, and several Redrums can be daisy-chained with the gate signals connected between each other. This example illustrates how this configuration is created. Only one Redrum actually plays samples. The other Redrums simply send gate CV messages to the first Redrum. The main Redrum has a simple 16-step drum pattern, while the other Redrums have different resolutions and shuffle settings. The pattern events layered in this manner can easily create complex rhythms.

1. Start with an empty rack. Set the tempo to 98 BPM and pattern shuffle to 99.
2. Create a reMix mixer and a Redrum Drum Computer.
3. Load the patch "Dublab BrushKit2.drp" from the Reason Factory Soundbank\ Redrum Drum Kits\Brush Kits directory.
4. Program the following pattern on "Redrum 1" pattern A1:

Redrum Pattern

	1	2	3	4	5	6	7	8	9	10	11	12	13	14	15	16
1	M						M									
2					M								M			
3					M								M			
4																
5																
6																
7																
8	M		S		M		S		M		S					
9																
10																

5. Bypass auto-routing and create a second Redrum.
6. Connect all Redrum 2 gate out CV sockets to the corresponding Redrum 1 gate in sockets.
7. Set the Redrum 2 pattern length to 12 steps and the resolution to 1/16T.
8. Program the following on Redrum 2 pattern A1:

Redrum Pattern (Edit Steps 1–12)

	1	2	3	4	5	6	7	8	9	10	11	12
1							S		S			S
2												
3												
4												
5												
6												

continued >

Redrum Pattern (Edit Steps 1–12)

	1	2	3	4	5	6	7	8	9	10	11	12
7												
8										S	S	Sf
9												
10												

9. Bypass auto-routing and create a third Redrum.
10. Connect all Redrum 3 gate out sockets to the corresponding Redrum 2 gate in sockets.
11. Set the Redrum 3 pattern length to 32 steps, resolution to 1/32, and enable shuffle.
12. Switch to edit steps 17–32.
13. Program the following on Redrum 3 pattern A1:

Redrum Pattern (Edit Steps 17–32)

	17	18	19	20	21	22	23	24	25	26	27	28	29	30	31	32
1					S											
2																
3													S			
4																
5								S								
6												S				
7																
8																
9																
10																

Pitch CV Modulation

Each Redrum channel has a pitch CV input, which modulates the playback pitch parameter. The parameter is bipolar, so the sample can be pitched up or down. A slight amount of pitch modulation adds character to a drum sample. The following examples describe different methods for configuring Redrum channels to modulate pitch.

Velocity CV Pitch Modulation

This is a simple method of using the Redrum gate CV value to modulate the pitch. The value of the gate CV signal varies depending on the dynamics of the step, and connecting the gate CV out to the pitch CV in alters the pitch as the dynamics change. This technique can be applied to all of the Redrum channels and the amount of modulation can be scaled using the pitch CV trim knobs.

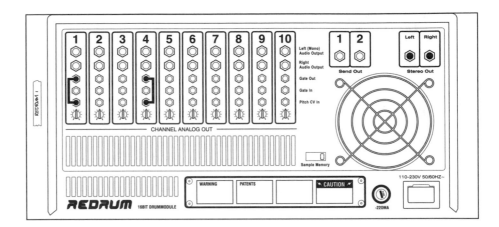

Figure 14-3
Redrum gate CV outputs connected to pitch CV inputs.

1. Start with an empty rack and set the tempo to 126 BPM.
2. Create a reMix mixer and a Redrum Drum Computer.
3. Load the patch "House Kit 02" from the Reason Factory Sound Bank\Redrum Drum Kits\House Kits directory.
4. Enable Shuffle on Redrum 1.
5. Connect the Redrum channel 1 gate out to the Redrum channel 1 pitch CV in.
6. Set Redrum channel 1 to gate mode 1.
7. Connect the Redrum channel 4 gate out to channel 4 pitch CV in.
8. Set Redrum channel 4 to gate mode 1.
9. On Redrum channel 1, set the level to 76, pitch to –24, and velocity-to-level to –26.
10. Program the following pattern:

Redrum Pattern

	1	2	3	4	5	6	7	8	9	10	11	12	13	14	15	16
1	S				M				M				M		H	H
2																
3																
4		M	H	S			S		S		S	H		S	M	S
5																
6																
7																
8																
9																
10																

▸ Run the Redrum pattern.

Global Pitch Control

Using several Spider CV splitters, a CV signal can be distributed to all of the Redrum channels. The pitch CV modulation is bipolar, so a Matrix pattern sequencer set in bipolar mode is a good choice to control the pitch of the Redrum samples.

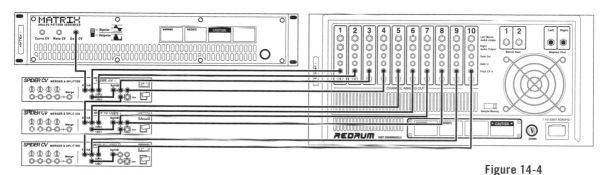

Figure 14-4
Matrix curve CV split ten times with three Spider CV modules connected in series.

1. In an empty rack, create a reMix mixer and a Redrum Drum Computer.
2. Load the patch "RnB Kit 03" from the Reason Factory Sound Bank\Redrum Drum Kits\RnB Kits directory.
3. Program the following pattern into Redrum pattern A1:

Redrum Pattern

	1	2	3	4	5	6	7	8	9	10	11	12	13	14	15	16
1	M															
2				M									M			
3																
4				M							M					
5																
6																
7	S	S	S		S	S	S		S	S	S	S	S	S		
8	M	M	M	M	M	M	M	M	M	M	M	M	M	M	M	M
9																
10																

4. Bypass auto-routing and create a Spider CV Merger & Splitter.
5. Connect the Spider split A output 3 to split B input.
6. Duplicate Spider CV 1 and connect Spider CV 1 split B output 3 to Spider CV 1 Copy split A input.
7. Duplicate Spider CV 1 Copy and connect the Spider CV 1 Copy split B output 3 to Spider CV 1 Copy 2 split A input.
8. Bypass auto-routing and create a Matrix Pattern Sequencer.

9. Set the Matrix to bipolar mode and connect the curve CV output to the Spider CV 1 split A input.
10. The Matrix curve CV is now split 13 ways through the three Spider CV splitters wired in series. Connect free outputs from the Spider CV splitters to each of the Redrum pitch CV input sockets.
▶ Run the sequence, and adjust the Matrix curve CV to globally change the pitch on the Redrum channels.

Envelope-Controlled Pitch Modulation

This example demonstrates using a Redrum channel gate CV output to trigger the envelope generator on a SubTractor. The envelope generator CV signal is then routed back into the Redrum channel pitch CV input to modulate the sample pitch.

1. Start with an empty rack, set the tempo to 90 BPM, and create a reMix mixer.
2. Create a Redrum Drum Computer and load the patch "Dublab BrushKit2.drp" from the Reason Factory Soundbank\Redrum Drum Kits\Brush Kits directory.
3. Set the Redrum channel 10 to gate mode 1.
4. Bypass auto-routing and create a SubTractor Synthesizer.
5. Connect Redrum channel 10 gate out to the SubTractor sequencer control gate input.
6. Connect the SubTractor filter env modulation output to the Redrum channel 10 pitch CV input.
7. Set the Redrum channel 10 pitch CV trim to 30.
8. Set the SubTractor polyphony to 1, enable low BW, and set filter envelope attack to 55 and filter envelope decay to 80.
9. Program the following on Redrum pattern A1:

Redrum Pattern

	1	2	3	4	5	6	7	8	9	10	11	12	13	14	15	16
1																
2																
3																
4																
5																
6																
7																
8																
9																
10	H			M	S				S		M	M		S	H	

▶ Run the Redrum pattern.

The signal from the gate CV triggers the SubTractor filter envelope. The contoured control voltage signal generated by the envelope then modulates the pitch on the cymbal, creating a decaying pitch modulation. Some of the Redrum channels feature pitch modulation control, but these lack the flexibility of the SubTractor envelope generator.

Samples

Redrum is a sample playback device that accepts a wide variety of formats. But for certain types of control over individual drum sounds, you should consider using an NN-XT Advanced Sampler instead. The Redrum patterns can be converted to sequencer note events, and the sequencer track can then be assigned to the sampler where the drum samples are mapped according to Redrum note values. Redrum channels 1 through 10 are triggered by note events on starting on C1 through A1. Mapping your sample zones accordingly creates a Redrum-compatible set in the sampler.

Monophonic Redrum Channel

In the example below, the gate output from the Redrum channel 1 triggers the NN19 sampler. The same sample has been loaded on the NN19, and the parameters match settings on the Redrum patch. The difference is that the short bursts of 32nd-note drum hits are monophonic. On the Redrum, the sample decay overlaps over the next sample attack. This configuration produces a very sharp and clear rapid-fire drum pattern.

Figure 14-5
Redrum channel 1 gate CV out connected to the NN19 gate input.

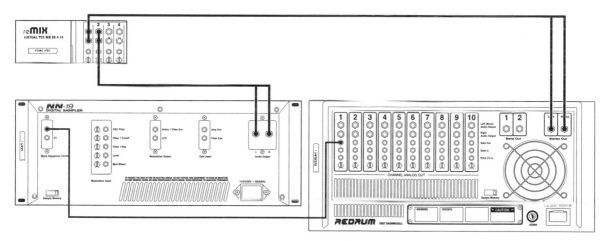

1. In an empty rack, create a reMix mixer and a Redrum Drum Computer.
2. Load the Patch "Hardcore Kit 02.drp" from the Reason Factory Sound Bank\ Redrum Drum Kits\Hardcore Kits directory.

3. Adjust the Redrum channel 1 level to 0 and mode to 1 (gate).
4. Set the Redrum pattern A1 resolution to 1/32.
5. Program the following on Redrum pattern A1:

Redrum Pattern

	1	2	3	4	5	6	7	8	9	10	11	12	13	14	15	16
1	M				M		M		M	M	M		M	M	M	M
2									M							
3																
4																
5																
6																
7																
8																
9																
10																

6. Create an NN19 Digital Sampler.
7. Use the NN19 sample browser to load "BD_Anarchy.wav" from the Reason Factory Sound Bank\Redrum Drum Kits\xclusive drums-sorted\01_BassDrums _directory.
8. Set the NN19 polyphony to 1, velocity F.Env to 16, and velocity amp modulation to 34.
9. Set the NN19 filter cutoff frequency to 97 and the filter envelope sustain to 127.
10. Set the NN19 amp envelope as follows: A 0, D 0, S 127, R 88.
11. Set OSC Pitch: 3, Semi: 8, Fine: 50, and KBD.Track: Off.
12. Patch the Redrum channel 1 gate out to the NN19 mono sequencer control gate in.
▸ Run the Redrum pattern.

REX Slices

Besides standard audio formats such as WAV, AIFF, and SoundFonts, the sample playback devices in Reason can load slices from ReCycle loops. This is a great way to add programmed rhythms on top of a ReCycle loop playing on the Dr.REX Loop Player.

1. Start with an empty rack, and set the pattern shuffle amount to 20.
2. Create a reMix mixer and a Redrum Drum Computer.
3. Enable shuffle on Redrum pattern A1, and enable channel 8&9 exclusive using the small button in the lower left corner of the panel.
4. Insert a Comp-01 Compressor/Limiter between the Redrum and the mixer.
5. Set the Comp-01 threshold to 14, attack to 50, and release to 0.

Sample Loading

6. Click on the sample browser button on Redrum channel 1 and open the file "Chm12_LoFi_125_eLab.rx2" in the Reason Factory Sound Bank\Dr Rex Drum Loops\Chemical Beats directory. The sample browser now lists the individual slices of the ReCycle file.

7. Load slice "Chm12_LoFi_125_eLab.rx2 [0]" on Redrum channel 1.

8. Channel 2: Chm12_LoFi_125_eLab.rx2 [5].

9. Channel 3: Chm12_LoFi_125_eLab.rx2 [6].

10. Channel 4: Chm12_LoFi_125_eLab.rx2 [2].

11. Channel 5: Chm12_LoFi_125_eLab.rx2 [15].

12. Channel 6: Chm12_LoFi_125_eLab.rx2 [14]. Set decay (length) to 32, pitch to –22.

13. Channel 7: Chm12_LoFi_125_eLab.rx2 [6].

14. Channel 8: Chm12_LoFi_125_cLab.rx2 [3]. Set velocity-to-level to 49, decay to 38.

15. Channel 9: Chm12_LoFi_125_eLab.rx2 [7].

16. Channel 10: Chm12_LoFi_125_eLab.rx2 [13].

17. Program the following pattern on the Redrum:

Redrum Pattern

	1	2	3	4	5	6	7	8	9	10	11	12	13	14	15	16
1	M															
2											S				S	
3					S								S			
4					S											S
5			S					S			S			S		
6		S								S					S	S
7																
8	M	S	M	H	M	S	M	S	M	S	M	H	M	S		S
9														S		
10																

▸ Run the Redrum pattern.

This Redrum patch should be saved so the sample and parameter information can be quickly recalled.

Reverse Samples

Reversing the playback of a sample is handy trick to create little transitions between drum hits. The Redrum playback engine cannot reverse the playback of a sample, but a Redrum step can be used to trigger the NN-XT sampler. The drum sample can be loaded into the NN-XT, where the playback direction can be reversed.

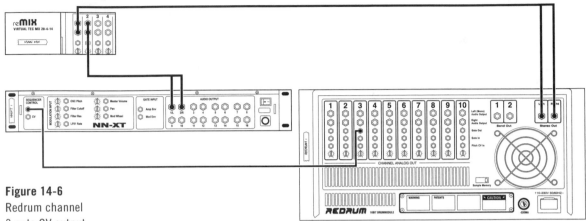

Figure 14-6
Redrum channel
3 gate CV output
connected to the
NN-XT gate input.

1. Start with an empty rack, set the tempo to 135 BPM, and create a reMix mixer.
2. Create a Redrum Drum Computer and load the patch "Techno Kit 04.drp" from the Reason Factory Soundbank\Redrum Drum Kits\Techno Kits directory.
3. Set Redrum channel 3 level to 0, length to 127, and decay/gate mode to 1.
4. Create an NN-XT Advanced Sampler and open the Remote Editor.
5. Load the Sample "Clp_Axis.wav" from the Reason Factory Soundbank\Redrum Drum Kits\xclusive drums-sorted\04_Claps directory.
6. Set the sample end position to 44.8% and the play mode to BW.
7. Adjust the NN-XT amp envelope release to 7.04 seconds, the velocity level knob to 40%, and pitch semitone to 4.
8. Connect the Redrum channel 3 gate CV output to the NN-XT gate input.
9. Program the following on Redrum pattern A1:

Redrum Pattern

	1	2	3	4	5	6	7	8	9	10	11	12	13	14	15	16
1																
2							M									
3	M															
4																
5																
6																
7																
8																
9																
10																

▸ Run the Redrum pattern.

The gate message from Redrum channel 3 triggers the NN-XT, which plays the sample backwards. This is the same sample being played by Redrum channel 2.

Dynamics

The dynamics of a drum pattern are important for creating a groove. Even when the timing is perfect, altering the dynamics adds feeling to the groove. Even with the limited variation between hard, medium, and soft dynamics, Redrum patterns have a more realistic feel when the dynamics vary. If higher resolution dynamics are necessary, the patterns can be converted to track notes and the velocity values can be edited in the sequencer.

One strategy for programming dynamics is to limit the basic pattern to soft and medium events. Even though the default event is set to medium, try programming the pattern using only soft dynamics. Go back through and change events on the downbeat and beat 3 to hard and events on beat 2 and beat 4 to medium. Once the base pattern is programmed, variations can be programmed using medium dynamics to create the feeling of hesitation or anticipation in a rhythm.

Redrum Accent Patterns

Many drum machines have a feature to accent a step in the pattern. The accent is a dynamic boost for the drum events on a particular step, and accents add dynamic change to static patterns. This example uses a Matrix Sequencer to trigger an envelope that modulates the Redrum master level. Keep in mind that this is not the way accents function in all drum machines. This technique is more like a pattern-controlled dynamic boost.

Figure 14-7
Redrum channel 10 gate CV triggers a SubTractor envelope. The envelope CV modulates the mixer level to add an accent to a Redrum step.

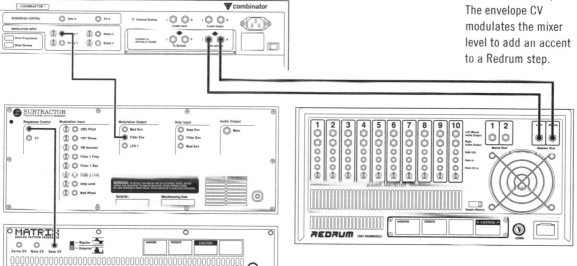

1. Start with an empty rack, and create a reMix mixer.

Redrum Accent Combinator Patch

2. Create a Combinator.
3. In the Combinator sub-rack, create a Redrum Drum Computer and load the patch "House Kit 08.drp" from the Reason Factory Soundbank\Redrum Drum Kits\House Kits directory.
4. Set the Redrum channel 10 level to 0. Channel 10 is used to program accents.
5. Program the following pattern on Redrum pattern A1:

Redrum Pattern

	1	2	3	4	5	6	7	8	9	10	11	12	13	14	15	16
1	M				M				M			M			M	
2					M								M			
3			M				M				M				M	
4																
5																
6																
7																
8																
9	M	M	M	M	M	M	M	M	M	M	M	M	M	M	M	M
10																

6. Still in the sub-rack, create a SubTractor Synthesizer.
7. Set the SubTractor polyphony to 1 and enable low BW.
8. Set the Filter Envelope as follows: A 0, D 53, S 127, R 39.
9. Set the amp envelope release to 39.
10. Connect the SubTractor filter env modulation output to the Combinator rotary 1 CV input.
11. Open the Combinator Programmer and assign rotary 1 to the Redrum master level, Min: 75 and Max: 127.
12. Set Rotary 1 to 0.
13. Create a Matrix pattern sequencer and verify its connection to the SubTractor.
14. Program gate events on Steps: 1, 5, 12, and 16.
15. Save the patch as "Redrum Accent.cmb."
  ▸ Run the sequence.

The SubTractor envelope decay and release values should be adjusted depending on the tempo of the track. Faster tempos require shorter decay and release times, while slower tempos need longer settings. The accent duration should not be longer than the duration of a step, but this can be adjusted to emphasize long samples.

Chapter 15
ReCycle Loop Techniques

The Dr.REX Loop Player is a sample playback device specifically designed for loops created with Propellerhead's ReCycle software. In order to synchronize a normal sampled drum loop with a sequence, either the sample pitch must be changed so that the playback duration matches the tempo, or some sort of time-stretch DSP must be used to change the length of the sample. ReCycle loops, in contrast, automatically synchronize without affecting the original pitch of the drum sounds and without adding time-stretching artifacts. ReCycle, which is a separate product, not included with Reason, converts ordinary drum loops into REX files usable with the Dr.REX. Included with the Reason Factory Sound bank are dozens of REX drum and music loops of various styles.

ReCycle takes a sampled drum loop, analyzes the locations of drum transients, and divides the loop into smaller sample slices. The drum loop slices are mapped to the keys of a sampler. ReCycle also generates a MIDI sequence based on the timing of the segments. The MIDI sequence is a series of notes that start on C1 and ascend chromatically so that each loop slice is on a different key. Along with tempo and time signature information, the sample and sequence data is stored in the ReCycle format (REX, RCY, or RX2). RX2 is the most recent version of the ReCycle 2.x file format, which supports stereo audio data. Regardless of tempo, the slices maintain the same relative spacing, keeping the groove and original pitch intact.

Using the Dr.REX Loop Player is a two-step process. First, load a ReCycle file, and then export the MIDI sequence data to a sequencer track. Pressing the To Track button exports the data to the selected sequencer track, where it appears as one or more groups. Slice events can be inspected in the "REX lane" in sequencer edit mode.

REX Slice Modulation

The heart of the Dr.REX Loop Player is a sample playback device much like the Redrum and NN samplers. There are parameters to control relative pitch, level, decay, and pan for each of the slices. The Dr.REX also has global parameters that control the overall sample playback level, pitch, filtering, and envelope settings. The individual slice settings are relative to the global parameters, and the global parameters can be modulated by external CV signals.

Velocity-Sensitive REX Slices

By default, the Dr.REX does not respond to velocity messages from the slice data on a sequencer track. One of the most useful modulation adjustments is to set the velocity-to-amp modulation to about 40. This will make the individual slices respond to velocity changes. The output level from the Dr.REX will decrease as the velocity-to-amp modulation is increased, and the slice velocity values (some of them, at least, depending on what sort of accent pattern you want to create) will need to be increased to compensate for the decrease in level. The Change Events box, accessed from the Edit menu, has a feature that will allow you to quickly increase the velocities of all selected notes on a Dr.REX sequencer track. In sequencer arrange mode, select all of the REX data groups, access the Change Events box, set the velocity add amount to 36, and click Apply.

REX Slice Parameters

ReCycle can process any kind of sound, which can then be loaded into the Dr.REX Loop Player. This example demonstrates how a simple loop of bass notes can be manipulated in Dr.REX. The original sample is a series of 16 notes playing the same pitch. Using the Dr.REX slice parameters, the note pitches will be adjusted to create a melodic riff. The original audio file is also monophonic, and by modifying the slice pan parameters, the mono loop will acquire some stereo movement.

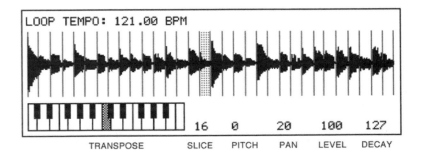

Figure 15-1
The Dr.REX slice parameter editor.

1. In an empty rack, create a reMix mixer and a Dr.REX Loop Player.
2. Load the ReCycle loop "Peff_Moog_16.rx2" from the *Power Tools for Reason* CD \ Dr.REX Loops directory.
3. Copy the REX slice data to the Dr.REX 1 sequencer track.

4. Adjust the REX slice parameters as follows:

Dr.REX Slice Parameters

sce #	1	2	3	4	5	6	7	8	9	10	11	12	13	14	15	16
ptch	−12	0	0	−2	0	0	−2	3	−12	0	0	−2	0	12	−2	0
pan	0	0	−64	0	0	63	0	0	0	−64	0	0	0	0	0	63
level	127	100	100	100	127	100	100	100	127	100	100	100	127	100	100	100
decay	127	127	127	86	127	127	127	86	127	127	127	86	127	127	127	86

▶ Run the sequence.

This example was created for this specific synthesizer REX file, but it illustrates a technique that can be applied to any REX loop.

Note CV Pitch Modulation

Dr.REX parameters can be controlled by various CV sources. This example illustrates using a Matrix pattern note CV to modulate the playback pitch of the Dr.REX. With the pitch CV sensitivity setting at 127, the note CV modulation is in chromatic increments. The note CV modulation requires a gate event on step 1 before the value.

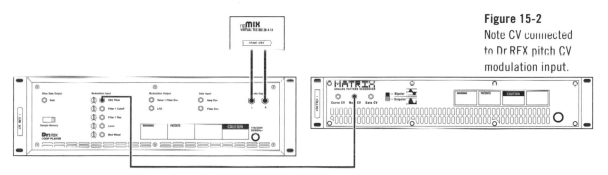

Figure 15-2
Note CV connected to Dr.REX pitch CV modulation input.

1. In an empty rack, create a reMix mixer and a Dr.REX Loop Player.
2. Load the ReCycle loop "090_RunningRhodes2_mLp_eLAB.rx2" from the Reason Factory Sound Bank\Music Loops\Variable Tempo (rex2)\Downtempo Loops directory.
3. Copy the REX slice data to the Dr.REX 1 sequencer track.
4. Set the Dr.REX transpose setting to −12 and the osc pitch octave to 0.
5. Create a Matrix Pattern Sequencer.
6. Connect the Matrix note CV output to the Dr.REX osc pitch modulation input.
7. Set the Dr.REX osc pitch modulation input trim to 127.
8. Draw F3 note events on steps 13 through 16, and draw a gate event on step 1.
▶ Run the sequence.

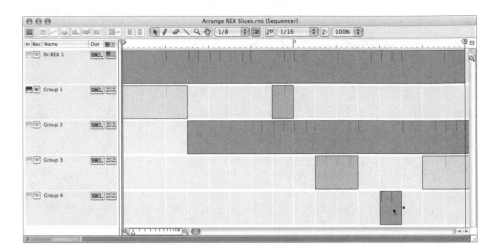

Figure 15-3
A Dr.REX sequencer track has been duplicated, and sections of the REX data have been segmented into shorter sections.

REX Slice Manipulation

Since Propellerhead introduced ReCycle, an entirely new method in electronic music production has evolved based on loop slices. The following examples demonstrate a variety of slice manipulation techniques useful for breakbeat and drum 'n' bass genres. These examples demonstrate a few ways the slice data can be manipulated in the sequencer to deconstruct and create completely different rhythms based on the original REX slice data.

Slice Rearrangement

This example demonstrates the basics of how complex drum 'n' bass loops are created using the Dr.REX Loop Player. The principle is to divide the REX data groups into smaller sections and move the sections around. Each of the smaller groups will contain a few slice events, and the timing among these events will not change, so in effect we'll be slicing the REX file into segments larger than a single slice.

1. Start with an empty rack, and set the tempo to 157 BPM.
2. Set the Loop Locators to 1.1.1 and 3.1.1.
3. Create a reMix mixer and a Dr.REX Loop Player.
4. Load the ReCycle loop "Drb28_StartUp_155_eLAB.rx2" from the Reason Factory Sound Bank\Dr Rex Drum Loops\Drum N Bass directory.
5. Copy the REX slice data to the Dr.REX 1 sequencer track.
6. Make three duplicates of the Dr.REX 1 sequencer track.
7. Rename the duplicate tracks "Group 1," "Group 2," and "Group 3." There should be four sequencer tracks, with the top track named "Dr.REX 1."
8. Mute the Dr.REX 1 sequencer track. This will be kept as a reference containing the original REX slice data.

9. Set the sequencer resolution to 1/8 and enable Snap to Grid.
10. Enable the selection tool.
11. Move the Group 2 region to start at position 1.2.3.
12. Move the Group 3 region to start at position 1.3.3.
13. Enable the pencil tool to draw new arrangement groups.
14. On Group 1, draw a group from position 1.2.3 to 1.4.3, and delete this group.
15. On Group 1, draw a group from position 2.1.1 to 3.1.1, and delete this group.
16. On Group 3, draw a group from position 1.1.1 to 2.1.3, and delete this group.
17. On Group 3, draw a group from position 2.2.3 to 2.4.1, and delete this group.
18. Duplicate the Group 3 sequencer track, and rename it "Group 4."
19. On Group 4, delete the region from 2.4.1 to 3.1.1.
20. On Group 4, draw a group from position 2.2.1 to 2.2.3, and delete this group.
21. On Group 4, select the region starting at 2.1.3, and change the start position to 2.3.1.
▸ Run the sequence.

Altering Notes

The Alter Notes feature, found in the Change Events window, is useful for creating variations of ReCycle loop sequences. This feature is different from randomizing note events, because the slice/note events are arranged in a different order. The feature only affects regions that are selected in either arrange mode or edit mode, so a small group of REX slices data can be altered rather than an entire loop.

1. In an empty rack, create a reMix mixer and a Dr.REX Loop Player.
2. Load the ReCycle loop "Chm13_Boutique_125_eLAB.rx2" from the Reason Factory Sound Bank\Dr Rex Drum Loops\Chemical Beats directory.
3. Copy the REX slice data to the Dr.REX 1 sequencer track.
4. Select the REX slice groups in the Dr.REX sequencer track.
5. Select Change Events in the Edit menu.
6. In the Change Events box, find the Alter Notes function and click on the Apply button.
7. Switch the sequencer to edit mode and view the REX slice data.
▸ Run the sequence.

Try experimenting with different selection ranges as well as alteration amounts. For example, select the last half measure of a REX slice sequence and apply the Alter Notes function. The first half will play normally while the second half plays a variation. Duplicate the Dr.REX sequencer track and experiment with the duplicate sequence. If the variations are a little too extreme, the original data can quickly be replaced from the original version.

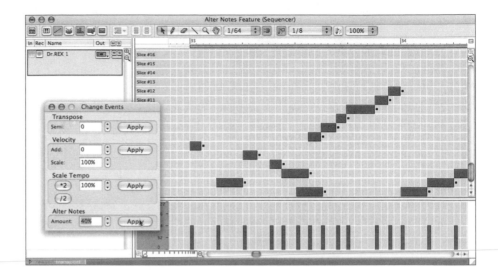

Figure 15-4
The Change Events window's Alter Notes feature.

Synchronizing ReCycle Grooves

Different REX drum loops will have different slice timings, especially when they originate from different styles of music. Slice data from one REX loop can be used as a quantization template to synchronize a different REX loop. Using the Dr.REX 1 REX data as a template, the Dr.REX 2 track can be quantized to conform and synchronize with the first track. Sometimes this function works flawlessly, but a lot has to do with the timing of the events and how close they are in relation to the other track. It works best if you use the track with more slices per measure as the template.

1. Start with an empty rack, and create a reMix mixer.
2. Create two Dr.REX Loop Players.
3. Set the loop locators to 1.1.1 and 9.1.1.
4. In Dr.REX 1, load the ReCycle loop "Hse08_Armand_135_eLab.rx2" from the Reason Factory Sound Bank\Dr Rex Drum Loops\House directory.
5. Select the Dr.REX 1 sequencer track, and copy the REX slice data to the track.
6. In Dr.REX 2, load the ReCycle loop "Tec02_BoneHat_130_eLAB.rx2" from the Reason Factory Sound Bank\Dr Rex Drum Loops\Techno directory.
7. Select the Dr.REX 2 sequencer track, and copy the REX slice data to the track.
8. In the sequencer arrange view, select a group from the Dr.REX 2 track.
9. Select Get User Groove in the Edit menu.
10. Select group regions 2 and 4 on the Dr.REX 1 sequencer track.
11. Click on the Quantize button.
  ▸ Run the sequence.

Selecting groups 2 and 4, but not groups 1 and 3, will allow you to compare the subtle differences in the quantization of the groove. Try listening both with the Dr.REX 2 track muted, and with it playing. Slowing down the tempo will make the differences easier to hear.

Matching grooves is not an exact science, but using REX slice data as a quantization template makes the process easier. The user groove can be applied to other parts of the sequence, such as a bass line. This will tighten up the timing between the bass line and the drum loop.

Averaging Grooves

Sometimes straight quantization of REX slice data is so dramatically different that the second loop does not fit. By applying a 50% quantization from one REX track to the other, then using the quantized track as the new template, you can create an average of the two grooves. Two REX loops with drastically different grooves will synchronize better with this technique. Applying the 50% quantization back and forth between the two different tracks will create an even smoother balance between the grooves, but it's always necessary to apply a 100% quantization to get the grooves in perfect sync.

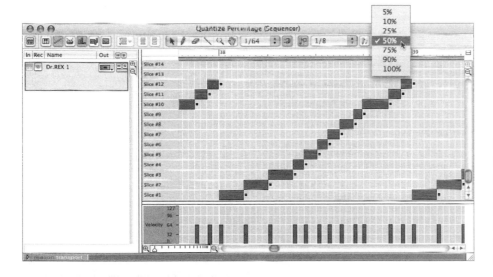

Figure 15-5
Quantization percentage control on the sequencer button bar. Choosing 50% applies a partial quantization to the selected note events.

1. In an empty rack, create a reMix mixer.
2. Create two Dr.REX Loop Players.
3. On Dr.REX 1, load the ReCycle loop "Hse10_Congas_125_eLab.rx2" from the Reason Factory Sound Bank\Dr Rex Drum Loops\House directory.
4. Copy the REX slice data to the Dr.REX 1 sequencer track.

5. On Dr.REX 2, load the ReCycle loop "Chm15_Funky_135_eLAB.rx2" from the Reason Factory Sound Bank\Dr Rex Drum Loops\Chemical Beats directory.
6. Copy the REX slice data to the Dr.REX 2 sequencer track.
7. In the sequencer arrange view, select a group from the Dr.REX 2 track.
8. Select Get User Groove from the Edit menu.
9. Select all groups on the Dr.REX 1 sequencer track.
10. Set the quantization amount to 50%, and quantize the events on the Dr.REX 1 track.
11. Select a group from the Dr.REX 1 sequencer track.
12. Select Get User Groove from the Edit menu.
13. Select all of the groups on the Dr.REX 2 sequencer track.
14. Set the quantization amount to 100% and quantize all the groups on the Dr.REX 2 track.
   ▸ Run the sequence.

Groove Tools

If there were a method of consistently creating a solid rhythm on any track, then the art of creating music would be a lot easier. Drum tuning, timbre, timing, and dynamics are the elements that create a solid groove. If one of these elements is not right, then a loop will lack that sparkle that moves listeners. This is why drum loops are so popular. Rather than painstakingly recreate grooves, they can be called upon in an instant with the Dr.REX Loop Player. The following examples are a little different from the standard audio processing tools because they are designed to take advantage of the natural feel found in sampled drum loops.

Groove Follower

This example uses a Scream 4 envelope follower to create a control voltage based on the dynamics of a ReCycle loop. The envelope follower signal is merged with the Dr.REX envelope CV to modulate the levels of a mixer channel. Using the envelope signal is optional, but without it, quiet sections of the loop will not open the mixer level CV enough for you to hear the Redrum pattern.

1. In an empty rack, create a reMix mixer and a Dr.REX Loop Player.
2. Load the ReCycle loop "Chm09_FatBoy_135_eLAB.rx2" from the Reason Factory Sound Bank\Dr Rex Drum Loops\Chemical Beats directory.
3. Copy the REX slice data to the Dr.REX 1 sequencer track.
4. Set the Dr.REX filter envelope sustain to 64 and the master level to 78.

Envelope Follower Section

5. Insert a Scream 4 between the Dr.REX and the mixer.
6. Disable Damage.

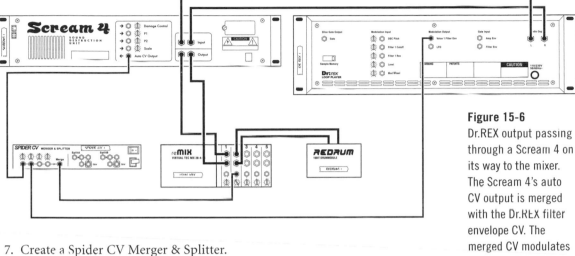

Figure 15-6
Dr.REX output passing through a Scream 4 on its way to the mixer. The Scream 4's auto CV output is merged with the Dr.REX filter envelope CV. The merged CV modulates the level of the Redrum mixer channel input.

7. Create a Spider CV Merger & Splitter.
8. Connect the Scream 4 auto CV output to Spider CV merge input 1.
9. Connect the Dr.REX voice 1 filter env modulation output to the Spider CV merge input 2.
10. Connect the Spider CV merger output to the mixer channel 2 level CV input.
11. Set the mixer channel 2 level CV trim to 58 and the fader level to 0.

Drum Pattern Section

12. At the bottom of the rack, create a Redrum Drum Computer.
13. Load the patch "House Kit 03" from the Reason Factory Sound Bank\Redrum Drum Kits\House Kits directory.
14. Program the following pattern:

Redrum Pattern

	1	2	3	4	5	6	7	8	9	10	11	12	13	14	15	16
1	M															
2				M									M			
3																
4				M							M					
5																
6																
7	S	S	S		S	S	S		S	S	S	S	S	S		
8	M	M	M	M	M	M	M	M	M	M	M	M	M	M	M	M
9																
10																

▸ Run the sequence.

The groove follower can be especially effective if the Redrum pattern is copied to the sequencer track and quantized based on the Dr.REX slice data. In many cases, the quantization will completely change the groove, and averaging the grooves will be more successful.

Beat Juggler

This technique was inspired by watching a DJ cut up beats on two turntables playing the same loop at different start times. The delay line creates a duplicate delayed signal of the original beat, and the Matrix modulates the mixer channels like a cross-switcher. Try adjusting the delay time to find different grooves, and then try creating different switching patterns on the Matrix. This is a fantastic way to give a simple drum loop new life and the energy of a live DJ.

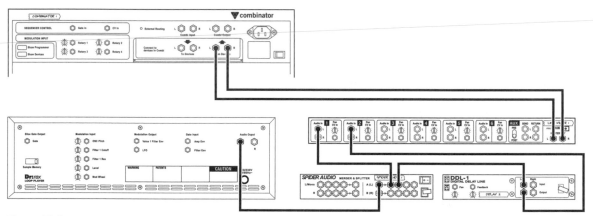

Figure 15-7
The Dr.REX output is delayed with a DDL-1. The original and delayed loop switched using the crossfader configuration established in the Combinator.

1. Start with an empty rack, and create a reMix mixer.

Beat Juggler Combinator Patch

2. Create a Combinator.
3. In the Combinator sub-rack, create a MicroMix Line Mixer.
4. Still in the Combinator, bypass auto-routing and create a Dr.REX Loop Player.
5. Load the ReCycle loop "Hhp07_BlackTalon_093_Chrnc.rx2" from the Reason Factory Sound Bank\Dr Rex Drum Loops\Hip Hop directory.
6. Copy the REX slice data to the Combinator 1 sequencer track.
7. Create a Spider Audio Merger & Splitter.
8. Bypass auto-routing and connect the Dr.REX Audio output left to the Spider Split A input. This patch will only use mono signals
9. Bypass auto-routing and connect the Spider split 1 output A to the MicroMix channel 2 left input.

10. Bypass auto-routing and create a DDL-1 Digital Delay Line.
11. Set the DDL-1 feedback to 0.
12. Bypass auto-routing and connect the Spider Split 2 output A to the DDL-1 audio input left.
13. Bypass auto-routing and connect the DDL-1 audio output left to the mixer channel 1 left input.
14. Bypass auto-routing and create a Matrix Pattern Sequencer.
15. Connect the Matrix Curve CV output to the Combinator rotary 1 CV input.
16. Set the Matrix to bipolar mode.
17. All of the curve settings in Matrix pattern A1 should be at minimum. Program maximum (63) curve settings on steps 3, 4, 7, 8, 11, 12, 15, and16.
18. Open the Combinator Programmer and set the following modulation routings:

Device	Source	Target	Min	Max
Line Mixer 1	Rotary 1	Channel 1 Level	0	100
Line Mixer 1	Rotary 1	Channel 2 Level	100	0
Delay 1	Rotary 2	DelayTime (steps)	1	6
Delay 1	Button 2	Step Length	0	1
Matrix 1	Button 1	Pattern Enable	0	1

19. Rename the Combinator controls and set the parameters as follows:

Control	Name	Default Value
Rotary 1	X Fade	63
Rotary 2	Delay Steps	68
Button 1	Matrix On	On
Button 2	16 – 8T	On

20. Save the patch as "Beat Juggler.cmb."
  ▸ Run the sequence.

Disabling the Matrix On button will stop the Matrix curve modulation of the X Fade modulation. By assigning the Combinator X Fade rotary to a knob or slider, you can tweak the mix in real time. Try different delay time variations by adjusting the steps and step duration controls.

Matrix Pattern REX Player

The Combinator can convert Note and Gate CV messages from a Matrix sequencer into MIDI data that can drive a Dr.REX Player. This establishes a new method of triggering ReCycle loop slices as if they were drum machine patterns. C1 is the note value of the first ReCycle Slice, so as a reference always start the ascending note slices from this value.

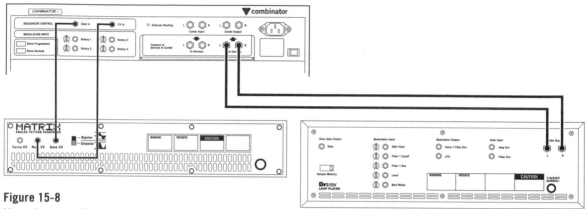

Figure 15-8
Matrix Note and Gate events patched to the Combinator sequencer CV inputs convert the data to MIDI events that trigger REX Slices.

1. Start with an empty rack and create a reMix mixer.

Matrix Pattern REX Player Combinator Patch

2. Create a Combinator.
3. In the sub-rack, create a Dr.REX Loop Player.
4. Set the Amp Envelope Release to 50.
5. Load the ReCycle loop "Gt_Wah_G7_04_115.rx2" from the Reason Factory Sound Bank\ Dr Rex Instrument Loops \Guitar Loops\Wah Wah 115 directory.
6. Do not copy the slice data to the Sequencer! A Matrix sequencer will be triggering the slices.
7. Still in the sub-rack, create a Matrix Pattern Sequencer. Verify that auto-routing has connected it to the Combinator's Gate and CV inputs.
8. Program the following Matrix pattern:

Matrix 1 (Steps 1–16)

Step	1	2	3	4	5	6	7	8	9	10	11	12	13	14	15	16
Note	C1	C#1	D1	D#1	E1	F1	F#1	C#1	D1	D#1	F1	F#1	G1	G#1	A1	A#1
Gate	H	H	H	H	H	H	H	H	H	H	H	H	H	H	H	H

9. Save the patch as "Matrix REX Player.cmb."

▸ Run the Combinator to hear the Matrix pattern trigger the Dr.REX slices. Enable the Select Slice Via MIDI button to see which slices are being triggered as the Matrix Pattern cycles. Also, try different ReCycle loops and patterns to find some interesting pattern and loop combinations.

Matrix-Triggered REX Playback

When the Dr.REX receives a note value of D0, it will begin a playback cycle of the entire loop from the first slice to the last. A Matrix can be used to exploit this feature for a unique loop trigger effect. Because the Matrix note CV range is limited to C1 and above, the curve CV is used generate a value equivalent to D0. The gate CV is used normally to send a note-on event to the Dr.REX through the Combinator. Finding the proper CV value is tedious, so the Matrix Pattern Sequence is partially prepared for this example.

1. Start with an empty rack, and create a reMix mixer.
2. Create a Combinator.
3. Load the Combi patch "15 – Matrix Trigger REX.cmb" from the *Power Tools for Reason* CD \ Combinator Patches directory. This patch includes a Matrix Pattern Sequencer with the curve CV value already set.
4. Verify that the Matrix curve CV output is connected to the Combinator CV in and that the Matrix Gate CV is connected to the Combinator gate in.
5. In the Combinator sub-rack, create a Dr.REX Loop Player.
6. Load the ReCycle loop "Hhp07_BlackTalon_093_Chrnc.rx2" from the Reason Factory Sound Bank\Dr Rex Drum Loops\Hip Hop directory.
7. Do not copy the slice data to the sequencer! The Matrix sequencer will be initiating loop playback.
8. On the Matrix, program gate events on steps 1, 17, 27, 28, 29, and 31.
▸ Run the Combinator to hear the Dr.REX loop triggered by the Matrix gate events. Experiment with different ReCycle loops and gate patterns to discover some new ways to manipulate the loop patterns.

You may notice that when you stop the Combinator patch, the loop continues to play until the end of the cycle. You can add a gate control that opens a mixer channel only while the Combinator is running. In the Reason Factory Sound Bank, there is a patch called "REXSelectoR.cmb" that demonstrates how this is achieved.

Chapter 16
Synthesizers

Synthesis is the process of creating sound electronically. A musician programming a synthesizer patch is like a painter developing his or her own colors and brushes for a work of art, or a composer building instruments exclusively for a new composition. The SubTractor and Malström are the primary Reason synthesizers, but the Redrum, NN-XT, NN19, and Dr.REX also have sound-shaping features. The main difference is that the latter group of devices uses audio samples as the source of sound waves.

Synthesizers use the audio and control voltage principles described earlier in this book, but modulation routings are fixed within the architecture of each device. This chapter discusses the practical side of adjusting parameters on the SubTractor and Malström synthesizers, and addresses some technical aspects of synthesis in these devices.

Software synthesis requires considerable computing power and speed, so it has only been within the last decade that advances in computer technology have made software synthesis accessible to owners of personal computers. The technology behind Reason's SubTractor and Malström synthesizers would not be possible without a computer's ability to perform complex processes in a tiny fraction of a second.

Sound Deconstruction

A friend passed on a bit of wisdom from her grandmother, who said, "If you can imagine every quality about a rose—the fragrance, the texture of the petals, the gentle colors—you have the skills to be a good cook." This charming analogy was my inspiration for understanding how to program synthesizers. Imagine the sound with as much detail as possible, and with the sound in mind, and deconstruct it into its basic qualities: voice, register, dynamics, timbre, and modulations. Understanding each of these elements of a sound and learning to recognize them is the first step in learning about programming synth patches.

The first characteristic of an instrument is its polyphony. This term refers to the number of simultaneous tones (also known as *voices*) that can be produced. A solo woodwind instrument has only one voice: It's a monophonic instrument. An electric piano has dozens of voices, making it a polyphonic instrument. Vintage analog synthesizers were typically limited in polyphony to between four and eight voices, but contemporary synthesizers typically range from 32 to 64 or more voices.

Most musical instruments typically only play a certain range of notes within the entire music scale. This range, or *register*, of pitches is the second key characteristic of a sound. Register is an important quality that helps the ear distinguish the difference between a bass guitar, a guitar, and ukelele. These are three similar stringed instruments, but they produce tones in different frequency ranges. Violin and picolo have registers higher on the musical scale, in the treble range of frequencies, while bass and tuba have low frequency characteristics.

The characteristic of *dynamics* refers to the loudness or amplitude of a sound, and how the loudness changes over time. For example, when a percussionist strikes a cymbal, the initial impact is loud, but over time the energy dissipates and the amplitude (loudness) decays back to silence. The changing loudness is described as the *envelope* of the instrument. In electronic instruments, envelopes have *stages*, sections that help shape the start, middle, and end of a sound. The stages are often described using the terms *attack, decay, sustain,* and *release.*

The term *timbre* (pronounced "tam-br") is what distinguishes one sound from another. For example, a piano, a saxphone, and a cello can play the same E note, but the instruments have different sonic characteristics. The pitch, or *fundamental*, is the same for all three instruments, but each instrument produces different harmonics. Harmonics are higher components of the sound (called *overtones* or *partials*) whose frequencies have a relationship to the fundamental. The amplitudes of the various overtones define the *harmonic content* of each instrument's tone, making each of them unique. Dull sounds have limited harmonic content, while bright sounds have more and higher overtones. A sine wave is the simplest timbre because it contains only one harmonic, the fundamental pitch, with no overtones. (There are technical differences in meaning between the terms "harmonic," "overtone," and "partial," but for synthesizer programming in Reason, the differences are not important.)

Most sounds change over time, depending on how long they last and on how loudly they are played. These transformations are referred to as *modulations*. Any type of pitch, timbral, or dynamic change is a modulation. Modulations add expressive elements and performance nuances. Common forms of modulation are subtle pitch variations called vibrato, or a sliding pitch called portamento or glissando. Another type of modulation is a variation in loudness called tremolo. Common timbral modulations take into account that sounds are brighter when played at higher registers or played loudly.

These chacteristics are the primary elements of a sound, and are the basis in the design of most synthesizers and samplers. The following sections describe how the parameters of SubTractor and Malström make use of these concepts.

Polyphony

The number of voices of sound is controlled by the polyphony parameter, which is featured on the Reason synthesizers, samplers, and Dr.REX loop player. The polyphony setting dictates how many simultaneous sounds can be produced. The default value of the polyphony parameter is usually eight voices. Eight to 24 voices are adequate for most patches.

Monophonic synthesizer patches are commonly used for bass and solo lead sounds, and require a polyphony setting of 1. If the device receives two note-on events, only one of the two notes is heard. Normally the more recent of the two notes takes priority. Whatever the polyphony setting, as successive notes are received the last note played takes priority. If there are not enough voices available to play all of the notes requested by the keyboard or the sequencer track, the oldest note(s) will be "stolen" to play new notes.

Each voice in a Reason synth uses all of the patch settings; thus a four-voice Malström patch (see Figure 16-1) has eight graintables, eight filters, and eight modulators running simultaneously. Using several Malströms at once may overtax the CPU. In this case, reducing the total polyphony of the sequence conserves processing resources. A bass patch may play one note, so it only requires a polyphony setting of 1. A pad patch might plays triads (three-note chords) and requires a polyphony setting of 3. If the triad patch has long envelope release times, however, a polyphony setting of 6 might be necessary to prevent notes from being chopped off as they die away.

KEY IN

Synthesizer programming is typically a trial-and-error process in which one sets a few parameters, plays some notes, and then adjusts more parameters until the sound is just right. The following examples will be easier to follow if you have a keyboard controller. If you don't have one, you can instead open the sequencer track in note edit mode and click on the piano keys on the left side of the window. Recording from these keys is also possible, but they always send the same MIDI velocity value (100).

Pitch Transposition & Range

Synthesizers potentially have a 128-note range that spans across a keyboard—far beyond the normal 88 keys of a piano. When creating a sound that plays in the register of a flute, focus on shaping the character of the sound in this register. Play notes that reflect the pitch characteristics you want. For a bass patch, play keys in the bass region, and for pads, play chords in both upper and lower registers.

● note on

polyphony

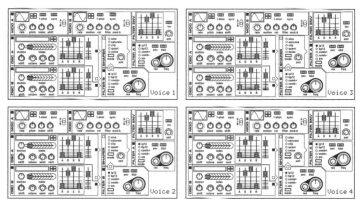

Synthesizer oscillators feature parameters to *transpose*, or offset, the pitch. The transposition controls are labeled Oct, which transposes the register up and down in octave increments, Semi, which transposes the pitch up in semitones, and Cent, which adjusts the pitch in cents (increments of 1/100 of a semitone). An incoming note played on Middle C can be shifted down several octaves to play in the bass register, or upward into the treble register.

Transposing SubTractor Oscillators

1. In an empty rack, create a microMix Line Mixer and a SubTractor Synthesizer.
2. On a keyboard controller, play notes around Middle C and adjust the OSC 1 Oct parameter to 2 to hear the register transposed downward.
3. Adjust the Semi and Cent parameters as well to see how these parameters modify the pitch. Instead of clicking on the Up/Down buttons, click and drag directly over the number values.
4. Save the song file as "Subtractor Synth.rns."

Figure 16-1
The polyphony control determines the number of voices that will be available for a synth patch. Each voice has its own oscillators, filters, modulators, and envelopes.

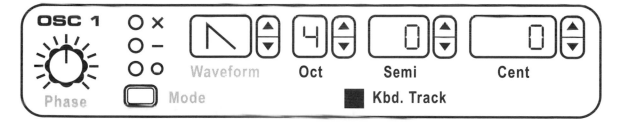

Fifth Intervals

1. Begin with the "Subtractor Synth.rns" song created above.
2. Select the SubTractor by clicking on it, and select Initialize Patch from the Edit menu. This restores the parameters to the inital settings.
3. Enable Osc 2.

Figure 16-2
The SubTractor oscillator transposition controls and keyboard tracking parameters determine the range of the synth patch.

4. Change Osc 2 Semi to 7. Seven semitones are a musical interval (offset) called a fifth.

▶ Play a few notes on a keyboard controller to hear the fifth intervals. One oscillator has the original pitch received from the keyboard, and the second oscillator is transposed up and two pitches are heard.

Keyboard Tracking

Incoming note events deterimine the pitch of the SubTractor synthesizer, but the register can be anchored to the range of a single note. The Kbd. Track button controls this mode. If Keyboard tracking is disabled, the oscillator always plays the same pitch regardless of the incoming note value.

1. Start with the "Subtractor Synth.rns" song file.
2. On Osc 1, disable Kbd.Track
3. Set the Oct to 3, Semi to 8, and Cent to 50. These transposition values adjust the Osc 1 pitch to C3 (Middle C).
4. Enable Osc 2.

Play a scale in the key of C (major or minor). Oscillator 1 has a fixed pitch tuned to C3, while Osc 2 responds normally to incoming note values. While this can have some musical value like always having a root key of C, this feature is more likely used to create a sound effect or percussion sound where tuning is fixed to one pitch.

Pitch-Bend

Pitch-bend control allows you to glissando pitch slides or create gestures like vibrato. This control is on all of Reason's sound modules. The pitch-bend modulation is set using the *Bend Range* parameter, usually indicated with a numeric display. Each step of the range is a half-step (semitone), so a setting of 1 limits the bend range to one semitone up and one semitone down.

Figure 16-3

Flow of pitch control values in the Sub-Tractor. CV/MIDI note values are shifted by the oscillator tranpostion parameters. These are combined with the pitch-bend value to determine the oscillator frequency before the portamento lag control. Modulation sources are summed with the pitch value after portamento.

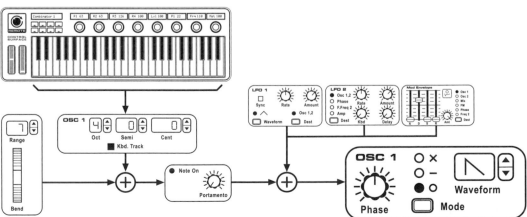

Portamento

Portamento is a pitch slide feature: The parameter controls the time it takes for the pitch to glide from one note to another. A short portamento time is commonly used for solo synth patches to give the notes an elastic feel as the pitches slide up and down the scale.

1. Start with the "Subtractor Synth.rns" song file.
2. Set Polyphony to one voice.
3. Set Portamento to 101.
4. Set the pitch-bend range to 24.
5. Play notes on a keyboard to hear the pitch slide between notes.
6. Play and hold a note until the pitch settles, and then adjust the pitch-bend wheel. Pitch-bend values are processed according to portamento lag time.
7. Play and hold a note until the pitch settles, and then adjust the Osc 1 octave transpose value. Again, portamento time affects the SubTractor transpose features.

Pitch modulation values from the SubTractor Mod Envelope and LFOs are not affected by portamento (see Figure 16-3). Modulation control voltages sum with the pitch value after the portamento stage. The NN-19 pitch control architecture is the same as SubTractor, but the Malström and NN-XT are different. On the Malström and NN-XT, portamento is only applied to incoming Note CV sources or MIDI note events.

Amp Envelope & Dynamics

The dynamics of a Reason synth sound and the shape of the amplitude are controlled primarily with the envelope ADSR parameters. Chapter 3 discusses envelopes extensively, but this section explores concrete examples of using envelopes to shape dynamics. The two factors that control envelopes are the envelope settings and the duration of the incoming note events. Synth patches feature other modulations that alter dynamics based on incoming note messages.

No Envelope

1. Start with the "Subtractor Synth.rns" song file, and initialize the patch.
2. Set the Velocity F.Env parameter to 0.
3. Set the amp envelope ADSR settings all to zero.
▸ Play some notes on a keyboard controller. With the AMP envelope settings set at zero, the dynamics of the patch occur as short percussive blips. The blip is the result of the envelope quickly rising to the maximum value and just as quickly dropping back to silence.

Attack Stage

4. Continue from the previous step with zero amp envelope ADSR settings.
5. Adjust the attack value to 51.

▸ Play a note or chord and hold it. The longer attack duration creates a loudness ramp that increases quickly from silence and peaks. At the end of the Attack period, the envelope drops back to silence creating a sharp bowing attack. Change the Attack value to 99 and hear a longer rising attack. Releasing the keys during the attack stage immediately stops the envelope before it peaks.

Decay Stage

6. Adjust the amp envelope ADSR parameters all back to 0.
7. Adjust the amp envelope decay value to 36.

▸ Play a note or chord and hold it. Increasing the decay value creates the opposite loudness ramp where the sound starts loud and diminishes to silence. Instead of short blips, the envelope plays short notes. Increase the decay parameter to 99, then play and hold some notes to hear a longer decrease in loudness.

Note duration also changes the behavior of decay. In order to hear the entire envelope, note events must be as long or longer than the total period set by the attack and decay values together. Releasing the keys in the middle of the decay ends the decay period.

Sustain Value

8. Adjust the amp envelope ADSR parameters back to 0.
9. Adjust the amp envelope sustain value to 63.

▸ Play a note or chord and hold it. You will hear the short blip of the zero attack and decay, then the sound maintains a loudness set by the sustain until the key is released.

Gate

10. Continue from the previous settings.
11. Adjust the amp envelope sustain value to 127.

▸ Play successive notes with different durations. The envelope with zero attack, zero decay and a sustain value to 127 to creates a gate envelope which simply opens and closes when notes are received.

Release Stage

12. Continue from the previous gate example.
13. Adjust the amp envelope release value to 63.

▸ Play a note or chord and quickly release it. When the note is released, the sound diminishes back to silence. This is different from the decay stage, which ends when the note is released. With a value of zero, the release stage instantly drops to silence, but when the value is greater, the envelope slowly, fades out. With the Release value set to 127, the sound can take several minutes to fade to silence.

Velocity Modulation

Incoming note events contain data that indicates how soft or hard a keyboard is played. This value is *velocity*, a unipolar gate value that ranges from 1 to 127. Velocity data can directly change the output level, adding dynamic expression to the patch.

1. Start with the "Subtractor Synth.rns" song file as before, and initialize the patch.
2. Set the Velocity F.Env parameter to 0, and boost the filter cutoff to 100.
3. Set the Velocity Amp amount to 32. This adds a positive velocity modulation so that soft notes are result in low volumes while hard notes result in high volumes.

▶ Play a series of notes or chords and change the intensity of the key strikes to hear Velocity modulation of the dynamics. Velocity can also change the envelope attack parameter. Continue with the following parameter changes:

4. Adjust the amp envelope settings as follows: A 89, D 0, S:128, R 48.
5. Adjust the Velocity A.Atk parameter to –42. This adds a negative velocity modulation to the amp envelope attack setting that decreases the duration of the attack time. High incoming velocity messages decrease the attack time significantly.

▶ Again, play a series of notes or chord progressions that gradually change in intensity from soft to very hard and fast. The soft notes are low with longer attacks, while the harder notes with larger velocity values are louder with sharp percussive attacks.

Figure 16-4

Velocity-to-amplitude modulation scales the amount of loudness modulation, and the Velocity A.Atk parameter scales the modulation applied to the amp envelope attack stage.

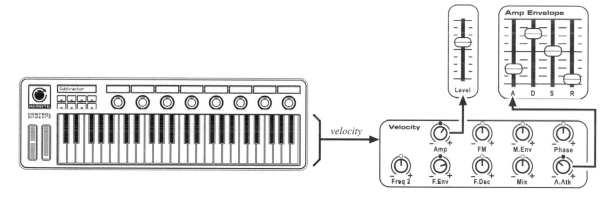

Legato Mode

The synthesizers and samplers have a mode switch which indicates "Legato" or "ReTrig/Legato." This parameter directly influences the amp envelope behavior as well as aspects of the other envelopes. In musical terms, *legato* means to play smoothly, so that the notes are connected. When a phrase is played legato, incoming note events overlap instead of having definite gaps between them.

1. Start with the "Subtractor Synth.rns" song file, and initialize the patch.
2. Set the polyphony to 1.
3. Adjust the amp envelope settings as follows: A 0, D 43, S 64, R 10.
4. Play a scale of notes and hold down the previous keys—this is playing the notes legato. As each key is pressed, a voice stolen from the previous note and the envelope quickly moves through the fast attack and decay stages.
5. Switch the mode from ReTrig to Legato.
6. Play the scale of notes again legato.

As a scale is played legato, the dynamics of the first note reflect the attack and decay settings, while subsequent notes skip those stages. Play the scale *staccato*, as short choppy notes with definite gaps between each note, and notes occur with the attack and decay stages. Legato mode simulates performance techniques used in some acoustic instruments. For example, when a clarinetist tongues a note, the attack has a sharp character that is not heard when the fingers are used to change the pitch without tonguing the note.

Legato is a feature of monophonic instruments, and the Malström automatically reduces polyphony to one voice. Create a Malström, play a chord on a keyboard controller, and switch the legato mode. Switching between modes causes the sound to change between a chord and a single note. Polyphony must be manually set for SubTractor patches; otherwise legato occurs only when the patch steals a voice.

Envelopes on Other Devices

Loudness envelopes and the velocity modulation routings are universal features in all Reason sound modules, and while the examples above describe the SubTractor synthesizer, they can be applied to the Malström synth and the samplers as well to shape dynamics. Short percussive or bass sounds have zero attack and a fast decay time of about 32. If the sound is a long drone or pad sound, then the attack and release times should be long. For plucked sounds, the attack and decay should both be fast (about 30 to 40), and the sustain level should be set low so the attack is louder than the sustain. Once the envelope characteristics are set, decide on velocity modulation over the dynamics. Sometimes no velocity modulation is required with for organs and synthetic drum patches, however it works well with expressive pads or solo sounds.

Generating Timbres with Oscillators

The *oscillator* is where a synthesizer's audio signals are born. This does not mean that all oscillators are the same. With analog synthesizers, the oscillator circuitry is similar from one instrument to another, so analog synths (as well as digital synths that are designed to emulate analog models) produce similar timbres. But digital synths usually have different sound generation systems. The SubTractor synthesizer uses digital wavetables to as a source of sound generation, while the Malström uses a hybrid of sampling and wavetables called graintable synthesis.

SubTractor Oscillators

The SubTractor oscillators are based on wavetables, which are digital snapshots of waveforms. The oscillator scans the wavetable—slowly for a low pitch, and more rapidly for a high pitch—and generates a signal at the specified pitch value. Each of the 32 wavetables produces a different timbre. The first four SubTractor waveforms (sawtooth, square, triangle, and sine wave) are classic waveforms that imitate the sound of analog synthesizers. The remaining wavetables are uniquely digital sounds with differing harmonic content that provide the basis for other types of sounds.

1. Start with the "Subtractor Synth.rns" song file, and initialize the patch.
2. Set the amp envelope as follow: A 0, D 0, S 127, R 0.
3. Set the Filter 1 cutoff frequency to 127. This opens the filter so that we can hear all of the harmonic content in each wavetable.
4. Adjust the Velocity F.Env parameter to zero.
5. Save this song as "Subtractor Osc.rns."
▸ Play and hold a note while adjusting the Osc 1 waveform parameter.

While switching through the wavetables, listen for the variations in timbre and harmonic content. On their own, the wavetables sound quite raw, and those with the higher harmonics can even be nerve-wrenching.

SubTractor Phase Offset Modulation

The oscillator mode switch adds timbral flexibility to the standard waveforms provided by SubTractor. There are two phase modes: subtract (–) and multiply (x). When the mode switch is set to "o" the feature is disabled. In subtract mode, the oscillator scans two values from the wavetable and calculates the difference. The result of the calculation becomes the new waveform. The second value is selected from an offset determined by the Phase parameter knob. In multiply mode, the two values from the wavetable are multiplied. This results in a new waveform, generally one that has more overtones.

1. Start with the "Subtractor Osc.rns" file, previously saved.
2. On Osc 1, set the phase mode to "–."
▸ Play and hold a note and adjust the Osc 1 phase knob.

Sweeping the phase offset control demonstrates how the harmonics change from silence when the phase offset is zero, to a thin tone, to a rich full tone when the phase offset is 127. When the phase offset is zero, the subtracted value equals the first value, causing the waveforms to cancel out. Next, switch the phase mode to "x" and adjust the phase knob to hear how the multiply mode affects the timbre. Multiply mode is actually ring modulation, which is discussed further on in this section.

LFO Phase Offset Modulation
Either LFO can be used to sweep the phase offset to create interesting shifting timbre effects in the SubTractor oscillators. Using the subtract mode with the sawtooth waveform creates an oscillator timbre called a pulse wave, and altering the phase creates an effect called pulse width modulation.

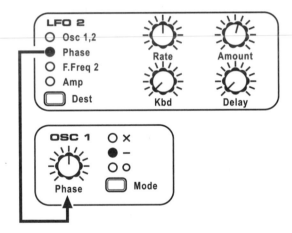

Figure 16-5
LFO 2 targets the oscillator phase parameter and applies a modulation to the phase offset.

1. Start with the "Subtractor Osc.rns" file, previously saved.
2. On Osc 1. Set the Phase Mode to "–."
3. Adjust the Osc 1. phase knob to 63.
4. Set the LFO 2 destination to phase.
5. Set the LFO 2 rate to 63 and amount to 75. These parameters initiate the LFO phase modulation.
6. Set the LFO 2 Kbd to 93. This changes the LFO rate based on keyboard tracking so that higher notes modulate faster than notes in the lower register.
   ▸ Play a chord and listen to the phase offset modulation from the LFO. Switch the Phase mode switch to "o" to compare it to the original waveform.

LFO 1 can also be used as a source by assigning the destination to Phase. LFO 2 only produces a triangle modulation wave, but LFO 1's alternate waveforms can be used to create different timbre modulation effects. Try one of the random waveforms to create unpredictable buzzing timbres.

Velocity Phase Offset Modulation

1. Start with the "Subtractor Osc.rns" file.
2. On Osc 1, set the Phase Mode to "x."
3. Adjust the Osc 1 phase parameter to 127.
4. Adjust the Velocity phase parameter to –54.
▸ Play notes at different dynamics levels and listen to how timbre changes.

Envelope Phase Offset Modulation

1. Start with the "Subtractor Osc.rns" file.
2. On Osc 1, set waveform to 23.
3. Set the phase mode to "–" and phase to 0.
4. Set the mod envelope as follows: A 46, D 66, S 0, R 0. Set its destination to phase and amount to 64.
▸ Play and hold a note to hear the mod envelope affecting the phase.

COUNT THE WAVES

To select a SubTractor oscillator waveform or a Malström Modulator waveform, click and drag up or down on the waveform graphic. When you do this, the ToolTip shows the number of the waveform. But because the parameter itself is zero-indexed (that is, the first waveform is number 0), the wave displayed as "5" in the SubTractor oscillators is numbered 4, "6" is actually waveform 5, and so on. The numbers used in this book correspond to the values shown on the ToolTips, not to the numbers displayed on the SubTractor panel.

With the phase knob set to 0 in subtract mode, the initial state is silent due to phase cancellation. As the attack stage of the mod envelope rises, the timbre grows in complexity. During the decay stage, the timbre diminishes as the modulation decreases.

Multiple Oscillators

The SubTractor has two oscillators which can be used simultaneously to layer two timbres. Combinations of waveforms blend the harmonic content from two sources, and when used with phase offset modulation, far more than 32 waveforms are possible. Explore waveform combinations along with phase offset modulation to discover the variety of timbral combinations.

Oscillator Detune

In a previous example it was demonstrated how the second oscillator can be used to create a second tuning for one-finger chord intervals. Instead of retuning one oscillator by several half-steps, slight tuning adjustments between two oscillators can be used to generate timbral modulations. Adjusting one of the oscillators out of tune, or *detuning* the oscillator, adds a subtle chorusing to the timbre.

1. Start with the "Subtractor Osc.rns" file.
2. On Osc 1, set the waveform to 3 (the sine wave).
3. Enable Osc 2, and set waveform to 3.
▸ Play a few notes and chords. Normally, Osc 2 increases the loudness of the sine wave. The two waveforms are synchronized so the amplitudes are added to

create a sine wave with a larger amplitude. Occasionally, however, Osc 2 will be out of phase with Osc 1, so adding a second sine wave without detuning may cause the sound to get softer due to phase cancellation.

4. Adjust the Osc 2 cent parameter to 20. This changes the pitch of Osc 2 just slightly and puts the two sine waves out of sync.

▸ Play and hold a note to hear the two oscillators with different tunings.

The peaks and troughs of the sine waves cause a phase cancellation effect called *beating*, which results in the warbling effect. Using identical waveforms creates a chorusing effect, but the slight beating is even apparent with different waveform combinations.

Envelope-Modulated Oscillator Mix

The Mix parameter crossfades between the outputs of Osc 1 and Osc 2, emphasizing one of the two timbres. When this knob is adjusted fully counter-clockwise, only Osc 1 is heard, and only Osc 2 is heard when the mix knob is adjusted fully clockwise to 127. The Mix parameter also be modulated to create a new variety of multiple-oscillator timbral variations.

1. Start with the "Subtractor Osc.rns" file.
2. On Osc 1, set the waveform to 3.
3. Enable Osc 2, and set the waveform to 5.
4. Adjust the mix knob to 0.
5. Set the mod envelope amount to113 and destination to mix.

▸ Play notes on a keyboard and listen to the modulation effect.

The Mod Envelope modulation on the oscillator mix parameter is actually a dynamics effect. Osc 2 is mixed in during the short decay stage, adding the complex timbres at the beginning of the note. The noise generator is on the same audio bus as Osc 2, and once enabled, it can be heard exclusively by disabling Osc 2 and setting the mix parameter to 127. Noise can add a percussive element using the envelope modulation technique.

Velocity-Modulated Oscillator Mix

Like the amp envelope, this mod envelope can be governed by velocity messages. This allows the mixture of timbres to change between low-velocity and high-velocity notes.

6. Continue from the Envelope-Modulated Oscillator Mix example.
7. Adjust the mod envelope as follows: A 0, D 0, S 127, R 0, Amt 0, Dest: mix.
8. Set the Velocity M.Env parameter to 38.

▸ Play notes at varying velocities to hear Osc 2 mixed in at different levels with Osc 1. The velocity modulation increases the level of Osc 2, adding the brighter harmonics of waveform 5 as notes are played harder. With this patch, the envelope stage parameters can be altered to feature both envelope and velocity modulation of the Osc 2 timbre levels.

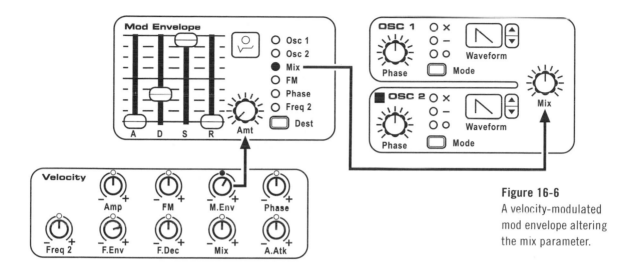

Figure 16-6
A velocity-modulated mod envelope altering the mix parameter.

Figure 16-7
The velocity modulation controls are bipolar. The center cetent indicates no modulation from velocity. Clockwise (positive) amounts add a positive modulation. Counter-clockwise (negative) amounts subtract the modulation. For example, a positive value for velocity to amp envelope attack increases the attack time with higher velocity values. A negative value for the same parameter shortens the attack time for notes with high velocity values.

Ring Modulation

Ring modulation is a process that requires two oscillator signals. The two signals are multiplied to create new harmonics. The sound can be similiar to the phase offset modulation in multiply mode. The tone from a ring modulator contains the sum and difference tones of all of the harmonics in the two inputs.

1. Start with the "Subtractor Osc.rns" file
2. On Osc 1, set the waveform to 3.
3. Enable Osc 2, and set the waveform to 3.
4. Adjust the Osc Mix to 127. The ring modulator tone emerges from the oscillator 2 side of the mix.
5. Switch on the Ring Mod button.

Play and hold a note then adjust the Osc 2 Octave and Semitone transposition parameters. Octave and fifth (semi: 7) offsets between the oscillators have the most musical results.

6. Change Osc 1 waveform to 6 (Display Waveform 7).
7. Change Osc 2 octave to 7.
8. Adjust the oscillator mix to 40.

▸ Play a note to hear the ring-modulated overtones layered with the original waveform of oscillator 1.

Ring-modulating different waveforms is another technique to add harmonics that create timbral complexity. Because the output of the ring modulator can be adjusted with the mix parameter, the oscillator mix modulation routings can be applied to create velocity- and envelope-controlled variations.

Ring Modulator Pitch Sweep

9. Continue from the previous example.
10. Adjust the oscillator mix to 127.
11. Set the Osc 2 octave to 5.
12. Set the mod envelope as follows: A 0, D 82, S 0, R 0, destination Osc 2, amount 116.

▸ Play and hold a note and listen as the pitch from oscillator 2 sweeps from a very high frequency downward. As the pitch decreases, you can hear the two resulting frequencies from the ring modulator. One tone is sweeping down while the other sweeps upward.

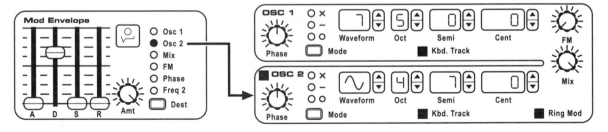

Figure 16-8

Mod envelope targets Osc 2 pitch to create the sweeping ring modulation effect.

This example is a very dramatic pitch modulation that results in an interesting sound effect, but the parameters can be altered to a short decay and small envelope modulation to create a metallic hammering timbre.

FM Synthesis

Frequency modulation synthesis (FM) requires both SubTractor oscillators. Oscillator 1 is called the carrier and oscillator 2 is called the modulator. The carrier oscillator generates the fundamental pitch of the note, while the modulator (Osc 2) changes the frequency. Vibrato is a basic form of frequency modulation: an LFO modulator imposes a pitch change, and the LFO amount parameter controls the intensity of pitch change. The FM amount parameter functions in the same way—FM amount controls the intensity of the pitch change imposed by the Osc 2. Low frequency modulations of pitch sound like slight warbling sounds, but when the modulator's frequency is in the audio range, FM adds harmonic overtones to the carrier timbre.

1. Start with the "Subtractor Osc.rns" file.
2. On Osc 1, set the waveform to 3.
3. Enable Osc 2 and set the waveform to 3.
4. Adjust the Osc Mix knob to 0. Osc 1 is the carrier signal.
▸ Play and hold a note, and then slowly increase the FM parameter. As the modulation increases, you hear the oscillator transform from a bare sine wave playing the fundamental to a bright, complex timbre.
5. Set the FM amount to 54.
▸ Play and hold a note and adjust the Osc 2 octave transpose downward to 0 and then upward to 9. As the modulator is transposed to 0, you hear the distinct sound of a warbled pitch modulation. At higher transposition values, the timbre has glassy or bell-like characteristics.

FM Envelope & Envelope Velocity Modulation
6. Continue from the previous example.
7. Set the FM amount to 0.
8. Set the Oscillator 2 Oct: 6, Semi 5.
9. Set the mod envelope as follows: A 0, D 64: S 0, R 77, Dest FM, Amt 2. This shapes the envelope stages that increase FM.
10. Set the Amp Envelope A: 0, D: 0, S: 127, R:77.
11. Set the Velocity M.Env: 39. This adds velocity modulation of the Mod Envelope.
12. Set the Velocity FM: 25. This adds direct velocity to FM modulation.
▸ Play notes at different velocities to hear the envelope and velocity modulation change the amount of frequency modulation. Higher velocities increase the modulation, which results in brighter timbres.

Wavetables & FM
FM synthesis was made popular by the Yamaha DX series of synthesizers during the mid-1980s. Each DX voice featured six sine wave oscillators that could be organized into various arrangements of carriers and modulators. It would take several (in some cases all six) sine waves oscillators to create the equivalent of one of the SubTractor wavetables. By using waveforms other than sine waves and adding phase offset modulation,

you can generate complex timbres that mimic complex multi-oscillator DX patches. The following creates a mellow bell/Rhodes DX sound:

13. Continue from the previous example.
14. On Osc 1, set phase mode to "–."
15. Set LFO 2 destination to phase, rate to 59, amount to 80, and keyboard tracking to 127.
16. Set the Osc 2 waveform to 8 (Display 9), oct to 7, semi to 7.
17. Set LFO 1 destination to Osc 2, rate to 31, amount to 12.

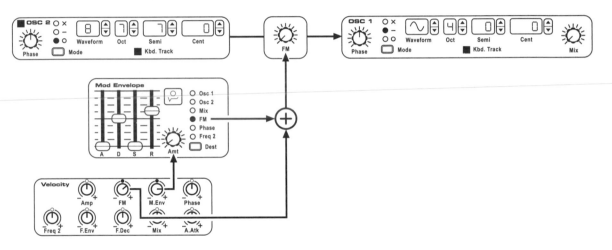

Figure 16-9
FM parameter controls the Osc 2 modulation amount of Osc 1. The modulation envelope and velocity-to-FM generate a combined value that increases the FM amount. Velocity also alters the mod envelope amount.

Shaping Timbre with Filters

The SubTractor name is derived from the term subtractive synthesis which uses filters to alter the harmonic content of the oscillator waveform. This allows us to start with one of the brash wavetables with those harsh high order harmonics and filter them down into something more palatable. By using the filter we *subtract* harmonic content to shape the timbre.

1. Start with the "Subtractor Osc.rns" file, previously saved.
2. Adjust the Osc 1 waveform to 15 (Display 16).
3. Adjust the filter 1 cutoff frequency to 56 and the resonance to 47.
   ▸ Play notes at different ranges from a keyboard controller. If the keyboard has a limited range, use the octave transpose keys to shift up into higher registers. As you play into the higher registers, notice that above note A3, the fundamental pitch is also attenuated by the lowpass filter. This is expected since the filter cutoff frequency is fixed to a value of 56. The default filter type is a 12dB lowpass filter, and switching to a 24dB lowpass makes the patch even darker.

Filter Keyboard Tracking

The Reason synthesizers feature keyboard tracking modulation of the filter so that the filter cutoff frequency can increase as the note pitch rises. This allows the timbre to remain more uniform from one end of the keyboard to the other.

4. Adjust the Filter 1 Kbd (filter keyboard tracking) parameter to 100.

▸ Again, play notes across the entire keyboard range and play in the upper register.

With the filter keyboard tracking modulation, notes higher on the scale sound brighter than before as the filter cutoff frequency increases to match the incoming notes and oscillator pitch.

Filter Envelope Modulation

At this point we have an uninspiring filtered wavetable patch, but this is where patch programming starts to get interesting: We're going to program the filter envelope to modulate the cutoff frequency. This adds dynamic timbral changes to the patch.

5. Adjust the filter envelope amount to 37.

6. Adjust the filter envelope decay to 54 and release to 0.

▸ Play a few notes to hear the filter being modulated by an envelope with a short percussive decay stage.

Velocity Filter Envelope Modulation

The filter envelope adds an initial impulse to the patch by quickly opening and closing at the attack. Like the amp envelope, the filter envelope responds to the duration of incoming notes and legato mode. Velocity can also control the filter envelope amount to add expressiveness.

7. Continuing from the previous example, adjust the filter envelope amount to 0.

8. Adjust the Velocity F.Env to 32.

9. Adjust the Velocity F.Dec to 24. This adds a velocity component to the filter envelope decay segment.

▸ Play a few notes at different dynamics to hear velocity modulating the filter.

The velocity modulation adds a timbral expression to the patch that sounds musical. The filter characteristics are starting to mimic acoustic instruments that sound brighter when played loudly and darker when played softly.

10. Increase the amp envelope release parameter to 81.

11. Play a few staccato notes and listen to the filter envelope abruptly close when the notes are released.

12. Increase the filter envelope release parameter to 81.

▸ Play staccato notes and chords and listen to hear the filter envelope release stage match the amp envelope.

Figure 16-10

A SubTractor filter used for subtractive synthesis, shaping the tone of the oscillator. Filter envelope and filter keyboard tracking combine to change the filter cutoff frequency. Velocity adds another stage of modulation based on performance dynamics, changing the behavior and amount of the filter envelope.

Now the patch has taken shape with a basic wavetable oscillator and filter configured with timbral modulation from the filter envelope. This has become a fairly nice digital polysynth patch. Let's finish by adding dynamic control to the patch:

13. Set the Velocity Amp modulation to 20.
14. Set Velocity to Amp Attack (A.Atk) modulation to –20.
15. Set the amp envelope attack to 28.
16. Save the patch as "Poly Wavetable.zyp."

This is a fairly complex patch with intricate velocity modulation routings that make it very expressive. While this much detail is not alway necessary when creating a custom patch that fits in your song, it's important to understand how the subtle modulation routings can affect the timbre. Having established the filter and modulation parameters for an expressive polysynth patch, scroll through the wavetables on oscillator 1 to see how the patch sounds with different wavetables or even more complex timbre generation like phase offset modulation. There is always a chance that the patch will be better with slightly more harmonic content.

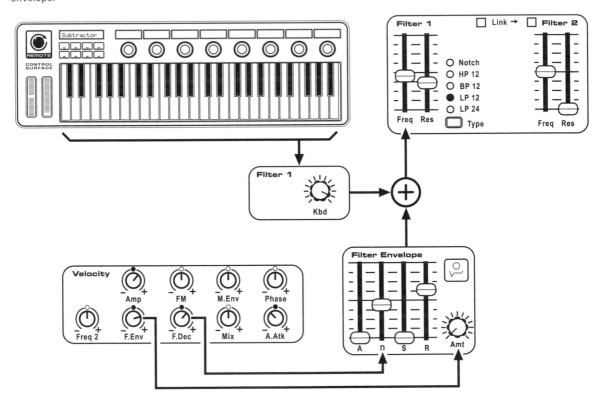

Malström Graintable Oscillator

The Malström graintable synthesizer creates timbres based on a method of synthesis that relies on sequences of wavetables. Each wavetable is a short segment called a grain, and the oscillator scans these grains to generate waveforms. Over the duration of the note, the oscillator cycles through a grain sequence, creating complex and changing timbres.

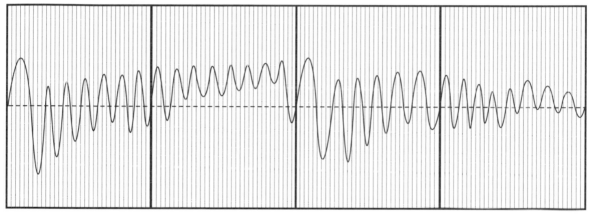

Grain Index 0   *Grain Index 1*   *Grain Index 2*   *Grain Index 3*

Figure 10-11
Each grain is, in effect, a separate wavetable. Grains segments form a sequence that progresses at the rate set by the motion parameter.

Motion

The oscillator sweeps through the set of grains, which changes timbre as the sequence progresses. The motion parameter controls the rate of the grain sequence sweep.

1. Start with an empty rack. Create a reMix mixer and a Malström.
2. Set Osc A to the Perc: AnvilHammer graintable.
3. Play and hold a note. Notice that the chime sound repeats. The grain sequence cycles through the graintable and starts back at the beginning.
4. While holding a note, adjust the motion parameter clockwise. The sequence rate increases and the cycle repeats at a faster rate.
5. Continue holding a note, and adjust the motion parameter to −26. Negative motion values decrease the rate.
6. Adjust the motion parameter to −64, and play a note. This value stops the grain sequence, and the oscillator scans only one grain. This is essentially a single wavetable.

The sequence varies depending on the graintable. Some cycle in one direction while some loop back and forth. Several motion sequences behave like sample loops: The sequence first plays through from index 0 to index 127 and then loops starting from an index point in between. Graintables like sine, square, sawtooth, and triangle are unaffected by the motion parameter.

Motion Modulation

Changing the oscillator motion rate with a modulator adds a time variant to the graintable that changes the timbre over the duration of the note. The following example demonstrates using a modulator ramp to alter graintable motion rate.

1. Start with an empty rack, and create a reMix mixer and a Malström.
2. Set Osc A to the Synth: AdditiveWave2 graintable. Play a note to hear the original graintable before changing the motion parameters.
3. Set Osc A motion to –64. This sets default motion to zero.
4. On Mod B, set the curve to 11, rate to 26, 1-Shot enabled, and motion to 63.
5. Play and hold a note to hear ramp alter the motion of the graintable. The initial attack stage of the timbre is complex. As the Mod B ramp decreases, the motion rate slows down and stops.
6. Adjust the velocity-to-mod setting to 37. This adds a velocity component to the motion modulation.

▸ Play and hold notes at different velocities. Low velocity notes have very little motion, and the high velocity events impose more motion modulation.

Velocity-to-modulator operates differently than an LFO on the SubTractor. The target modulation amount (Modulator B to Motion) and the velocity-to-modulator parameters must both be set.

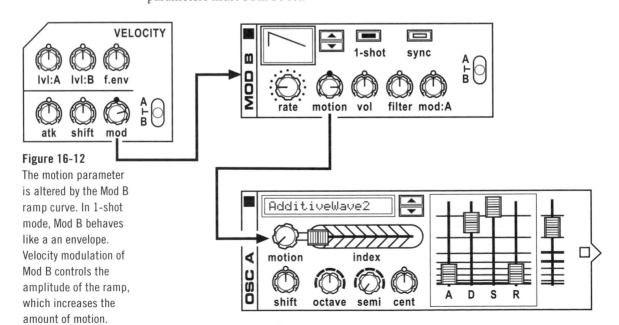

Figure 16-12
The motion parameter is altered by the Mod B ramp curve. In 1-shot mode, Mod B behaves like a an envelope. Velocity modulation of Mod B controls the amplitude of the ramp, which increases the amount of motion.

Index

The simple waveform graintables like sine, square, and sawtooth, are single-cycle waveforms, but most of the others have longer durations and are composed of hundreds of grains. The index parameter allows you to offset the start of the grain sequence, or, if motion is set to –64, to select a single grain to use as a waveform.

1. Start with an empty rack, and create a reMix mixer and a Malström.
2. Set Osc A to the Perc: AnvilHammer graintable. Set motion to –64.
3. Hold a note and slowly adjust the index slider on Oscillator A from 0 to 127. As the index advances, different percussive events of the graintable are heard.
4. Slide the index parameter slowly backwards from 127 to 0. You hear the percussive events backwards.

The actual number of grains varies depending on the original sample, so the index parameter is a relative control rather than a precise indicator of the actual grain position. Some graintables contain hundreds of segments while others only have a few grains.

Grain Index Modulation

When the graintable motion parameter is stopped (–64), interesting segment combinations can be generated by altering the index parameter with the Malström Modulator A. The following example demonstrates reversing grain playback.

5. Continue from the previous example, and set the index value to 0.
6. Set the Modulator A to curve 11, rate 32, 1-Shot enabled, and Mod A to index 21.
▶ Play and hold a note to hear the Modulator ramp cycle backward through the grain indices. Disable the 1-shot mode and change the modulator curve to hear different ways the grains can be altered.

Velocity Index Modulation

Velocity can control the index position by using Mod A with curve 32 and the velocity to modulator amount knob. Mod A controls the index position, while velocity changes the output value from the modulator. With the graintable motion disabled, the oscillator plays a different grain depending on the incoming velocity value.

1. Start with an empty rack, create a reMix mixer and a Malström.
2. Set Osc A to the Synth: SweepingSaw graintable.
3. Play a note to hear the graintable. Notice that the timbre starts with a bright saw sound, then a lowpass filter sweep gradually cuts out the higher harmonics.
4. Set the Osc A motion to –64 and index to 127.
5. Set the velocity to modulator amount to 63.
6. Set the Modulator A curve to 31 and modulator to index amount to –64 or 63.
▶ Play notes at different velocities to hear the modulation of the grain index.

This particular sweeping saw graintable has different timbral qualities at each grain point, so the velocity modulation sounds like velocity to filter cutoff. Experiment with other graintables to see how this velocity index modulation can add an expressive element in a synth patch.

Index Velocity Modulation

The following example is similar to the velocity index modulation, but the motion parameter is set to 0 for normal playback. With graintables that cycle in one direction, the attack timbre changes with an index offset.

1. Starting with an empty rack, create a reMix mixer and a Malström.
2. Set Osc A to the Bass: ThumbBass graintable and index to 64.
3. Set the Modulator A curve to 31 and modulator to index amount to –44.
4. Set the velocity-to-modulator amount to 63.
▸ Play notes at different velocities to hear the index shift further back to 0.

High-velocity events set the offset to index 0, and the graintable plays through the original attack. Lower velocity events start in the middle of the graintable, and the attack timbre is skipped. Adjust the velocity to level A parameter to 12 to add dynamic modulation.

Modulated Shift

The shift parameter controls the playback pitch of each grain segment. The center zero value is the normal pitch of the grain. Adjusting the parameter to a positive value increases the pitch, and counter-clockwise decreases the pitch. Graintable shift is different than changing the oscillator pitch. When the grain pitch is changed, the segment is resampled, then scanned by the oscillator. The result is an increase or decrease in harmonic content that changes the timbre.

1. Start with an empty rack, create a reMix mixer and a Malström.
2. Set Osc A to the Misc: Tampura graintable.
3. Play and hold a note, and sweep the shift parameter from –64 to 63. Listen as the timbre changes from dark to bright.
4. Set the Osc A shift to 0.
5. Set Mod A rate to 60, Curve to 12, 1-Shot enabled, mod to shift 21.
▸ Play and hold a few notes to hear the modulator ramp increase the shift value. This increasing shift adds higher harmonics to the timbre.

Velocity-Modulated Shift

1. Starting with an empty rack, create a reMix Mixer and a Malström.
2. Set Osc A to the Perc: FingerCymbal graintable.

3. Adjust Osc A shift to −18, octave to 3, and release to 78. The long release stage is added to lengthen the sound duration. Play a few notes to hear the patch at this stage.

4. Set the velocity-to-shift modulation to 39.

▶ Play a few notes at different velocities to hear the timbre shift. Velocity shift modulation adds a level of expressiveness to Malström patches.

Malström Dynamics

Each oscillator has a dedicated amplitude envelope section, so each timbre can have unique dynamic characteristics. Obviously, you can have two layered graintables with the same envelope characteristics to create a thicker sound, but the envelopes allow you to stage each oscillator so that one is used for the attack stage, and the second is used for the sustain and release stages.

1. Starting with an empty rack, create a reMix mixer and a Malström.

2. Set Osc A to the Perc: Tabla graintable.

3. Set the Osc A envelope as follows: A 58, D 100, S 127, R 86.

4. Enable Osc B, and select the Perc: TubeSlap graintable. Set index to 7 and octave to 5.

5. Set the Osc B envelope as follows: A 0, D 68, S 0, R 0.

▶ Play a few notes to hear the tubeslap attack blended with the tabla body.

Velocity Modulation

The lvl:a and lvl:b parameters assign velocity modulation to each of the oscillators. Having two controls allows you assign different sensitivity curves to each oscillator.

6. Continue from the previous example.

7. Set the velocity to level A to 22, and velocity to level B to 36.

▶ Play a few notes at different velocities to hear the combined layers with different velocity scaling amounts. The TubeSlap attack stage is more sensitive to velocity message while the Tabla sustain and release stages linger.

Attack Rate Modulation

The velocity "atk" parameter modulates the attack stages of the oscillator envelopes, not the filter envelope. The A/B switch directs the velocity to attack and velocity to shift modulation. The center position assigns the modulation target to both oscillators, while A and B positions target the respective oscillators.

8. Continue from the previous example.

9. Set the velocity to attack to −28, and velocity target to A.

10. Set the Osc A attack to 65.

▸ Play notes at different velocities to hear the attack rate modulation add more of the tabla attack layered with the tubeslap attack.

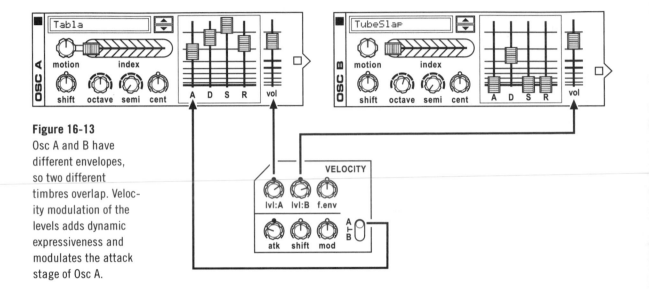

Figure 16-13
Osc A and B have different envelopes, so two different timbres overlap. Velocity modulation of the levels adds dynamic expressiveness and modulates the attack stage of Osc A.

Waveshaping Synthesis

The Shaper section can apply a type of modulation that distorts the timbre generated in the oscillators. This type of distortion synthesis is also called waveshaping synthesis. Waveshaping is dependent on the amplitude of the incoming signal. Each mode is a shaping function that alters the shape of the waveform by changing the momentary output amplitude of the signal.

1. Start with an empty rack, and create a reMix mixer and a Malström.
2. Enable the Shaper and set Shaper amount to 127.
3. Enable the Osc A to Shaper routing.
4. Disable Filter A.
5. Play and hold a note to hear the sine wave distorted by the sine shape function. Adjust the mode to hear the other shape functions, and set the mode back to sine.

By adjusting the Osc A. volume slider, the waveshaping intensifies with loudness. At louder levels the harmonics become more complex, creating a brighter timbre. Waveshaping introduces another method of altering timbre based on dynamics.

6. Continuing from the previous example, set velocity to lvl:A to 47. This adds a velocity to loudness modulation that affects the waveshape function.

7. Set Osc A Graintable to Wave: Triangle, set its volume to 100, and set its envelope generator to A12, D 73, S 84, and R 81.

▸ Play notes at different velocities to hear the waveshaping synthesis alter the timbre.

Using simple waveforms illustrates the potential of waveshaping synthesis because it is a form of distortion, but try other graintables with the velocity modulation parameters set to become familiar with other combinations. Some combinations of graintables and shaper functions work well together.

Because the amount of waveshaping depends on the loudness of the input, modulating oscillator volume can embellish the timbre. Add a Mod B to volume modulation with curve 21 cycling at a slow rate. Also try using two oscillators with different envelope settings that over lap for time based waveshaping effects.

Stereo Malström Timbres

The Malström has a stereo output bus and each oscillator and filter can be discretely directed to the individual outputs using the *spread* control. At the minimum spread setting both outputs carry the same signal, and at the maximum setting the output bus is at full separation. To establish a stereo timbre, the oscillators must have slightly different settings—for example, shift, index, motion, or detune.

1. Starting with an empty rack, create a reMix mixer and a Malström.
2. Enable Osc B and set the graintables on Osc A and Osc B to Wave: Square*16.
3. Set the spread parameter to 127.
4. Set the Osc B index to 21. This creates an index offset between the two oscillators.

▸ Play a few notes to hear the stereo timbre created by an index offset. Slide the Osc B index parameter back to zero to hear the sound become monaural.

5. Set the Osc B index to 0 and set the shift to 6. This creates a shift disparity between the oscillators.

▸ Hold a note and sweep the shift parameter from minimum to maximum. Notice that the stereo effect sounds best with very small shift offsets.

6. Set the Osc B Shift to 0, and set the motion to 2.
7. Set the Osc A motion to –2.

▸ Play a few notes to hear the motion offset between the oscillators.

8. Set the motion to zero on both oscillators.
9. Set the Osc B cent to 4. This creates a stereo timbre through oscillator detune.

▸ Play a few notes to hear the detuned stereo timbre. Also, try switching to different graintables and explore synthesizing stereo timbres with a combination of these techniques.

Malström Filters

The lowpass and bandpass filter modes allow you to apply subtractive synthesis techniques to Malström patches to further shape the harmonic content of the sound. A set of routing controls allows you to direct the oscillator outputs into the dual filter system. Audio signals generated in Oscillator A can be routed to either Filter A or Filter B, while Oscillator B can only be directed through Filter B.

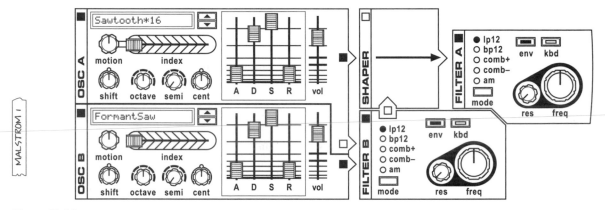

Figure 16-14

Osc A output routed to the Shaper (disabled), which directs the signal through Filter A. Osc B output routed into Filter B.

Subtractive Synthesis

1. Starting with an empty rack, create a reMix mixer and a Malström.
2. Set the graintable on Osc A to Wave: Sawtooth*16.
3. Set the Osc A envelope release to 60.
4. Route Oscillator A to the Shaper. With the Shaper disabled, the signal passes through into Filter A.
5. Set the Filter A resonance to 52 and enable kbd (keyboard tracking). Keyboard Tracking is not scalable on the Malström, and the toggle switch simply turns on the fixed keyboard-to-filter-cutoff modulation.
6. Adjust the velocity-to-filter envelope parameter to 25. This applies a filter envelope modulation controlled by incoming note velocity.
7. Adjust the Filter Envelope release stage to 81.
▸ Play a few notes to hear the basic subtractive synthesis patch created with the graintable oscillator as the timbre generator. The velocity and filter envelope modulation function in the same manner as subtractive synthesis techniques applied with the SubTractor.
8. Continue from the previous example, disable the routing of Oscillator A to Shaper, and enable the routing of Oscillator A to Filter B.
9. Route Filter B to the Shaper. This establishes a series connection between the filters. Oscillator A's output goes to Filter B, then through the shaper into Filter A.

10. Set the Filter B resonance to 52, and enable keyboard tracking.
11. Set the mod wheel to filter amount to −25. This adds a control to modulate both filters' cutoff frequency simultaneously.

▶ Play a few notes to hear the filters working in series to create a 24dB lowpass filter with velocity and filter envelope modulation. While playing, move the mod wheel to sweep the filter cutoff frequency. The negative mod wheel modulation closes the filters to darken the tone.

Stereo Filtering

Oscillator A can be routed to both filters in parallel, and setting different filter parameters creates a stereo effect. The parallel filter configuration is only available with Oscillator A as a source.

1. Starting with an empty rack, create a reMix mixer and a Malström.
2. Enable and set the graintables on Osc A to Wave: Sawtooth*16.
3. Set the Osc A envelope release to 60.
4. Adjust the velocity to filter envelope amount to 25.
5. Adjust the filter envelope release stage to 81.
6. Route Oscillator A to the Shaper and also to Filter B.
7. On Filter A and Filter B, set mode to comb+, resonance to 23, env on, kbd on.
8. Set Filter B freq to 60, and Filter A freq at 64.
9. Set the spread to 127.

▶ Play a few notes to hear the comb filters create a stereo effect. The output from a single oscillator splits and connects in parallel to both filters. The differing filter frequency values create the stereo shift between the two channels. Add a slow modulation to the filter to create a sweeping flange effect, experiment with different graintable sources, and try mixing different filter modes.

Stereo Subtractive Synthesis

Using two oscillators as sources for a stereo timbre requires that the filters processing the two channels have identical settings. In this example, the filters shape the timbre of their respective oscillators exclusively. This routing path is depicted in Figure 16-14.

1. Starting with an empty rack, create a reMix mixer and a Malström.
2. Enable Osc B and set the graintables on Osc A and Osc B to Wave: Sawtooth*16.
3. On both oscillators, set the release time to 75.
4. Enable the routing of Osc A to Shaper and the routing of Osc B to Filter B. This establishes a dual oscillator/filter configuration.
5. On both filters, set frequency to 42, resonance 22, env enabled, and kbd enabled.

6. Set the filter envelope stages as follows: A 73, D 0, S 127, R 81.
7. Set the velocity to filter envelope modulation to 63.
8. Set velocity to shift modulation 4, target Osc B. This initiates the stereo difference effect with the Osc B shift.
9. Set the spread parameter to 127.
10. Set Mod B curve to 31 and Mod B to filter 16.
11. Set velocity to modulator 34. This adds a direct velocity to filter cutoff modulation in addition to the filter envelope.

▸ Play a few notes at different velocities to hear the stereo timbres shaped by the lowpass filters. The velocity to oscillator B shift modulation creates the offset in sounds for the stereo effect, while both filters have the same filtering characteristics.

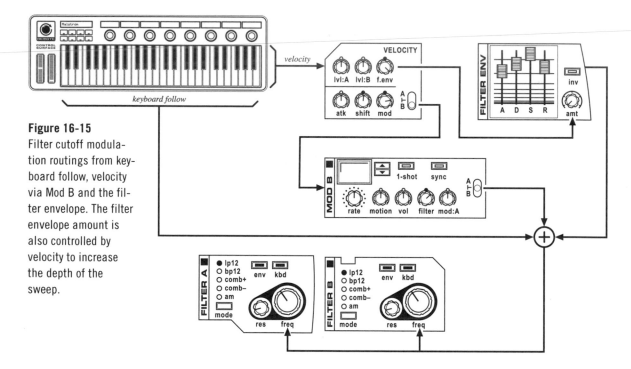

Figure 16-15
Filter cutoff modulation routings from keyboard follow, velocity via Mod B and the filter envelope. The filter envelope amount is also controlled by velocity to increase the depth of the sweep.

12. Continue from the previous patch, select the Malström and choose Combine in the Edit menu.
13. Assign rotary 1 to the Filter A and Filter B frequency parameters.
14. Assign rotary 2 to the Filter A and Filter B resonance parameters.

▸ Play a few notes through the Combinator and adjust the rotary 1 and rotary 2 knobs to make simultaneous adjustments to the filters running in parallel. The Combinator allows convenient control over the dual filter section.

Mod Wheel

The modulation wheel adds real-time performance control to a synthesizer, and the routing knobs scale the modulation amounts. The mod wheel controls a variety of parameters depending on the device. On the Subtractor, the mod wheel routings include filter cutoff and resonance, LFO amount, oscillator phase, and FM amount. On the Malström, the routings include oscillator index and shift, filter cutoff frequency, and modulator amounts.

SubTractor LFO Vibrato

A common type of mod wheel control is an LFO-to-oscillator-pitch modulation that adds vibrato: The intensity of the vibrato increases as the mod wheel is moved further. On the SubTractor, the LFO 1 mod wheel amount parameter duplicates the LFO 1 amount parameter. With SubTractor patches, set LFO 1 amount to zero when adding a mod wheel LFO modulation unless you want some LFO modulation to always be in the preset.

1. Start with an empty rack and create a reMix mixer.
2. Create a SubTractor.
3. Set the filter frequency mod wheel amount to 0.
4. Set the LFO 1 mod wheel amount to 31.
▶ Play and hold a note, and adjust the mod wheel to hear the LFO pitch modulation.

In this example, LFO 1 targets the SubTractor oscillators 1 and 2, and the mod wheel controls the modulation amount. Changing the LFO 1 destination routing will assign mod wheel LFO modulation to a different section. It should be noted that the NN-19 Sampler mod wheel controls function in a similar manner.

Malström Mod Vibrato

The Malström mod-wheel-to-modulator parameter functions differently than in the SubTractor. In addition to the mod-wheel-to-modulator setting, the modulator amount values must be set for their targets.

1. Start with an empty rack, and create a reMix mixer.
2. Create a Malström Synthesizer.
3. Set Mod A to pitch to 33.
4. Set a mod-wheel-to-modulator value of 63.
▶ Play and hold a note, and adjust the mod wheel to hear the pitch modulation.

These settings function like the SubTractor example above: There is no initial pitch modulation. The mod sheel scales the modulation amount that has been set in the modulator itself; if the mod wheel is set to maximum, then the modulation amount is equal to the value set in the modulator.

6. Set the mod wheel itself to 0.

7. Adjust the mod-wheel-to-modulator parameter to 55.

8. Play and hold a note. Initially a subtle pitch modulation occurs. Move the mod wheel and the pitch modulation intensity increases.

9. Continue holding the note, and adjust the mod-wheel-to-modulator knob. Sweep the value between 0 and 63. As this value increases, the pitch modulation decreases.

Unless the mod-wheel-to-modulator value is 63, a slight modulation is always audible when the wheel is at zero. Negative values of this parameter will invert the mod wheel control. When the wheel is at zero the maximum modulation is occurring, and when the wheel is at 127, no modulation is occurring. This architecture of mod wheel control is used in the NN-XT Advanced Sampler for both the mod wheel and the external control wheel.

Controllers

The SubTractor features controller modulation parameters that allow for a second set of real-time control settings, but these are only available if the MIDI keyboard control features include aftertouch (A.touch), an expression pedal, or a breath controller. Aftertouch is a pressure-sensitive control that engages when a key is depressed. Pressing down further on a held note sends a MIDI aftertouch value that ranges from 0 to 127. An expression pedal is the footpedal version of a mod wheel. A breath controller is a device that responds to air pressure exerted through the mouthpiece. (Many MIDI controller keyboards can send breath controller and expression pedal data from front-panel sliders.)

The SubTractor patch can select one of these three sources and apply modulation routings, which function in the same manner as with the mod wheel. The external modulation also includes an amplitude parameter, so an expression pedal or breath controller can control the dynamics. The Malström does not feature routings for external controllers, but the NN-19 and NN-XT samplers feature parameters for these modulation controls.

Chapter 17
Samplers

Since the invention of recording technology, experimental artists have explored composing with recorded sound. Many of the early pieces used tape machines or phonographs as instruments. These experiments in recorded sound, called *musique-concrète*, eventually evolved into the modern technology of sampling. A sampler is a versatile sound playback device that uses digital audio recordings as sound sources.

Many of the programming principles outlined in the synthesizer chapter apply to both Reason samplers. The sampler oscillators load pre-recorded sounds, but other parameters are the same: The modulation routings, filters, and amp envelopes are like those used for subtractive synthesis on the Malström and SubTractor. Sampler parameters are saved as patches that contain parameter settings and information about the audio files to load.

The NN19 and NN-XT can only play back audio samples. Samples are recorded using third-party recording or editing applications. The Apple and Microsoft operating systems include basic recording software, and most sound cards include audio recording programs bundled with their audio drivers. There are also recording applications available that you can download from freeware and shareware websites.

Loading Audio Samples

Before a sampler can generate any sound, an audio sample must be loaded into the device. The procedure is similar on the NN-19 and NN–XT samplers, but if you're planning to use samples with a high word length and sample rate, it's recommend that you use the NN-XT.

1. In an empty rack create a reMix mixer and an NN-19 Sampler.
2. Open the sample browser window by clicking on the blue folder button above the mapping editor on the NN-19.
3. Load the sample "Loopmasters-DRMLP_120.WAV" from the *Power Tools for Reason* CD \ Audio Samples directory.

▸ Play and hold a note. Listen as the sampler plays the loop. When the end of the recording is reached, playback stops. Play different keys and you will hear the tempo of the loop change depending on the key. The original tempo of the recording is heard when you play a note on C3. When you play notes higher, the speed increases, while lower notes play at a lower speed.

1. In an empty rack, create a reMix mixer and an NN-XT Sampler.
2. Expand the NN-XT Remote Editor and open the sample browser window by clicking on the Load Sample button.
3. Load the sample "Loopmasters-DRMLP_120.WAV" from the *Power Tools for Reason* CD \ Audio Samples directory.

▸ Play and hold a note to hear the sampler play through the loop. Again, play different notes to hear the pitch speed up and slow down. Play C3 to hear the loop at the original pitch and speed—this is the *root key*. Adjust the root key parameter to C2 and again play C3. With the root key assigned to an octave lower, playing a note on C3 doubles the pitch and tempo.

Play Modes

An audio file loaded into the sampler is assigned to a *key zone*. A zone has parameters for the basic elements like root key, range, and play mode. The play mode indicates the playback characteristics. The NN-19 has three play mode options: normal forward (Loop OFF), forward loop (Loop FW), and forward-backward looping (Loop FW-BW). The NN-XT play modes include these three modes as well as backwards playback and a special forward looping sustain (FW-SUS) mode. The following example demonstrates the behavior of each play mode.

1. In an empty rack, create a reMix mixer and an NN-XT Sampler.
2. Load the sample "Loopmasters-Filter_125.WAV" from the *Power Tools for Reason* CD \ Audio Samples directory.
3. Play and hold a note on C3 to hear the original sample playback.

4. On the NN-XT remote editor, select the key zone by clicking on the sample name "Loopmasters-Filter_1" or the key zone block. Once the zone is selected, you will see the zone parameters appear at the bottom of the display.

5. Change the play mode to FW-LOOP.

▸ Play and hold C3 to hear the sample loop. The loop plays in the forward direction until the key is released.

6. Change the Play Mode to FW-BW.

▸ Play and hold C3 to hear the sample loop. You will hear the loop play forward, then backward, then forward again.

7. Change the Play Mode to BW.

▸ Play and hold C3 to hear the sample loop. The loop plays in reverse and then stops.

8. Change the Play Mode to FW-SUS.

9. Set the Loop End to 12.5% (21084 Frames). Hold the shift key for fine adjustment of frames.

10. Set the amp envelope release stage to 7.11 seconds.

▸ Play and hold C3 to hear the first beat loop. Release the key to hear the remainder of the loop play through the release stage of the envelope.

When the sampler is triggered, playback begins at the position indicated by the start parameter for all modes except backwards. If a loop mode is not selected, then playback will end at the position indicated by the end parameter. In backwards mode (BW), playback begins at the end position and ends at the start position.

Looping

In order to create a sampler instrument patch that can sustain long notes, it will be necessary to use samples that use the loop play modes. Audio Files in WAV and AIFF formats can include loop points. These points indicate the exact position where looping begins and ends. Precise looping is best achieved with a sample editing program. Setting loop points is one of the most tedious tasks in developing sample patches, which is why many people rely upon sample libraries produced by professionals.

1. In an empty rack, create a reMix mixer and an NN-XT sampler.

2. On the NN-XT remote editor, open the sample browser and navigate to the *Power Tools for Reason* CD \ ReFills \ Lapjockey directory.

3. Enter "MinePad1.aif" in the search field, click Find, and load the sample.

4. Click and select the "MinePad1" key zone. Notice the loop start and loop end parameters, which are set to 45.9% and 93.7%.

5. Play and hold a note or chord to hear the loop. The sample loops continuously and smoothly until the key is released. This is a properly looped sample!

6. Change the loop start value to 0.0%.

7. Play and hold a note. As the note loops you will hear a noticeable pop or click at the loop transition point.

8. Double-click on the "MinePad1.aif" sample field to open the sample browser and load the "MinePad1.aif" sample again. When the sample is loaded, the original loop points are restored.

The loop start and loop end parameters define the region where the loop occurs. Normally, the loop start position occurs after the sample start, but the sample start can occur in the middle of the looped section. If the sample start position is later than the loop end position, then sample playback begins at the loop start marker.

Looped audio samples are timbre generation sources, similar to wavetables. Like a wavetable oscillator, the sample zone has tuning and keyboard tracking parameters. Certain tones reproduce quite well when transposed to higher and lower registers relative to the root key, but others will sound unnatural as the harmonic content changes with pitch transposition. Instead of using a single sample mapped across the keyboard, complex sampler patches use several different samples recorded in smaller musical registers, a technique called multisampling.

MultiSampling

The earliest sample playback instrument was the Mellotron, a keyboard instrument that uses recorded sounds as a sound generator. The Mellotron housed a rack of tape strips, and each strip was mounted so it could be drawn across a playback head. When a key was pressed, a spring mechanism pulled the tape across the playback head. Each key had its own tape strip and playback mechanism, so the samples were dedicated to individual tape strips. The Mellotron introduced the concept of the multisampling, in which each key is assigned to a different source sound. The individual notes of a pre-recorded instrument like a flute or violin could be reproduced by playing the keys on the Mellotron keyboard.

Modern digital samplers, including the NN19 and NN-XT, feature multisampling: Each key zone is like a Mellotron tape strip, and different samples can be assigned to different keys or key ranges. The LCD displays on the NN19 and NN-XT are used to program the *key map*. The key map sorts incoming note messages and initiates playback of the correct sample. A different sample can be mapped to each of the 128 MIDI notes. In order to build the multisample patch, the first step is to load the samples.

1. Start with an empty rack, and create a reMix mixer and a NN-XT sampler.

2. Open the sample browser and navigate to the Reason Factory Sound Bank \ NN-XT Sampler Patches \ Reed and Pipe \ MTRon Flute Samples directory.

3. Select all of the audio files in the directory. Use shift-click while selecting the files, or the select-all keyboard shortcut.
4. Click OK to load the samples.
5. You will see eleven sample zones loaded.

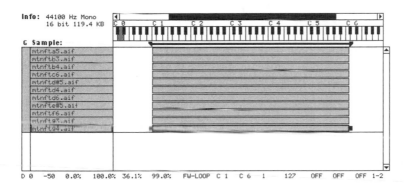

Figure 17-1
Multiple samples loaded into the NN-XT. Zones are mapped to the entire keyboard range.

The horizontal bars that correspond to each sample indicate the range of keys that will trigger the sample. Notes from any key between C1 and C6 will trigger all of the zones. When the samples are first loaded, they're all assigned by default to the full keyboard range. Before the patch can be used, each zone must be mapped.

Pitch Detection & Auto-Mapping

The NN-XT features a utility for quickly mapping multisamples. Two items in the Edit menu will automatically set the root key and map the zones across the keyboard. There is a specific procedure for automatically mapping samples to different key zones.

6. Position the cursor in the Group (G) column and click to select all zones.
7. On the Edit menu, select Set Root Notes from Pitch Detection.
8. On the Edit menu, select Automap Zones. You will see the zones mapped across the keyboard with ranges that do not overlap.
9. Save the Patch as "Mellotron Flute.sxt."
10. Enable the Select Zone Via MIDI button.
 ▶ Play a scale across the keyboard and watch as each zone is selected when keys assigned to it are received.

Having the samples mapped, you can see how these Mellotron flute samples are distributed over several different regions of the scale. Each sample is recorded from a different note on the Mellotron keyboard. (Unlike the original Mellotron, this version doesn't have a separate sample for each key.) The pitch detection features automatically sets the root note of each sample to provide the auto-mapping feature with the information it needs to position each sample.

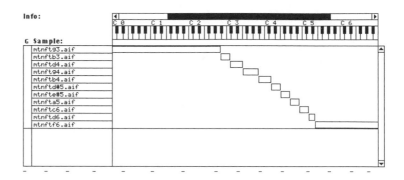

Figure 17-2
The key map shows that the zones are mapped to different ranges.

The automatic pitch detection is not always perfect, and some editing may be required, but you'll find that many of the samples and key zones are arranged properly. One little issue is that the automatic pitch detection will adjust the tuning of the sample zone. Sometimes the slight tuning adjustment actually helps. If the zone is improperly mapped, then the automatic pitch detection did not successfully analyze the sample, and the zone will require manual adjustment. You can click on the zone and drag the handles to change the key range.

Quick Sample Key Maps
Another use of multisampling is to create a sample palette, such as a collection of percussion or sound effects. With this type of patch, the samples play back at the original pitch and the range of the zone is limited to one key. The NN19 automap feature is suited for making this task simple.

Figure 17-3
The NN19 auto-map feature automatically assigns loaded samples to one note range zones indicated by the segments above the keyboard. Drag tab markers if necessary to adjust zones.

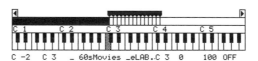

1. In an empty rack, create an NN19 Digital Sampler.
2. Use the sample browser to load the first 15 samples from the Reason Factory Sound Bank\Other Samples\Chords-Phrases-Pads-Stabs directory.
3. Disable KBD.TRACK. The samples will not be transposed based on keyboard pitch.
4. Set the oscillator pitch octave to 3, semi to 8, and fine-tune to 50.
5. From the Edit menu, select Automap Samples.

6. Save the patch as "StabPallete.smp."

▶ Play notes across the keyboard to trigger the samples.

NN-XT auto-mapping does not assign zones to individual keys, so building the sample map in the NN19 is more efficient. The NN19 patch can be saved, and opened in an NN-XT. Note that if the samples have root keys assigned within the audio file, this process may not work properly. The root notes for the sample palette must all be set to C3.

Synth Parameter Programming

The key difference between the two samplers is the architecture of the synth parameters. The NN19 architecture is similar to the SubTractor: It has an oscillator timbre source, a filter, and filter and amp envelopes. On the NN-XT Advanced Sampler, each sample zone can be given its own pitch, filter, dynamics, and modulation settings.

Programming the sampler synth parameters is virtually the same as programming a SubTractor or Malström patch. Dynamics and timbre controls are featured in the amp envelope and filter sections of the NN-XT Remote Editor and the NN19 interface. For example, if you change the filter cutoff frequency on the NN19 Stab-Palette patch, the filter will affect all of the samples. On the NN-XT, filter settings apply to each zone individually, as do the velocity, LFO, and envelope modulations.

Group Parameters

When developing multisampled instrument patches, you will most often apply the same parameter settings to each of the zones. The first step is to select all of the zones in the NN-XT remote editor. If only one zone is selected, parameter changes will only be applied to a single zone.

1. Start with an empty rack, and create a reMix mixer and a NN-XT sampler.
2. Load the "Mellotron Flute.sxt" patch created earlier.
3. Open the NN-XT remote editor.
4. Position the cursor in the Group (G) column and click to select all zones. Parameter changes will affect all of selected zones.
5. Set the amp envelope as follows: A 1.32 s, H off, D 60.0 ms, S 0.0 dB, R 2.71 s.
6. Set the filter mode to LP 24, frequency to 92Hz, resonance to 22%, and key track to 100 cent/key.
7. Set the mod envelope as follows: A 1.03 s, H off, D 3.07 s, S 0%, R 2.0 s.
8. Set mod envelope to filter at 50%. This adds a filter sweep to the patch.
9. Set velocity to F.Freq (filter frequency) to 50%.
10. Set velocity to level at 34%. This adds velocity to dynamics modulation.
11. Set the amp envelope spread to 75%. This adds keyboard track to panning modulation, a feature found in Reason only in the samplers.

12. Save the patch as "MelloFlutePad.sxt."

▸ Play a few note at different velocities through different registers of the keyboard to hear the flute's panning based on key position.

Layering Samples

The NN-XT can trigger several different samples from a single MIDI note event. This can be used to create layers of timbres and even different multisample groups. This example demonstrates how to layer several different samples to create an "ensemble" of samples. When a key is pressed, all of the samples will play back simultaneously.

1. In an empty rack, create a reMix mixer.
2. Create an NN-XT Advanced Sampler and open the Remote Editor.
3. Load the sample "135_Vocode_mLp_eLab.aif" from the Reason Factory Sound Bank\Music Loops\Fixed Tempo (wave, aiff) directory.
4. Set the Group Key Poly to 1.
5. Select Add Zone from the Edit menu. The parameter settings below are for the new zone being created.
6. Load the sample "CYM1V10HSH.aif" from the Reason Factory Soundbank\Redrum Drum Kits\xclusive drums-sorted\06_Cymbals directory.
7. Set the velocity level amount to 40%.
8. Set the pitch keyboard track to 0.
9. Set the amp envelope release to 1.53 seconds.
10. Select Add Zone from the Edit menu. The following parameter settings are for the new zone being created.
11. Load the sample "BD1Dub.aif" from the Reason Factory Soundbank\Redrum Drum Kits\xclusive drums-sorted\01_BassDrums directory.
12. Set the velocity level amount to 59%.
13. Set the pitch keyboard track to 0.
14. Set the amp envelope release to 1.05 seconds.
15. Select Add Zone from the Edit menu.
16. Load the sample "SN2br.aif" from the Reason Factory Soundbank\Redrum Drum Kits\xclusive drums-sorted\02_SnareDrums directory.
17. Set the velocity level amount to 47%.
18. Set the pitch keyboard track to 0.
19. Set the pan to −22%.
20. Save the NN-XT patch as "Loop&Drums.sxt."

▸ Play notes on a MIDI keyboard to hear the ensemble patch.

Layering samples can also be used to stack different waveforms, as in a multi-oscillator synthesizer patch. Each zone contains a sample of a different basic waveform and each timbre can be assigned unique dynamics and filter parameters, or they can be grouped together like a single timbral source.

Velocity Mapping

Most acoustic instruments like a piano or guitar sound differently depending on dynamics. To account for these changes, the instrument is recorded at different dynamic levels (sampled while being played softly, moderately, and loudly). Once the samples are loaded and set into key zones, each zone is mapped to velocity messages.

1. Start with the "Loop&Drums.sxt" patch in the previous example.
2. Click on the "CYM1V10HSH.aif" sample zone to select it.
3. Adjust the Lo Vel to 98. This adjusts the lower range of the velocity map so that it will only respond to velocity messages of 98 or greater.

▸ Play notes on C3 at different dynamics. Slowly increase the velocity until you hear the cymbal sample triggered along with the loop and kick drum.

This is a very simple form of velocity mapping, similar to the example in the Combinator chapter. To get an idea of a complex velocity map, inspect the mapping on the NN-XT patch "A Grand Piano.sxt." (Use the Patch Browser Search function.) This patch has four velocity layers that were each programmed with specific parameter settings for each zone. Another complex NN-XT patch is "–T RHODES MK I.sxt," which is part of the ElectroMechanical ReFill available on the Propellerhead website. This Rhodes sample patch has eight velocity layers, and each layer has 26 zones. Creating this single NN-XT patch involved recording, editing, looping, and mapping over 200 samples.

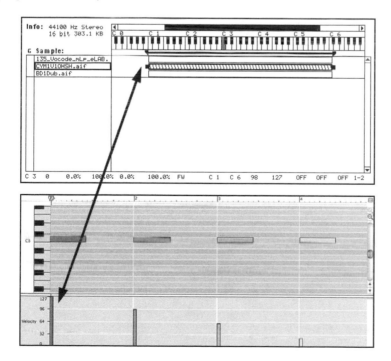

Figure 17-4
A velocity map sorts incoming note events and directs them to trigger different samples. The cymbal sample is triggered when velocity is 98 or greater.

Stereo Timbres

Any monophonic sample can be made into a stereo timbre source within the NN-XT. The technique is based on using two identical samples with slight differences in parameter settings.

1. In an empty rack, create a reMix mixer.
2. Create an NN-XT Advanced Sampler and open the remote editor.
3. On the Reason Factory Sound Bank, use the Browser Search feature, and load the sample "DasModel-05_D4.wav."
4. Select Set Root Notes from Pitch Detection from the Edit menu.
5. Set the Pan to –100%.
6. From the Edit menu, select Duplicate Zones. This duplicates the sample to create two timbre sources—one zone for each stereo channel.
7. On the duplicate zone, set the pan to 100%, LFO 2 rate to 0.11 Hz, and LFO 2 to pitch to 9 cents.

  ▸ Play a note or chord and listen to the stereo effect. The slight pitch modulation causes the second zone to detune, causing the stereo separation. If pan is not adjusted on this patch, the pitch modulation will create a flanging effect.

The stereo timbre source takes advantage of the NN-XT's ability to assign different parameter settings to each sample zone. This procedure can also be applied to groups of zones, so a monophonic multisample can be duplicated, panned, and adjusted to induce a stereo effect.

Layering Patches

Entire patches can be layered in a single NN-XT. This allows you to stack several multisampled instruments, which will be playable from a single keyboard or sequencer track. This example illustrates a popular technique of layering a female vocal multisample to create an atmospheric choral sound on top of a string orchestra.

1. In an empty rack, create a reMix mixer and an NN-XT Advanced Sampler.
2. Bypass auto-routing and create another NN-XT.
3. On NN-XT 1, load the patch "VNS+VCS+BSS.sxt" from the Orkester Sound Bank\Strings\String Combinations directory.
4. On NN-XT 2, load the patch "FEMALEAHHH.smp" from the Reason Factory Sound Bank\NN19 Sampler Patches\Voice directory.
5. Expand the remote editor panel on NN-XT 2.
6. On NN-XT 2, click on the first group area to select the key zones, and click on Copy Zones in the Edit menu.
7. Expand the remote editor panel on NN-XT 1.
8. Select Paste Zones in the Edit menu. The zones from NN-XT 2 are now layered with the zones on NN-XT 1.

9. While the pasted zones are still selected in the NN-XT 1 remote editor, set the group amp envelope gain level to –11dB, and set the velocity-to-amp envelope attack modulation to –22%.

10. Delete NN-XT 2.

11. Enable MIDI on the NN-XT 1 sequencer track and play notes from a MIDI controller to audition the layered patch.

Audio Manipulation

Manipulation of recorded audio is one of the most interesting aspects of using samplers. The audio data can be tweaked much as if it were being played by a synthesizer. The pitch can be modulated with an LFO, short segments of a sample can be used as a waveform, and sample playback can be reversed. A wide variety of effects can be applied to samples to create unique timbres. The following examples illustrate a few ideas that you may find inspiring and that may lead you to further experimentation.

Envelope-Modulated LFO Rate

The NN-XT is the only device in Reason that allows CV control over the LFO rate. This can be used to create unusual pitch modulation patterns. In the example below, the Matrix pattern sequencer CV/gate signals are split to trigger both the SubTractor and the NN-XT. The SubTractor's filter envelope signal modulates the LFO rate on the NN-XT.

1. Start with an empty rack, and create a reMix mixer.
2. Create a Matrix Pattern Sequencer and a Spider CV Splitter & Merger.
3. Connect the Matrix note CV output to the Spider CV split A input.
4. Connect the Matrix gate CV output to the Spider CV split B input.
5. Pencil in tied gate events from step 1 through step 8 on the Matrix.
6. Bypass auto-routing and create a SubTractor synthesizer.
7. Connect Spider CV split B output 1 to the SubTractor sequencer control gate input.
8. Set the SubTractor polyphony to 1, enable low BW, and set the filter envelope decay to 75 and filter envelope release to 45.
9. Create an NN-XT Advanced Sampler and open the NN-XT Remote Editor.
10. Load the sample "CYM1 1OHSH.aif" from the Reason Factory Soundbank\Redrum Drum Kits\xclusive drums-sorted\06_Cymbals directory.
11. Set the NN-XT amp envelope release to 7.06 seconds, and the LFO1 pitch modulation amount to 1350 cents.
12. Connect the SubTractor filter env modulation output to the NN-XT LFO1 rate CV input.

13. Connect Spider CV split A output 1 to the NN-XT sequencer control CV input, and Spider CV split B output 2 to the NN-XT sequencer control gate input.
14. Set the NN-XT LFO1 rate CV trim to 93.
▸ Run the sequence.

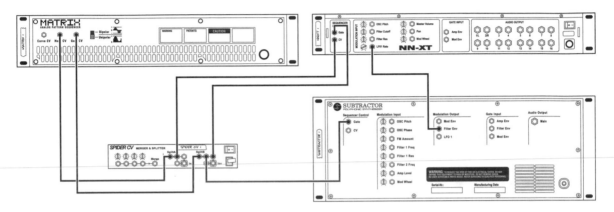

Figure 17-5
A Matrix triggers both the NN-XT and SubTractor. The SubTractor envelope controls NN-XT LFO rate.

Turntablist

A turntablist is a DJ who uses the turntable as an instrument. The effect described below is quite extensive and requires a lot of fine-tuning, but the results are astonishing. This effect emulates the sound of a vinyl record being scratched on a turntable by triggering samples that play forward and backward. The modulation envelope controls pitch and filter settings that create the sound of the sample accelerating and decelerating.

1. Start with an empty rack, set the tempo to 84 BPM, and set the pattern shuffle amount to 29.
2. Create a reMix mixer.
3. Create an NN-XT Advanced Sampler.
4. Using the sample browser, load the sample "Peff_BrassAction.aif" from the *Power Tools for Reason* CD \ Audio Samples directory.
5. Duplicate the sample zone "Peff_BrassAction.aif" five times.
6. Set the NN-XT group parameters as follows:

NN-XT Group Parameters	
Key polyphony	1
Mode	Legato
Portamento	36

The NN-XT sample zones all have the same name, so they are referenced from their order from top to bottom. Only adjust the parameters indicated in the charts.

Only parameters of the selected zone selected will be modified, so click on the sample name before editing the parameters. Start with the NN-XT sample parameters found along the bottom of the Remote Editor display:

NN-XT Sample Parameters

Zone	Root	Start	End	Play Mode	Lo Key	Hi Key
1	C3	0.0%	100.0%	FW	C3	C3
2	D3	35.6%	100.0%	FW	C#3	D3
3	E3	0.0%	74.4%	BW	D#3	E3
4	F3	0.0%	40.4%	BW	F3	F#3
5	G3	0.0%	14.9%	BW	G3	G#3

Two zones are used for forward playback and three are set for reverse playback. The start positions are offset to recreate scratching at varying points of the record. The sample end parameter is actually the sample start position for zones set in BW play mode. Each sample zone in this patch has specific parameters, so be careful not to select the group or more than one sample zone. Start with the velocity modulation parameters:

NN-XT Synth Velocity Parameters

Zone	Mod Dec	Sample Start
1	–9%	56%
2	–22%	44%
3	11%	0%
4	31%	0%
5	25%	0%

Samples in BW play mode play from the end position sample parameter, and because the playback duration will be short, modulation of the sample start parameter will be insignificant.

The modulation envelope is assigned to the sample playback pitch with very short ramps to create the sound of the record speeding up and slowing down. Set the following Mod envelope parameters:

NN-XT Synth Mod Envelope Parameters

Zone	Attack	Hold	Decay	Sustain	Release	Pitch	Filter
1	48.5ms	Off	1.13 s	0%	44.8ms	2269 cents	44%
2	0.10 s	Off	36.4ms	0%	20.6ms	1875 cents	44%
3	7.2ms	Off	0.30 s	0%	0.14 s	379 cents	44%
4	22.7ms	Off	0.20 s	0%	0.36 s	1517 cents	44%
5	48.6ms	Off	0.36 s	28%	20.6ms	2269 cents	44%

The filters are given a dynamic character from the envelope modulation source. Verify that all zones have their filters enabled, and set the filter parameters shown in the table on the next page.

NN-XT Filter Parameters

Zone	Freq	Res	Mode
1	547Hz	0%	LP 6
2	1.3kHz	50%	LP 6
3	3.2kHz	41%	LP 12
4	707Hz	25%	LP 12
5	28.2kHz	0%	LP 6

The amp envelope parameters are the same for all of the sample zones, and can be applied to the entire group of zones.

7. Select the group of zones by clicking on the group region on the remote editor display.

8. Program the following amp envelope parameters:

NN-XT Synth Amp Envelope Parameters (Group)

Zone	attack	Hold	decay	sustain	Release
Group	0.5ms	Off	60ms	0.0dB	19.1ms

For those who are new to programming NN-XT patches, this patch is probably a long task. It's recommended that you now save the NN-XT patch to a convenient location on your hard drive.

The playback of the sample patch can be rather unpredictable, so it's necessary to add some compression and equalization to the NN-XT outputs:

9. Insert a Scream 4 distortion unit between the NN-XT audio outputs and the mixer channel 1 inputs.

10. Connect the Scream 4 auto CV output to the P1 CV input.

11. Set the P1 CV trim to 34.

12. Program the following settings on the Scream 4:

Scream 1 Settings

Damage: *on*	Damage control	30
	Algorithm	Tape
	P1	24
	P2	99
Cut: *on*	Lo	−26
	Mid	42
	Hi	5
Body: *off*	Reso	
	Scale	
	Auto	
	Type	
	Master	

Pattern Control Section

While this effect can be controlled via MIDI, a Matrix pattern sequencer is the most convenient way to trigger the scratch events on the NN-XT. Scratching is a very rhythmic process, and the configuration is designed to take advantage of all three Matrix control voltage outputs:

13. Create a Matrix Pattern Sequencer and switch it to bipolar mode.
14. Connect the Matrix note and gate CV outputs to the NN-XT sequencer control CV and gate inputs.
15. Connect the curve CV output to the NN-XT osc pitch modulation input.
16. Adjust the NN-XT osc pitch CV trim to 14.

Scratch Pattern Programming

This is probably the most difficult part of the Turntablist effect. Keep in mind that the samples on C3 and D3 play forward while the samples on E3, F3, and G3 play backward. Alternating between forward and backward requires separate gate and note events. The Matrix curve CV controls the oscillator pitch, and this should be varied for each gate event. Scratching does not have a consistent pitch, so varying this control value adds more realism.

The velocity modulation on the NN-XT is set to mimic the push and pull speed. With the forward playback sample zones, velocity will also shift the start position. Gate events with high velocity settings will start these samples at a point further from the original start position. Velocity will also change the rate of the modulation decay. This creates the variation in acceleration/deceleration speeds. Mixing up the gate velocities is another way to add realism to the effect.

17. Select Matrix pattern A1, set the pattern resolution to 1/32, and enable shuffle.
18. Program the following on Matrix pattern A1:

Matrix Pattern

Step	1	2	3	4	5	6	7	8	9	10	11	12	13	14	15	16
Curve	0	0	20	20	−32	−32	63	−64	32	0	0	0	15	20	36	50
Note	C3	C3	F3	F3	D3	D3	G3	C3	F3	C3	G3	D3	E3	E3	E3	E3
Gate	L		L		L		H	M	M	H	L	H	TM	TM	TM	

▸ Run the Matrix pattern.

NN-XT REX Loop Player

Reason samplers can load ReCycle loops by opening them through the patch browser. The various modulation features of the NN-XT Advanced Sampler make it a very powerful ReCycle loop player. When the ReCycle loop is loaded, the slices are automatically mapped across the keyboard.

NN-XT REX Playback Procedure

In order to extract REX slice data to the sequencer track, you need to use a Dr.REX. Once this data is exported to the sequencer, the Dr.REX can be deleted. Keep the sequencer track even when the device is deleted. You may need this sequence for other purposes—as a user groove quantization template, for instance. The configuration below is no different from using a Dr.REX Loop Player, but features on the NN-XT allow you to manipulate the REX slices in ways not possible with the Dr.REX. The next few sections will illustrate the power of using the NN-XT as a ReCycle loop player.

1. In an empty rack, create a reMix mixer.
2. Bypass auto-routing and create a Dr.REX Loop Player.
3. Load the ReCycle loop "Chm19_Funkiest_130_eLAB.rx2" from the Reason Factory Sound Bank\Dr Rex Drum Loops\Chemical Beats directory.
4. Copy the REX slice data to the Dr.REX 1 sequencer track.
5. Create an NN-XT Advanced Sampler.
6. Using the NN-XT patch browser, load the same ReCycle loop.
7. Copy the REX slice groups from the Dr.REX 1 track to the NN-XT 1 track.
▸ Run the sequence, and save the file for use with the next example.

Reverse REX Slice Playback

By changing the play mode on certain slices of the ReCycle loop, you can generate some nice variations. Reverse hits can be used as little transitions between phrases, or as variations to the drum pattern. The sound of a reversed slice can also create elastic sounds with a completely different feel from the original loop.

8. Start with the NN-XT REX player created in the previous example.
9. Open the NN-XT remote editor panel.
10. On the first slice, assigned to note C1, change the play mode to BW.
11. Change the play mode to BW on slice 5 (E1) and slice 13 (C2).
▸ Run the sequence.

Looped REX Slices

The short loop times of the slices create a very distinctive sound, similar to granular synthesis. The loop length set by the loop start and loop end parameters on each NN-XT zone can be either percussive for longer times, or harmonic with very short times. The results are very esoteric and are the roots of new electronic styles of music.

12. Start with the NN-XT REX Player described above.
13. Set the loop markers in the sequencer to loop only one measure, from 1.1.1 to 2.1.1.
14. Open the NN-XT remote editor panel.

15. On the NN-XT, make the following edits to the REX slice zone parameters (empty means no change):

Slice # / Root Key	Loop End	Play Mode
1 / C1		
2 / C#1	5.5%	FW-LOOP
3 / D1	5.6%	FW-LOOP
4 / D#1		
5 / E1		
6 / F1	28.6%	FW-LOOP
7 / F#1	14.4%	FW-LOOP
8 / G1	5.9%	FW-LOOP
9 / G#1		
10 / A1	4.4%	FW-LOOP
11 / A#1		
12 / B1	0.8%	FW-LOOP
13 / C2		
14 / C#2		BW

▸ Run the sequence.

This technique is similar to the drum programming used to create "drill" rhythms. Using looped drum samples in conjunction with a fast sequence containing 64th-notes will create completely new textures.

Velocity-Switching REX Slices

The ReCycle loop sample zones in the NN-XT can be quickly duplicated and layered. The layered zones can be assigned to respond to different velocities so that forward and reverse samples can be changed by changing the velocity in the sequence.

16. Start with the NN-XT REX player described above.
17. Set the loop markers in the sequence to loop two measures from 1.1.1 to 3.1.1.
18. Open the NN-XT remote editor panel.
19. Select all NN-XT slice zones by clicking on the group (G) area of the editor window.
20. Adjust the group low velocity to 64.
21. In the Edit menu, click on Duplicate Zones, and then select Group Selected Zones.
22. Scroll to the bottom of the NN-XT remote editor window and select the second group of zones if it isn't already selected.
23. Adjust the low velocity to 1 and high velocity to 63 for the second group.
24. Change the play mode to BW on all of the zones in the second group. You must do this individually for each zone. There is no group adjustment for this parameter.

25. Change the sample end (not loop end) markers for each of the second group zones according to the following chart. This must be done manually for each zone.

Slice #/Root Key	End
1 / C1	42.0%
2 / C#1	75.6%
3 / D1	78.1%
4 / D#1	82.6%
5 / E1	49.7%
6 / F1	81.4%
7 / F#1	76.8%
8 / G1	69.1%
9 / G#1	56.8%
10 / A1	73.7%
11 / A#1	75.4%
12 / B1	68.4%
13 / C2	30.4%
14 / C#2	74.4%
15 / D2	68.6%
16 / D#2	76.1%
17 / E2	63.4%
18 / F2	69.9%
19 / F#2	34.5%
20 / G2	60.0%
21 / G#2	76.0%
22 / A2	42.1%
23 / A#2	83.5%
24 / B2	86.5%
25 / C3	69.8%
26 / C#3	67.2%
27 / D3	73.7%
28 / D#3	40.0%
29 / E3	59.1%

26. Switch the sequencer to edit mode and enable the REX and velocity lanes.
27. Enable the pencil tool and modify the velocity values to less than 64 for the following slices: 2, 4, 6, 8, 10, 14, 18, 22, 27, and 29.
28. Save the NN-XT patch, and then run the sequence.

Chapter 18
MIDI Sequencing

MIDI is an acronym for Musical Instrument Digital Interface. Developed in the early 1980s as a standardized method of communication between electronic music instruments, MIDI establishes a digital network that connects synthesizers, other sound generators, and computer sequencers. Data transmitted along the network of cables can trigger synthesizers and samplers to play notes, change patches, and synchronize timing and tempo. After all these years, MIDI is still the basis of current sequencing applications, including Reason.

The MIDI sequencer revolutionized music creation. Even before the invention of the sequencer, artists could use multitrack audio tape, which allowed a single person to record every part of an arrangement. The musician would have to play all of the parts without mistakes, however. Using synthesizers and a sequencer, composer/performers can freely edit their tracks after recording—fixing the timing, transposing the part to a new key, or using an entirely different timbre, for example. Changes to a sequenced track are instantaneous, offering amazing flexibility.

At the heart of each Reason song is a MIDI sequence, in which note events are recorded, arranged, and routed to the devices in the rack. The sequencer's edit mode features the tools necessary for making microscopic adjustments to MIDI events, and the arrange mode is used to structure the entire song. This chapter will focus on methods that make arrangements easier to handle, and hopefully will improve your productivity when developing tracks in Reason.

Sequencer Tracks

Each time a sound generator module is created in the Reason rack, a corresponding sequencer track is added. This is a convenient feature, but it can also lead you to work in a manner that is somewhat narrow-minded. Just because Reason adds one sequencer track per device does not mean you have to work with only one track per device. In fact, using multiple tracks per device can be more efficient. This has already been demonstrated in previous chapters, where multiple tracks are used to rearrange REX slices. The next few sections discuss more ways of using multiple sequencer tracks.

Recording Multiple Takes

One method of developing musical ideas is to experiment with layering and alternate versions. This is achieved by creating several duplicate sequencer tracks assigned to the same device. After creating a synth or sampler and loading the patch, find the associated sequencer track in the track list. Drag-duplicate the sequencer track several times and keep them grouped together so that you can move to the next track quickly. After recording a part that you're not sure about, mute the track and try another take on a second track.

To layer a complex part, select the MIDI focus on the first track and begin recording a passage in loop mode. When the transport cycles back to the beginning, switch to the next track and continue recording new note events. After recording, try assigning each of the tracks to a different sound module. If the tracks are recorded in different registers, then they may layer nicely with the right selection of synth or sampler patches.

If you have a remote-compatible keyboard control surface with buttons, check to see if a pair of buttons or a rotary encoder control is assigned to the Target Track function. Click on Additional Remote Overrides in the Options menu. Once these are assigned, the sequencer record track can be changed directly from a rotary encoder or a set of scroll buttons. This eliminates the need to manually navigate track changes with a mouse.

Automation Tracks

Rather than recording automation data to the same track as the MIDI note events, create a separate track exclusively for automation. Having the automation controls on a separate track allows you to disable parameter automation quickly by muting the track. By Option/Alt-clicking or using the contextual menu item, you can go directly to the sequencer track display containing the automation data. If you have MIDI knobs or sliders assigned to parameters on different devices in the rack, you can record automation data simultaneously for each device on different tracks by arming record all of the automation tracks at once. Reason will intelligently route the correct controller data to the correct track.

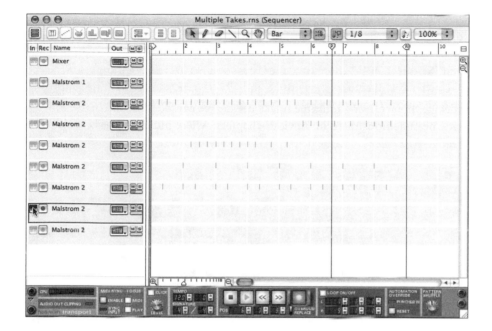

Figure 18-1
Having several empty tracks assigned to a single instrument allows you to quickly add a part or modify a sequence.

A measure or group of measures containing controller data can be duplicated to repeat through the course of the sequence from the arrange view. This can also be achieved by selecting and duplicating individual blocks of controller lane data, but it's much faster to use the arrange window. In effect, the sequencer track containing the controller data becomes a more flexible version of a Matrix curve CV pattern.

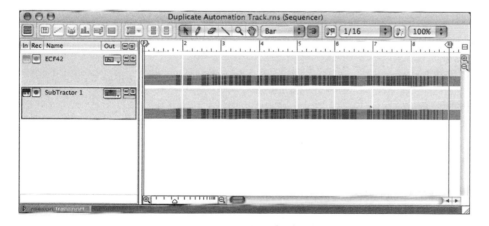

Figure 18-2
Filter events recorded on an ECF-42 automation track duplicated and routed to a SubTractor.

Certain parameters, such as the mod wheel, pitch bend, filter cutoff frequency, and volume, function in the same manner on various devices. Controller automation of these parameters can be assigned to other devices by duplicating the automation track and changing the destination device. For example, if the master volume level of a Malström is used to create a swell in dynamics for a pad sound, the level automation track can be duplicated and applied to any of the sound modules in Reason. ECF-42 filter cutoff and resonance parameter automation can be duplicated and will control the Dr.REX and NN-19 filters, filter B of the Malström, filter 1 of the SubTractor, and the NN-XT global filter control. In version 3.0, it's also possible to copy controller data freely from one automation lane to another throughout Reason.

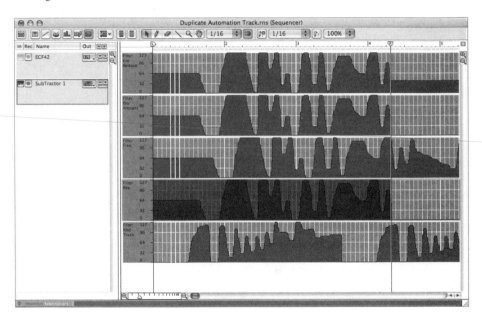

Figure 18-3
Automation events recorded into one lane can be freely copied into any other lane.

Splitting Note Events

In an effort to get a new song started as quickly as possible, you may record polyphonic events consisting of bass octaves played in the left hand and triads (or more) played in the right hand. This is useful for developing chord progressions, but the resulting track can sometimes overwhelm a mix. Naturally, this sequence is recorded live, but with a little editing, it can be distributed over several tracks.

1. Duplicate the original track twice, and mute the original track.
2. Enter edit mode to view the key lanes of the first duplicate track.
3. Zoom out the sequencer view to see all of the note events.
4. Select and delete all of the bass octave note events.
5. Switch to the second duplicate track.
6. Select and delete all of the right-hand chords.

Having the chord progression split to two different tracks allows more flexibility in changing the voices of the sequence. The bass octaves might be assigned to a synth pad played on a Malström, while the chords might be assigned to a choir multisample on the NN-XT. Alternatively, you might elect to delete the bass part entirely in favor of a more active, syncopated line. The separation of tracks also makes arrangement easier since the chord events and bass octave events can be deleted or duplicated as separate groups in the arrangement window.

If you like to sketch new progressions this way, check out the Performance Patches folder in the Combinator Patches folder in the Reason Factory Sound Bank. Many of these patches are set up as keyboard splits, with bass in the left hand and a chording sound in the right hand.

Left-Hand Controller Overdubs

Overdubbing pitch-bends and mod wheel moves into a track that already contains some of the same type of data is a bit tricky in Reason, because the program treats these controllers like other types of automation. While in record mode, once you touch the left-hand wheel you're overdubbing, Reason will erase any other data of this type in the track as the play cursor moves over it.

The solution is to overdub new controller moves on a separate track assigned to the same synth. Once you have the modulation moves the way you want them, you can cut them from the overdub track and insert them at a corresponding point in the main synth track.

Redrum Tracks

Pattern-based Redrum programming has its advantages because it's gratifying when a drum groove is programmed quickly. Using multiple Redrum patterns and the pattern lane to develop an arrangement is simple. One problem with this method is that it's not easy to make specific pattern changes. The occasional crash cymbal can be added to the drum lane of a Redrum sequence track, but a snare hit can't be removed from a particular bar without going through a number of steps to record a mute event or duplicate and reprogram the pattern and then edit the pattern automation.

Once a programmed drum arrangement has been established for the structure of a song, it can be converted to MIDI sequence events that trigger the Redrum channels. Pattern changes are easily recognized, as pattern groups will be assigned different colors. Set the left and right loop locators to the boundaries of the track region where pattern A1 is playing, copy the pattern to the track, move the locators to the next pattern region, and so on. Do this once for each pattern. Once all of the patterns have been copied to the track, switch off Enable Pattern Section on the Redrum. Then use group duplication in the track view so each pattern will play in the sections where it's needed.

Sometimes starting with a single Redrum pattern used as a metronome track is useful. The base pattern can be modified in edit mode, while percussive embellishments like snare rolls or crash cymbals can be programmed on separate sequencer tracks so that they can be quickly identified in the arrangement window. This provides a better overview of the entire drum arrangement.

Redrum patterns converted to MIDI sequence events can be split in the same manner as tracks with note events. For example, a converted Redrum pattern may use six different channels: bass drum, snare drum, rim shot, open hi-hat, closed hi-hat, and crash cymbal. Each of these elements can be split into its own track. One drum arrangement technique, especially with programmed drums, is to mute out different elements for a certain period. Having each of the drum events on its own sequencer track makes this process more efficient, because the data can be deleted from the arrangement wherever the drum sound should be silent.

Once the Redrum is triggered from sequencer tracks, you can freely add snare "ghost notes" to individual measures, humanizing the track. This can be difficult in a Redrum pattern because the clock resolution of the pattern is fixed (to sixteenth-notes, for instance). Another advantage of copying Redrum patterns to tracks is that the drum sounds are no longer limited to three velocity levels. Each note can be given its own velocity with the pencil tool, and you can draw smooth crescendos and diminuendos with the line tool.

Groups

Most music is repetitive by nature, and elements of a music arrangement often recur throughout a track. Repetitive elements of a sequence can be recorded once and then duplicated for each instance where they occur. The key to arranging and duplicating musical phrases in a sequence is to use the group features. Regions of a track can easily be grouped using the pencil tool in the arrange view, or by selecting a range of measures with the arrow tool and selecting the Group command in the sequencer edit menu. A single group can be moved by selecting it and dragging it to a different position on the sequencer track, and the same can be done with several selected groups.

Arrangement groups add a visual element to the structure of a sequence. Not only does this provide a method of quickly moving to different parts of the sequence by dragging the position marker, the loop locators can quickly be set at the boundaries of a long group so you can work on a section of the music while listening to it.

Inserting Measures
The name of the Insert Bars Between Locators command in the sequencer Edit menu is somewhat misleading, because it is not restricted to full measures. The loop

locators can define a space of any length, and the insert command will shift events to the right by exactly the distance between the locator markers. Using the snap-to-grid feature with the resolution set to Bar will ensure that the space inserted is exactly on a measure; otherwise it may end up being less than a full measure.

Sometimes inserting a half- or quarter-measure space between passages can add a dramatic pause to a track. The are several pitfalls to be aware of when using this technique, however: Groove, shuffle, and user quantization will be useless in the section after the break, and if Matrix or Redrum patterns are used, special 4-step or 8-step patterns may need to be programmed to occur during the break. It's a lot of work to add this timing shift to a track, but the effort is sometimes worth it. It may be easier to insert a one-measure gap, then shorten the gap using an audio editor after the song is finished and mixed.

Splitting All Groups

When you start moving individual groups around in the arrangements, the group regions will usually start and end at different measures. The Insert Bars Between Locators command can be used to insert a split point across all groups at a specific point in the sequence. Set the right and left locators to the same position, and then use this command. A space of zero measures is created, which splits all of the groups. This can be performed at another position to mark the start or end of the region, and the various groups in between can then be selected and grouped as a single phrase.

Chapter 19
Reason Accessories

Reason alone provides everything necessary to compose and produce music, but other software applications can expand the production possibilities. Discussed in some detail in earlier chapters is ReCycle, the application that creates REX loops. Registered Reason users can also download Reload from the Propellerhead website. Reload converts Akai sample libraries for use with Reason. ReBirth RB-338 users can integrate the 303 synth bass and drum machine patterns from ReBirth into a Reason production (for more details, visit www.rebirthmuseum.com). And using the ReWire protocol, Reason interfaces with other software applications, which will allow you to record audio tracks and use plug-in synthesizers and effects from other manufacturers.

Reload

Reload is a utility that converts Akai S1000 and S3000 sampler libraries into samples and patches that are usable in Reason. Reload will convert data from sample CD-ROMs and removable storage media. The application extracts and converts the audio data into AIFF format, and converts the Akai sampler patch information into SXT patches that are usable in the NN-XT sampler. Hundreds of commercial sample libraries are available for Akai samplers, and Reason users have convenient access to this vast collection. It's important to note that Reload will only run on Apple Mac OS X or Microsoft Windows XP operating systems. If you need an operating system upgrade in order to use Reload, please research all of the implications of the upgrade before performing it. Older software, including audio and MIDI device drivers, may become unusable under the new OS.

Using Reload is quite simple. When the application launches, it waits until an Akai format CD-ROM or other removable storage media is mounted. After the verification process, Reload gives you the option of either extracting the data into a folder or packing the data into a ReFill file. If the CD-ROM has many small individual samples, the extraction process takes longer than if there are a few large samples. It can take as long as 45 minutes to convert a standard CD-ROM on a slow computer. The process can take still longer if you opt to pack the folder into a ReFill. After the extraction process, Reload will launch the ReFill Packer utility to create the ReFill.

Extracting the Akai format media to a folder is useful for direct access to the individual samples. Perhaps only one partition or patch is needed, so the rest can be discarded. If you want to modify certain samples, then it's necessary to have access to the AIFF files. Packing an Akai CD-ROM into a ReFill is useful if you want to take advantage of the ReFill file compression feature. ReFill can compress sample data with around a 2:1 ratio, and this will definitely economize hard drive space. The latest version of ReFill Packer must be installed if you intend to create ReFills from sample libraries imported using Reload.

Custom Patch Directory

The NN-XT patches converted from Akai patches are located in the same directory as the sample files. Navigating through the folders can be a little confusing, mainly because the names given them will be "Partition A," "Partition B," etc. Patches of certain sample banks that you find useful should be saved in a separate directory so that they are easily found. If you have extracted the Akai media to a folder, then create an NN-XT Patches directory in this folder, or in some other convenient location on your system. Load the patch into the NN-XT, then save the patch into the NN-XT Patches folder. You can't copy the NN-XT patch file from the partition directory into the NN-XT Patches folder, because if you do, the file pointers to the samples will point to the wrong folder.

ReFill Packer

ReFills are add-on files that contain samples, ReCycle loops, patches, and songs usable by the different devices in Reason. The Reason Factory Sound Bank and Orkester files are the ReFill libraries installed with the Reason application, but dozens of commercial ReFill libraries are available. In the Reason user community, there exists a subculture surrounding the ReFill Packer utility. Several users produce ReFills that can be downloaded from the Internet and used freely.

Before creating a ReFill, you should organize the directory layout in a manner similar to creating a project folder for song projects. All sample and patch content must go into this folder before packing. The *Power Tools for Reason* CD contains a directory named "ReFill Production Template," which provides an example of how to structure the directory hierarchy. You can duplicate this folder to your hard drive, rename it, and move the content into the appropriate directories within it.

Two other files must be included in the ReFill project folder—the info.txt and splash.jpg files. The splash.jpg is a small image that brands the ReFill. The file must be in jpeg format, and must have the exact dimensions of 64 × 64 pixels. If the image does not meet these requirements, ReFill Packer will reject the file and abort the packing process. The info.txt file is a text file that contains information about the ReFill: its name, copyright, and any comments. The name indicated in the info.txt file is extremely important, because Reason is sensitive to ReFill names. If two different ReFills have the same name indicated in the info.txt, one or both may be rejected when Reason looks for them.

Move the ReFill packer application into the same directory as the Reason Factory Sound Bank. When preparing to compress the project folder, ReFill Packer requires access to the Reason Factory Sound Bank.rfl file. If it can't find the Reason Factory Sound Bank, a prompt will appear asking for the Factory Sound Bank CD.

Samples & File Paths

Samples and patches that are associated with the samples can be copied into the ReFill project folder, but patch and audio sample files must reside in the same directory. The NN-XT, NN-19, and Redrum patches contain information about file paths that tell Reason to look for the sample in a specific location on a hard drive. ReFill Packer checks this information to verify that the audio file locations link properly with the patches.

Once the sample and patch data is copied into the ReFill project folder, open the patches, and resave them into the patch folders. Once resaved, the patch contains updated file path information. Simply moving the patch files will not work, because the file path is not updated, and ReFill Packer will abort when it discovers the problem.

Production Strategy

In order to build a ReFill, you must have a Reason song file open in which you can open and resave patches to update the file path data. This song file should be saved in the ReFill project folder so that it can be easily accessed. Reason song files are also affected by the file path information, and if the samples load properly into the song file, then they will function properly as part of the ReFill package. Developing content around a song is an effective technique for creating a complementary palette of samples, loops, and synth and Combinator patches. When the different elements work in harmony, using the content is much easier for the end user.

ReWire

Reason can be connected to other software applications using ReWire. This is a protocol that shuttles audio, MIDI, and synchronization data back and forth between ReWire-compatible programs. The current versions of applications such as

Digidesign Pro Tools, Apple Logic, Ableton Live, Steinberg Cubase and Nuendo, Mark of the Unicorn Digital Performer, Cycling '74 Max/MSP, and others support ReWire. Using ReWire, Reason can be incorporated into larger productions that require audio recording, plug-ins, and hardware synthesizer sequencing.

The ReWire system is hierarchical: One application acts as a ReWire host while another functions as a ReWire slave. (Some people prefer the word "client" to "slave.") Before enabling ReWire between Reason and a ReWire host, quit both applications. The ReWire host application must be launched first, and ReWire channels to Reason must be enabled. After enabling ReWire on the host application, launch Reason. If the connection is properly established, the ReWire lamp will illuminate on the Reason Hardware Interface. After the session, Reason must be shut down before the ReWire host application can quit. Some applications, such as Pro Tools, are scripted to automatically launch and quit Reason in the proper order.

Once the connection is established, MIDI data can be sent from the host application to the devices in the Reason rack, and the audio from the Reason devices can be routed through the mixing suite and plug-in effects of the host application. The transport, tempo, and loop controls synchronize between Reason and the host application.

Preparing for ReWire

Using Reason with a ReWire host application does present more flexibility, but the added features can be a bit cumbersome. A large part of a piece of music can be created using Reason alone, after which the host application will only be necessary before mixdown. Using the audio inputs on the Reason Hardware Interface, 64 individual audio signals can be connected from Reason to the host application.

Prepare the ReWire connection by using Spider Audio splitters to split the mixer input signals. Audio signals can be split so each signal is connected both to the mixer and to the Reason Hardware Interface. The host application can directly access signals from Reason. The mixer master outputs should stay connected to input 1 and input 2 on the hardware interface as a way to monitor while you're working in Reason alone. During the mixdown stage, add plug-in effects as needed in the host application.

Another useful technique is to bus signals from the Mixer 14:2 into the host application through aux send outputs. The aux send outputs can be connected to the Reason Hardware Interface inputs, and different groups of input signals can then be directed to the busses using the aux send attenuation controls.

Reason Adapted

Reason Adapted is a limited version of the full Reason application. It's customized specifically for third-party distribution, and is based on features in Reason 2.5. There are several different versions of Reason Adapted and the features may differ, but typically the program contains a fixed set of devices, such as a mixer, a few effects devices, a synthesizer module, a sampler, a Dr.REX, a Matrix, and a Redrum. The devices themselves function in the same manner as in the full version.

When a new Reason Adapted song is created, the rack components are already created and can't be changed. Fortunately, cabling can still be modified, so Reason Adapted users can manipulate the signal paths. The sequencer tracks are also fixed, but one is assigned to each of the devices so automation is still available, and all of the devices will respond to MIDI.

Reason Adapted usually comes with a limited sample set packed in a special ReFill sound bank. The sampler and Redrum can load audio samples from a hard drive, but Reason Adapted can't access ReFills created for the normal version. The same applies to sampler, Redrum, synthesizer, and effect patches, and patch saving is not available.

Reason Adapted users should still develop the habit of creating project folders to keep samples and backup song files organized. Song files created with Reason Adapted will open in the full version of Reason. Users who upgrade to the full version of Reason will be able to open their old song files, which can then be further modified.

Index

On the CD-ROM

Reason provides many useful tools for creating music, and it's very easy to use Reason alone to create complete instrumental productions. The real power of Reason lies in using the application as a creative conduit to shape your compositions by transforming the palette of timbres as needed. The CD-ROM contains samples, demo songs, and example patches that illustrate this concept. Several projects in this book refer to files found on the *Power Tools for Reason* CD-ROM. Use of these files is important in achieving the expected results. These files function with the full version of Reason 3.0.4, and include the following types: Combinator patches (.cmb), audio samples (.aif and .wav), and ReFill (.rfl), and ReCycle (.rx2) files.

The demo songs are in Reason Song File format and require the full version of Reason 3.0.4. The diversity of styles demonstrates the flexibility of the application. The CD-ROM also showcases the talents of many people who contributed audio samples, engineering, and graphic design. Refer to the "CD-ROM Info.html" file for photos and biographies of the artists, musicians, and engineers who participated in this project and for links to their websites.

Examples in the book often refer to Combinator patches found on the CD-ROM. Load these patches directly from the CD-ROM in order to access audio samples and ReCycle loops included in the package. To use these patches from your hard drive, copy the entire CD-ROM contents without renaming or changing the directory structure.

Readers can expand their sample libraries with the ReFills included on the CD-ROM. The ReFills include a variety of samples ranging from bizarre electronic effects and sampled acoustic instruments to palettes of musical riffs and bass loops produced specifically for this book. Those interested in developing their own Reason sample libraries should refer to the ReFill Production Template. This folder can be copied to a local hard drive, where custom samples, loops, and patches can be saved into the appropriate subdirectories.

The Song Project Template folder contains a directory structure recommended for organizing song files, samples, patches, and back-up data. For each new song project, copy this folder to a local hard drive and rename the directory.